MW00445458

The
Sustainable
Rose
Garden

The Sustainable Rose Garden

A Reader in Rose Culture

Edited by Pat Shanley, Peter Kukielski, and Gene Waering

with drawings by Maria Cecilia Freeman

NEWBURY BOOKS

Philadelphia and Newbury

Published in the United States of America and
Great Britain in 2010 by
Newbury Books
(An imprint of Casemate Publishers)
908 Darby Road, Havertown, PA 19083
and
17 Cheap Street, Newbury, Berkshire, RG14 5DD

Copyright 2010© The Manhattan Rose Society. Individual authors
retain copyright to their contributions.

ISBN 978-1-935149-16-3

Cataloging-in-publication data is available from the Library of
Congress and the British Library.

All rights reserved. No part of this book may be reproduced or
transmitted in any form or by any means, electronic or mechanical
including photocopying, recording or by any information storage and
retrieval system, without permission from the Publisher in writing.

10 9 8 7 6 5 4 3 2 1

Printed and bound in the United States of America.

For a complete list of titles please contact:

CASEMATE PUBLISHERS (US)
Telephone (610) 853-9131, Fax (610) 853-9146
E-mail: casemate@casematepublishing.com

CASEMATE PUBLISHERS (UK)
Telephone (01635) 231091, Fax (01635) 41619
E-mail: casemate-uk@casematepublishing.co.uk

Mixed Sources
Product group from well-managed
forests and other controlled sources
www.fsc.org Cert no. SW-COC-002283
FSC © 1996 Forest Stewardship Council

DEDICATED TO

John J. Shanley (1943–2009)
for his unfailing support of the mission of
Manhattan Rose Society and his ability to see
the dream and to believe that nothing is impossible —
the impossible only takes a little longer.

Contents

Drawings by Maria Cecilia Freeman

Of all flowers
methinks a rose is best.

—JOHN FLETCHER (1579–1625)

Foreword

The 21st Century is an exciting time to grow roses. Granted, there have been other exciting "eras" for roses, perhaps beginning when the Chinese and Persians first brought roses in from the wild and cultivated them in their gardens. Much later, in the late 18th and early 19th centuries, the Empress Josephine made it fashionable to grow roses, and helped to encourage the breeding of new varieties under her patronage at Malmaison. Heightened interest in roses during the 19th Century resulted in increased hybridizing efforts, discoveries and beginnings, new rose introductions, and also new groups of roses—the Hybrid Perpetuals,

> *"He who would have beautiful Roses in his garden must have beautiful Roses in his heart. He must love them well and always."*
>
> —FROM *A BOOK ABOUT ROSES* BY DEAN S. REYNOLDS HOLE

Noisettes, Hybrid Musks and others. The Royal National Rose Society (RNRS) of Great Britain was founded in 1876 and the American Rose Society (ARS) followed in 1892. Dean S. Reynolds Hole (1819–1904) began his book, *A Book About Roses*, with this now well-known sentiment: "He who would have beautiful Roses in his garden must have beautiful Roses in his heart. He must love them well and always." Dean Hole spoke—and speaks—for many!

Marilyn Wellan, with Bailey.
PHOTO: MYRON WELLAN

Throughout the 20th Century, the art and science of growing roses developed to magnificent proportions. Dedicated rosarians have endeavored to live by Dean Hole's mandate. The rose was recognized as the national floral emblem in several countries including England and the United States. Roses were praised as the world's favorite flower. The number of local ARS rose societies grew to nearly 400; the RNRS grew to over 115,000 members and it gained the patronage of England's Royal Family. Both organizations were able to occupy new headquarters, and installed rose gardens on their properties. Botanic gardens everywhere planted important collections of roses, further encouraging more gardeners to grow roses at home. The great rose nurseries of the world thrived as rose offerings for home and public gardens became more and more colorful, exciting and plentiful. Amateur rose hybridizing became a favored hobby, and great new roses came from those efforts.

As the popularity of roses grew, so did the desire by some to grow the most "perfect" roses they could grow. Rosarians who exhibited roses competitively did so with a natural passion for exhibition-quality blooms, and they freely shared information on the subject with new and less-experienced growers in their neighborhoods, local societies, and through published articles. Perhaps over time, the available reading material and programming taught us more than casual rose gardeners needed to know. Growing roses that might measure up to the blooms grown for exhibition appeared to be too difficult and costly for many. To keep these roses totally free of disease—the bane of the average rose gardener—was a daunting task. According to the "experts," it required the use of harsh chemicals, and it took a lot of work. Many gave up the battle in favor of a garden that was easier to manage, or chose not to garden with roses at all.

I came into the hobby in the 1980s with a mighty passion for roses and for the rose society. I absorbed all I could about "proper" care and feeding of my roses, and became somewhat of a spokesperson for growing roses to all who would listen. I remember how eagerly I shared everything I knew about rose products and the newest varieties with a neighbor, a seasoned farmer who had long maintained and enjoyed a beautiful rose garden in front of his farmhouse without any help from me. After a time he let them go, and I still cringe with regret for perhaps depriving him of the enjoyment he found in his rose garden all those years—and in growing them his way.

The idea—the goal—of the sustainable rose garden movement is to show the way to growing beautiful roses with less pressures from disease and with less effort on the part of the grower.

Yes, collectively, we showed everyone how difficult it was to grow roses. In retrospect, I believe this may have contributed to the declining popularity of the rose and reduced membership in rose societies and revenues for rose nurseries that we have witnessed in the last several decades. Of course, this may not have totally caused the waning popularity of rose culture. Fashions come and go, if growing roses can be considered a fashion. Economies ebb and flow. Societal pressures demand lifestyle changes. All these things may have contributed.

For the past 10 or 12 years, rose organizations and the rose industry have begun to respond to the will of people who love roses and want to grow them, but without the level of care that was previously advocated. I experienced this revolution in my own garden, mainly because I wanted a beautiful garden of roses and didn't want to work as hard, and as a leader of the American Rose Society, which needed to gain and retain members more than anything else. We came to the realization that we must alter our horticultural practices for the sake of the environment and our health, and change the way we grow roses if we are to encourage others to grow them. The message needed to be ... and became ... "Yes, you can grow beautiful roses." For the past decade or longer, there has been an increasing level of interest in sustainable rose gardening where the emphasis needs to be—in the rose industry which is motivated by economics, and among the rose organizations of the world which are motivated by the desire to survive and thrive.

Pat Shanley, Peter Kukielski, and Gene Waering are advocates of sustainable rose gardens, and together they have put together a notable collection of articles by some of today's esteemed "champions" of the rose world. A number of experts and witnesses to the efforts being made in attaining the sustainable rose garden were invited to contribute. According to Gene Waering, the "Reader" is modeled—to use a phrase from Stephen Scanniello—on the "rose culture writ large" nature of the (highly collectible) American Rose Annuals, so ably published for the American Rose Society by its President Emeritus J. Horace McFarland (1859–1948) for 29 years from 1916 to 1945. The editors have achieved that goal with the varied mix of outstanding essays and articles within this publication.

For the past 10 or 12 years, rose organizations and the rose industry have begun to respond to the will of people who love roses and want to grow them, but without the level of care that was previously advocated. I experienced this revolution in my own garden ...

The idea—the goal—of the sustainable rose garden movement is to show the way to growing beautiful roses with less pressures from disease and with less effort on the part of the grower. So many have seen the need for this information, and are making it available to the rose gardeners of America. Rose hybridizers internationally, including David Austin in the United Kingdom, William Radler (to name but one) in the United States, Wilhelm Kordes in Germany, and Viru Viraraghavan in India among others, are leading the way, introducing more disease-resistant and disease-free roses which make sustainability possible. Nursery owners including Pat Henry, Janet Inada, Bill Patterson, Gary Pellett, and Ron Robertson—again, among many others—offer new disease-resistant varieties, but also the older proven varieties that have been around for years *because* they are sustainable. Directors of gardens where the public often discovers roses for the first time are keenly aware of the pitfalls and prohibitions against the use of harsh chemicals; the popular rose gardens that Clair

Martin, Marjorie Marcallino, Karl Mckoy, Barbara Oliva, Jill Perry, and Peter Kukielski maintain for visitors helps to "show *and* tell" the sustainability story. The Earth-Kind® Rose Trials introduced by Dr. Steven George and promoted extensively by Gaye Hammond, are internationally known, and that story has brought much needed attention to the sustainability effort. Rosarians who make sure the science of rose culture is available to all of us include some who are featured in this book: Alice Flores, Michael Marriott, Dan Mills, John Starnes, Billy Styles, Alan Talbert, Vance Whitaker, and David Zlesak. Where would we be without the writers and story tellers who inform us and keep the rose mystique alive, including the Tea Ladies of Australia, James Delahanty, Bill Grant, Jeri Jennings, Ellen Spector Platt, Allison Strong, Betty Vickers, Heritage Rose Foundation President Stephen Scanniello and American Rose Society President Jeff Wyckoff? The *Sustainable Rose Garden*, already rich with rose culture, is made even richer by including exquisite illustrations by acclaimed botanical artist Maria Cecilia Freeman and a lovely touch of poetry by Emily Dickinson and others.

Can one book—or one idea—bring about a revolution in the way roses are created and grown? Probably not. But with each new effort by the professionals, the organizations, the gardens, and individual rose growers, we will gradually achieve the sustainable rose garden for those who will only grow easy roses. Once those new rosarians become devoted to their roses, we hope that each and every one finds a way to contribute to roses outside their own garden: by writing, teaching, sharing, encouraging others to grow roses, collecting and preserving heritage roses, and by contributing to and helping to strengthen the rose societies and organizations that pull it all together.

Yes, the 21st Century is an exciting time to grow roses. There is much to be done, through science, education, and dedication to the mission, to be sure, but the rose world has awakened, and has already begun to take up the challenge. Let this excellent publication inspire you to be a part of the effort.

Alexandria, Louisiana   MARILYN WELLAN
September 2010

Buds have an interest all their own: Top, left to right: 'Lady Hillingdon', Double Knock Out®, 'Slater's Crimson China', 'Abraham Derby'; bottom, left to right, 'Michele Meilland', *Rosa banksiae banksiae*.

Introduction
Winston & Roses

PAT SHANLEY

We live in a world where our environment is constantly threatened by a variety of sources, including the chemicals we spray in our gardens. For years, rosarians—exhibitors and nonexhibitors alike—have followed regular spray programs in order to get good results with their roses. The available varieties we planted were subject to pests such as blackspot, powdery mildew, rust and the like. We had one good blooming at the beginning of the season, and after that our roses languished unless we sprayed them with harsh and caustic chemicals. I am among those who sprayed regularly in order to maintain a beautiful garden and exhibit successfully. But when I began my rose garden, we didn't suspect how harmful those complex chemicals would turn out to be.

Diseases such as cancer are at epidemic proportions. How many of us don't know at least one person with cancer? How many of us have lost friends and family to this dreaded disease, and how many of them were rosarians who sprayed their roses with chemicals for many years? One thing we do know for certain is that whatever we spray in our gardens eventually finds its way into our ground water and into the food chain.

My personal journey toward a sustainable rose garden began one beautiful sunny Sunday in July, about 10 years ago. My husband and I were having breakfast on the patio, and my Great Dane, Winston, was enjoying

Winston in his prime. His sudden loss made me reconsider my approach to using synthetic chemicals in my rose garden.

a romp in the grass. We had a good-sized pond in our backyard, and Winston loved to race around the pond, full speed, until he wore himself out. That morning was no different, and we watched in amazement as Winston ran and ran and ran ... and then came over to lie beside me with his big silly grin that said, "Look what I can do!"

After breakfast, I put Winston in the house and proceeded to spray my roses with Daconil for blackspot prevention. I waited the requisite time, according to the instructions, to allow the spray to dry before I let Winston out again. Later that afternoon, Winston began to feel unwell and as the gastrointestinal symptoms developed, I knew he was in serious trouble. I rushed him to the emergency animal hospital near my home. One hour later Winston was dead. Dogs are notorious for eating all kinds of things they shouldn't, such as leaves, grass, and twigs. Can I prove that Winston died from ingesting Daconil? No, I cannot. But in my heart of hearts I will always question what took the life of a beautiful, healthy dog so quickly. It was then I realized Queen of Show was not worth risking health and life.

The Sustainable Rose Garden: A Reader in Rose Culture is a follow-up volume to our 2008 publication, a little paperback of the same title. This volume expands on the original work. When we first discussed publishing a small book in conjunction with the 2008 Great Rosarians of the World Lecture Series—East Coast, it was our intention to put together a synopsis of the panel discussion, "The Sustainable Rose Garden," that was a part of the lecture series, so our audience would have something to take away with them. Maria Cecilia Freeman's cover artwork was so lovely, and the book so full of timely information, that we thought it might appeal to a larger public. So we took an ad in *American Rose* magazine—the official publication of the American Rose Society. The response was overwhelming. Requests for the book came in from all over the world. Clearly, the rose-loving public was clamoring for information on how to grow their beloved roses without polluting the environment and risking the health of future generations.

A call has gone out for disease-resistant roses in recent years, and it has been heard around the world as hybridizers and nurserymen alike do the research and put up the money to produce roses that can be grown successfully without the use of harsh chemicals. Today, we recognize names such as Bill Radler, Keith Zary, Tom Carruth, Griffith Buck, Ping Lim, Wilhelm Kordes, III, as pioneers in leading the way toward sustainability in the rose garden. We hear the expression "Earth-Kind® Roses" and know it signifies a way of growing roses without chemical intervention and in the most earth-friendly way in order to preserve this planet for our children and our grandchildren.

The American Rose Society has recognized the need for sustainability, too, and this was evidenced in the creation a few years ago of the Good Earth Rose Committee, a national standing committee which is working toward the future of growing roses without chemical intervention. There is also a column in every issue of *American Rose* magazine called "Good Earth R.O.S.E—Responsible, Organic, Simple, Earth-Friendly" dedicated to growing roses organically. A test garden for disease-resistant Hybrid Tea (exhibition form) roses has been established at the

In my heart of hearts I will always question what took the life of a beautiful, healthy dog so quickly. It was then I realized Queen of Show was not worth risking health and life.

American Rose Center, which houses the gardens of the American Rose Society, in Shreveport, Louisiana. It is dedicated to identifying these roses for the exhibitor. Clearly, the need for growing roses without degrading the environment has been recognized and addressed by the American Rose Society, our national umbrella association dedicated to educating the public on all aspects of the Rose, which has been the National Floral Emblem of the United States since 1986, including its cultivation and preservation.

The hobby of growing our beloved roses can either survive and prosper—or fade away. If we can give the rose-growing public roses they can grow safely, it will in all likelihood prosper. The very future of the rose and organizations such as the American Rose Society, the Heritage Rose Foundation, the Heritage Roses Group and hundreds of local rose societies, together with the many nurseries that produce the roses, hangs in the balance.

We have come to a crossroad in that future. Whatever the challenges ahead, we need to take the road toward a better and healthier world to live in, that allows us the opportunity to grow beautiful roses and still preserve this planet for our children, our grandchildren and all the generations to come.

A call has gone out for disease-resistant roses in recent years, and it has been heard around the world as hybridizers and nurserymen alike do the research and put up the money to produce roses that can be grown successfully without the use of harsh chemicals.

My personal quest for roses that would thrive and bloom without spraying has been a long one. For the first few years after Winston died, I watched my roses as they became covered in blackspot or decimated by Japanese beetles and had to fight the urge to return to a spray program. But today, I am happy to report my garden consists of varieties—both new and old—that are healthy and disease-resistant—such as those named and described within these pages—and the garden is lush and beautiful once more.

That being said, we must remember that sustainability is a relatively new concept in the world of roses and there is much work to be done in this arena. Therefore, the methods advocated and roses recommended in these pages are not 100% foolproof but rather a basis for further dialogue and testing. Depending on where you live, the rose varieties mentioned in this book may or may not live up to your sustainable expectations. An important key to growing roses sustainably is to plant *the right rose in the right location*, taking into account varying weather and other conditions.

The information presented to you here is not the final word on this subject, but is meant to be a guide to help you with your sustainable journey. It is my hope that this book will help you to begin or continue that journey toward a beautiful and satisfying sustainable rose garden. Is it possible to grow great roses without using harsh chemicals? The answer, in my opinion, is a resounding Yes! The Sustainable Rose Garden is no longer a dream. It is a reality.

We are most grateful to Marilyn Wellan, Past President of the American Rose Society and Great Rosarians of the World 2009 co-honoree, for writing the Foreword to this book.

We also extend our heartfelt thanks to all of the contributing authors who so generously gave of their knowledge and their time. Their very willingness to contribute their efforts has given greater credibility to this cause. Thank you also to Maria Cecilia Freeman for once again offering beautiful illustrations.

To Peter Kukielski, Rockefeller Curator of The Peggy Rockefeller Rose Garden, The New York Botanical Garden—co-editor of this book, Rosarian Extraordinaire and dear friend—thank you for taking the time to help edit this book, in particular the photography section, and for sharing your wisdom and experience.

To David Farnsworth and Steve Smith at Casemate Publishing, thank you for seeing the merit of our work and making our dream of an expanded, hardcover version of *The Sustainable Rose Garden* a reality.

To Sue Tomkin of Tomkin Design, thank you for creating a wonderful design to present the contents of the book. Thank you Kelly Waering for copy-editing the manuscript.

Many thanks to the Board of Directors of Manhattan Rose Society for believing in this cause and for your continued support.

And once again, last but not least, thank you to Gene Waering, Vice President and Program Chairman of Manhattan Rose Society, and a co-editor of this book. Thank you for all that you do to make ALL of our projects and events so successful. You are a driving force behind Manhattan Rose Society, and this book would not exist without your tireless efforts and dedication to the Rose.

More buds: Top, left to right: Golden Threshold™, *Rosa gigantea*, 'Hawkeye Belle', *Rosa moschata;* bottom, left to right: *Rosa roxburghii, Rosa fedtschenkoana.*

Growing Tea Roses

Reprinted with minor edits from
Tea Roses: Old Roses for Warm Gardens
by permission of the authors

LYNNE CHAPMAN, NOELENE DRAGE, DI DURSTON,
JENNY JONES, HILLARY MERRIFIELD, BILLY WEST·

CLIMATE

In temperate climates, the Teas are among the most adaptable and forgiving of roses, and with a little care and attention they will reward you with garden shrubs of great distinction and beauty. The general guidelines for rose growing apply but we would like to add more about the particular needs of Tea roses drawing on our own observations and experience.

Living in a Mediterranean-type climate in south-western Australia, we are able to grow Teas in almost ideal conditions, with flowers being produced for much of the year. Most of the rainfall occurs in winter, when heavy showers are interspersed with lengthy fine periods. Apart from an occasional frost in some areas, it is rarely cold for long enough to inhibit growth and many varieties flower well at this time. Late spring and autumn produce magnificent displays, with flowers of large size and fine colour. The summers are hot and dry and, if the temperature remains over 32 degrees Celsius for some weeks, there is a noticeable decline in the number and size of the blooms and some of the Teas do not flower again until the weather becomes cooler.

Although Tea roses prefer warm conditions, they survive surprisingly well in cold climates if they can be planted where they are sheltered from cold winds and prolonged frosts, and given protection over the winter months. This will vary according to the region and help can be sought from local rose societies or from books that deal with the problem of winter survival. One of the best ways to grow Teas in very cold climates is to plant them in large pots, as was once the custom, moving them outside in the summer and placing them under cover to avoid the ravages of winter.

PLANTING

Because many Tea roses grow into large bushes that can live for a long time, it is worthwhile spending extra time and effort on preparing planting sites. Where soils are heavy and drainage poor, it may be well to consider raising the beds, as Teas will not tolerate wet feet. Regardless of soil type, the prior addition of organic matter is beneficial, while surface mulching with pea or lucerne hay, straw or similar materials helps to insulate the roots from extremes in temperature.

Teas ... vary in size and spread, and lend themselves to being used in many different situations, making a valuable contribution to the garden. Many of the nonclimbing varieties become medium-to-large bushes and can be used to great effect as shrubs in mixed garden plantings.

In time, Teas tend to become tall and spreading, so allow plenty of space between the individual plants. On the whole, they do not take kindly to transplanting and may take years to recover their vigour and flower size. Take this into consideration if the transplanted rose is to play an important role in a garden scheme, as it may sometimes be better to purchase a new plant of the same variety.

GROWING CONDITIONS

Although a situation in full sun is usually recommended for roses, Teas will also do well where sunlight is filtered through deciduous trees, while some of the darker varieties benefit from afternoon shade in very hot summers. Planting in shady areas may lead to taller, more spindly growth.

Tea roses do not have a natural dormancy period and if they receive a regular supply of water and fertiliser they will flower and grow almost continuously in warmer areas. If young plants are regularly watered for several years until their root systems are well developed, they will then survive on a stricter watering regime. Established bushes are capable of withstanding harsh conditions, but bloom quality and quantity will suffer if little water is available. When planting, the use of slow-release fertiliser mixed into the soil under the rose has been found to be beneficial, and the application of subsequent nutrients will need to be balanced with the available water supply—when water is limited, feed sparingly.

PRUNING

In 1931, Australian horticulturist George Knight wrote, 'Tea roses, to obtain the best results, should not be pruned heavily at any time; only a very light pruning is necessary. In fact, I think it advantageous to occasionally miss a season altogether', and this advice still holds good. Almost all Teas resent hard pruning. If they are pruned in the same severe manner as Hybrid Teas, the plants may take several years to recover, or may not recover at all!

There are many accounts of huge old Tea roses happily growing and blooming despite not being tended for many years. However, in most gardens some trimming is necessary to keep them to a manageable size, remove dead wood and encourage a more compact growth habit.

Because the beautiful foliage of Tea roses is as important a feature as the blooms, they should be trimmed between flowering flushes as you would other decorative shrubs, but with a light hand. Regular deadheading encourages continuous blooming, and shortening the stems by about three eyes when removing spent blooms and hips will produce a well-shaped plant.

Almost all Teas resent hard pruning. If they are pruned in the same severe manner as Hybrid Teas, the plants may take several years to recover, or may not recover at all!

Potted Teas need to be trimmed often to maintain the required shape and size, and those grown in gardens with limited space will also respond well to this treatment. Climbers may take three to five years to form their framework and flower to their full potential so it is best not to cut them back too hard when young.

Whether trimming a Tea rose between flowering flushes, or cutting back a large, old unpruned plant, the general rule of thumb is that no more than one third of the bush should be removed at any one time.

PROPAGATING

Most Tea roses strike easily from cuttings and grow well on their own roots. The taking of cuttings is an ideal and inexpensive way of increasing your own stock and making sure foundlings do not disappear altogether. Another alternative is to collect budwood in the summer and then contact your local rose nursery for their assistance in budding it on, if you do not feel confident about doing this yourself.

Cutting-propagated Teas may take a little longer to establish but soon catch up with budded roses. However, mainly for economic reasons, most of the Teas available today in Australia are grafted plants. Commonly used rootstocks that are all compatible with the Teas are the spring-flowering climbers *Rosa multiflora* for acid soils and 'Dr Huey' in alkaline situations, with 'Fortuneana' (*R.* x 'Fortuneana') widely used in south-western Australia's deep, sandy soils. Interestingly, the strongly growing 'Fortuneana' is being used in the United States in similar climates and soil conditions. *R. indica major*, 'Manettii' and *R. canina* were popular as rootstocks in earlier times in Australia and these roses can often still be seen growing in old gardens and in the countryside. Other stocks such as *R. rubiginosa* ('Eglantine') and 'Gloire des Rosomanes' ('Ragged Robin') were also used.

If there is any doubt about the compatibility of a stock with the soil or its scion, plant the rose with the graft about 10 centimetres below the ground surface to allow it to form its own roots.

RECOMMENDED VARIETIES

Teas are among the most versatile of roses. They vary in size and spread, and lend themselves to being used in many different situations, making a valuable contribution to the garden. Many of the nonclimbing varieties become medium-to-large bushes and can be used to great effect as shrubs in mixed garden plantings. They are also effective as hedges or screens, using roses of the same variety or a mixture of plants of similar growth habit. Have patience, as they can be a little slow to take off, but once they do you will be rewarded by their health and vigour, profusion of repeat bloom, and the beauty of their widely varying subtle colours.

Of the Teas featured in this book, the following are the varieties and their sports that we have found to be the most reliable and rewarding (double inverted commas indicate unidentified found roses and roses with incorrect names).

'Anna Olivier' and 'Lady Roberts'

'Comtesse de Labarthe' ('Duchesse de Brabant') and 'Mme Joseph Schwartz'

'G. Nabonnand' and 'Peace'

'Général Galliéni'

'Hugo Roller'

'Lady Hillingdon'

'Madame Antoine Mari'

'Madame Lambard'

'Maman Cochet' and 'White Maman Cochet'

'Marie Van Houtte'

'Monsieur Tillier'

'Mrs B. R. Cant'

'Mrs Dudley Cross'

'Papa Gontier'

"Papillon" (as sold in Australia; seen in U.S. as 'Beauté Inconstante')

'Rosette Delizy'

"Souvenir d'un Ami" (as sold in Australia and New Zealand)

TEAS SUITABLE FOR PARTICULAR SITUATIONS

Large pots	The best choice is a well-foliaged Tea rose which repeat-flowers quickly, such as 'Comtesse de La-barthe' ('Duchesse de Brabant'), 'Mme Antoine Mari', 'Marie Lambert' and 'Papa Gontier'
Usually thornless	'Alexander Hill Gray', 'G. Nabonnand' and 'Peace' (1902), 'Hugo Roller', 'Molly Sharman-Crawford' and 'Mrs Dudley Cross'
Winter blooms	'G. Nabonnand' and 'Peace' (1902), 'Général Scha-blikine', 'Lorraine Lee', "Octavus Weld", 'Papa Gontier', 'Safrano' and 'Isabella Sprunt'
Hot weather blooms	'Devoniensis', 'Étoile de Lyon', 'Général Galliéni' and 'Rosette Delizy'
Cut flowers	'Étoile de Lyon', 'Général Galliéni', 'Hugo Roller', 'Maman Cochet', 'Mrs B. R. Cant', "Triomphe du Luxembourg" (as sold in Australia) and 'William R. Smith'

A Close Look at Tea Roses

Adapted from the GROW-East Presentation at
Queens Botanical Garden, New York, June 13, 2010

LYNNE CHAPMAN, HILLARY MERRIFIELD AND BILLY WEST

Tea roses are derived from several repeat-flowering garden hybrid roses imported to Europe from China in the early 1800s at a time when there was a fascination for all things oriental. Originally called Tea-scented China Roses, these hybrids not only brought with them an exotic, multi-layered scent and novel colours, but together with other China roses were reliably repeat flowering. They were called the loveliest of roses for their elegance and subtle colours, and breeders produced over 2,000 Teas from 1820 to 1920. (SEE PLATE 4) But fashions changed, and after the First World War there was a gradual decline in popularity of the Teas, worldwide, until, by the 1950s they had all but disappeared.

The revival of interest in old garden roses in the second half of the 20th century saw a number of Teas being re-discovered. By then, Teas were rare in catalogues, and most of those we know today were found in old nursery gardens, public and private gardens, cemeteries and the sites of old homes. Of the 2,000 or so Teas that were bred, less than 200 are now listed in nurseries and collections worldwide. Unfortunately, over time, confusion in naming has occurred, and among these Teas are many wrongly named roses and many duplicates, and the actual number of extant Teas is even lower.

ACCORDING TO R. E.
"BOB" EDBERG, EDITOR
OF THE ONGOING
*ENCYCLOPAEDIA OF
ANTIQUE ROSES*, WHICH IS AN
ANNOTATED REPUBLICATION
OF THE ROSE PLATES IN
JOURNAL DES ROSES, "THE
FRENCH *JOURNAL DES ROSES*,
ISSUED CONTINUOUSLY EVERY
MONTH FROM JANUARY, 1877,
THROUGH AUGUST, 1914, WAS
THE SINGLE MOST IMPORTANT
CHRONICLE OF ANTIQUE ROSES
EVER PUBLISHED." FOR MORE
ABOUT THE *ENCYCLOPAEDIA OF
ANTIQUE ROSES* VOLUMES AND
PROJECT, SEE www.oldroses.
com/encyclopaedia.htm.
　　　　　　　—EDITORS

When starting *Tea Roses: Old Roses for Warm Gardens* (SEE PLATE 4) in 2000, we envisaged a small handbook describing all the Teas available in Australia at the time but, as we collected these, we realised there were problems with many of the names: one rose being sold under several names and several varieties being sold under one name, and roses that, when compared with the original descriptions, were clearly misidentified. We then had a major research project on our hands as, although we agree that a rose is beautiful no matter what it is called, we do believe that finding the correct name is important. It establishes a living connection with history and, from a practical point of view, provides information about what to expect of the rose—colour, growth habit and where it would do best in a garden.

Investigating the identity of our old Teas, we quickly became aware that very often we were not dealing with roses that had come down through time with an unbroken link to their original names. Many were re-identified foundlings, sometimes given a name on the strength of little more than a hunch. Right from the beginning we were rigorous in our approach to rose identification. We needed to become Tea rose detectives—scientific in our approach—putting up hypotheses on the identity of each of the Teas and then looking at all the evidence we had accumulated for or against.

As our research progressed, we became increasingly aware of just how much rose literature and catalogue description is derived from earlier writings rather than from first-hand observation and experience. For this reason, we determined to limit ourselves to the varieties we could personally grow and observe.

If we were asked to designate one characteristic shared by all Teas, it would probably be variability, variability and more variability. Teas, with their ever-changing colours and flower shapes, are never the same from one season to another, or even from day to day. Colours can vary over an extraordinarily wide range. Petal numbers can double up when the flowers develop more slowly in cold weather, prickles can be shed as the wood ages and even the fragrance can change over the course of a day and as the flower matures.

This variability is part of their charm for Tea rose aficionados. But it also presents enormous challenges when trying to recognise or identify them. So how did we make decisions?

We had to get to know our roses extremely well. There are no shortcuts in this sort of work and having six authors/growers enabled us to closely observe the roses in different locations and compare our findings. Our Teas were grown in gardens of different soil types, and they needed to be observed, photographed and recorded over the seasons and over the years, as flowers on young bushes can look quite different from those on mature plants. We designed special Tea rose data sheets on which we entered not only descriptions of all parts of the rose but also preserved specimens, photographs and scans of living material. The completed data sheets were eventually correlated to produce the Distinguishing Features tables which accompany the descriptions of roses in the book.

Early editions of the *Journal des Roses* often contained detailed descriptions of Teas.

Accurate and detailed descriptions are an important part of our book but unfortunately not common in much of the literature we consulted. Some early descriptions in rose journals and books are very detailed, for example those in earlier editions of the *Journal des Roses,* but others consist of just a few words or sentences, often sparse and unhelpful, for example "full," "pink," or "large, fine and very full." While many catalogues simply repeated the introducers' descriptions, there were a number that provided invaluable first-hand observations.

We therefore needed to compare our Teas with descriptions and portraits in the rose literature of the past, translating this where necessary. The results of our wide-ranging literature searches were compiled into chronological tables which were of great assistance in seeing if descriptions of Teas had remained the same or changed over time, as in the case of 'Triomphe du Luxembourg'. The rose described at the time of its introduction in the 1830s is clearly completely different from the one re-introduced under this name in the 1980s.

Our Teas were grown in gardens of different soil types, and they needed to be observed, photographed and recorded over the seasons and over the years, as flowers on young bushes can look quite different from those on mature plants.

Old nursery catalogues were an important source of information about which Teas had come to Australia (about 1,000 in all). Information from the catalogues was compiled to show the dates Tea varieties were sold by nurseries, known to be in private collections, or referred to as living specimens in journals and books. This showed us the distribution of Teas and gaps caused by loss of popularity and if and when they were re-introduced. The source of the re-introductions was also noted. (A small section of this work, relevant to the Teas in the book, can be found in Appendix IV of the book, and the full document is available on request from the authors.)

Comparing Teas in interstate and overseas gardens with those we grew in Western Australia was also important, especially if we could see reliably named specimens. We travelled widely, and sometimes overseas experts came to us in Australia. We would like to acknowledge the valuable assistance given to us by rose experts, nurserymen and gardeners in Australia and around the world, who generously shared their opinions, knowledge, research material and photographs with us.

When researching the identity of old roses, much of the time we dealt, and are still dealing today, with incomplete information, with ambiguities and contradictions. The work is often a slow and painstaking puzzle, piecing together the small amounts of material accumulated over time. But if the research is approached with rigour—applying basic scientific processes of inquiry, the testing of hypotheses, sorting fact from opinion—we can arrive at a point of certainty, even if sometimes this means we are certain that we do not have enough information to decide the correct name of a particular rose.

Take the cover rose on our book, 'Comtesse de Labarthe'—or is it 'Duchesse de Brabant'? Actually, it is both, one rose with two names. We know from early records that the original name was 'Comtesse de Labarthe', 1857 and, as this name has precedence, and also because the rose was always known under this name in Australia (eventually shortened to 'Countess Bertha'!), we used 'Comtesse de Labarthe' in the book. If we had been living in the United States we probably would have used 'Duchesse de Brabant', as this name has been in use there since the early 1870s.

We have found out a lot about this rose, including that in recent times it has been designated as an Earth-Kind™ rose and in the past, as detailed in a letter from Mrs Roosevelt[1] that it was Colonel Theodore Roosevelt's favourite rose. But we have not found out why the name changed in the U.S. We do have some theories, including that in 1854 a pink Centifolia was released called 'Duc de Brabant' which seems to have become 'Duchesse de Brabant' by 1859. So, could it have been confused with a Tea rose of the same colour?

The Duchesse de Brabant in question is Marie Henriette, Duchesse de Brabant from 1853 when she married the Belgian Duc, Leopold, to 1865 when he became King. Marie-Henriette—known to have been fonder of roses than of her husband—may, as Brent Dickerson has suggested,[2] have expressed a liking for this rose and, as these things do, it morphed from the Duchess de Brabant's favourite rose to 'Duchesse de Brabant'.

That is quite plausible. But it does not explain why the renaming was only widespread in the U.S. In Europe, the rose remained 'Comtesse de Labarthe', although 'Duchesse de Brabant' was listed as a synonym from the 1880s[3]. This is an unusual problem which we hope continued study will be able to resolve.

Most of the Teas in our book came into one of five categories:

1. Teas that were correctly identified. Fortunately, this is the largest group, although at times we questioned the identity of all the Teas we grew. How did we verify that the names were correct? (Much of this work was done in an Australian context, but the methods are applicable elsewhere). We started with the only three Teas to remain in commerce in Australia from the time of their introduction up to the present day: 'Lady Hillingdon', 1910, 'Mrs Herbert Stevens', 1910, and 'Lorraine Lee', 1924. Now mistakes can happen. Roses in commerce can get muddled over time. So we checked these against descriptions and portraits from the time they were first introduced and found they matched and, if we needed more proof, each has a climbing sport with which it tallies in all but habit.

The above are later Teas, while an early Tea, the superbly fragrant 'Devoniensis', 1838, also has a climbing sport. It was well-documented, especially in English-language publications, including Henry Curtis's *The Beauties of the Rose*[4]. (SEE PLATE 5) 'Devoniensis' was absent from nursery catalogues for a time but continued to be known and grown in Australian gardens. So, (1) it has survived as a named rose, (2) it matches early detailed descriptions and paintings and (3) it has a sport that is identical in all but habit. If a rose can tick all these boxes we are satisfied it is correctly identified.

Another early Tea that ticks all the boxes is 'Safrano', 1839. Although it opens to a fairly loose flower, the half open bud is beautiful. This rose was very popular as a cut flower over a century ago. This is another rose with a continuous history in Australian gardens, and it is also a well-documented rose. Not only do we have portraits but also quite detailed descriptions. (SEE PLATE 8)

And also a sport, not climbing this time but a colour sport , the lemon yellow 'Isabella Sprunt' which was noted by the Reverend James Sprunt of Kenansville, North Carolina, in 1855. In a letter to Henry Ellwanger[5], Reverend Sprunt describes how he pruned back his large bush of 'Safrano' and, the early summer being very dry, the top of the bush died. However, six or eight strong shoots grew up from ground level and one differed from the rest in that it produced "fine yellow flowers." This sport he named for one of his daughters. A cutting was sent to Isaac Buchanan, Florist and Nurseryman of New York, who introduced 'Isabella Sprunt' into commerce in 1865. It went on to become one of the most popular Teas for use as cut flowers.

If we had had any doubts about these roses, they would have been dispelled when, in 2003, Lynne Chapman's bush of 'Isabella Sprunt' reverted to 'Safrano'!

The ultimate Tea verified by its sports is 'Maman Cochet'. Not only does it have a climbing sport but also a colour sport, 'White Maman Cochet', which itself has a climbing sport. There are also several red sports, and, interestingly, 'Maman Cochet' produced sports in both the United States and Australia at around the same time[6].

By contrast, 'Alexander Hill Gray', 1911, has neither a sport, nor an early plate that we have been able to find. And there are none of the detailed botanical descriptions in journals that accompanied the early Teas. Descriptions are usually brief—"deep lemon yellow" or "soft yellow, fragrant, double,"—which could apply to many, many

'Maman Cochet' from R.G. Elliott. *The Australasian Rose Book,* c. 1920, Melbourne: Whitcombe and Tombs, p. 49.

roses. Even its tendency to thornlessness is not mentioned, but we are confident that 'Alexander Hill Gray' is correctly named. It was a popular exhibition rose and grown under glass in cooler climates. Awarded the British National Rose Society's gold medal soon after its release, it was still being recommended for exhibition purposes in Australia in the 1950s.

When an unnamed yellow rose was found in an Australian cemetery 30 years later, nurseryman Roy Rumsey was able to identify it as 'Alexander Hill Gray'. Roy had a lot of experience with roses, firstly at the leading

Australian rose nursery Hazelwoods when he was very young, then at Hilliers in England and later while training at Kew. Back in Australia, he worked for his father for a while and then started a rose nursery with wife Heather. He had handled thousands of plants of the very popular 'Alexander Hill Gray' throughout his career, so was delighted to see it again and was able to introduce it back into commerce in Australia in the 1980s. In the U.S., 'Alexander Hill Gray' was reintroduced from a plant bought from nurseryman Roy Hennessey.

If we were asked to designate one characteristic shared by all Teas, it would probably be variability, variability and more variability. Teas, with their ever-changing colours and flower shapes, are never the same from one season to another, or even from day to day.

So it is possible to positively identify a rose if you have access to a reliable authority with firsthand knowledge, such as the two Roys, Hennessey and Rumsey, but unfortunately that does not often happen.

Even very detailed descriptions have not stopped mistakes being made, which leads to the second category:

2. Impostors incorrectly called Teas. A climber masquerading as a Tea is "Sombreuil". That this is not a Tea has been known for many years but how long does it take to get a message across? When the Australian rosarian David Ruston conducted a pleblecite in 2009 to find the world's top ten Tea roses, what came in at No. 6? This rose, superb, but not a Tea! The true Tea, 'Sombreuil', or 'Mlle de Sombreuil', is a shrub that can make a fine pillar rose, but it is not a climber.

Another climber that is not a Tea has been sold for many years as the Tea, 'Monsieur Tillier', 1891. It was sourced by Graham Stuart Thomas from a Paris garden, probably the Roseraie de l'Haÿ, as 'Monsieur Tillier'. It was marketed by L. Arthur Wyatt in the early 1970s through his English nursery and later sold by the Peter Beales Nursery, again as 'Monsieur Tillier'. Now the Tea 'Monsieur Tillier' is a shrub and unlike some Teas it does not have a climbing sport; but a rose widely sold under this name is most definitely a climber, and it is in our book under the study name "Monsieur Tillier ex Beales".

Ongoing research has shown that this rose is in fact the Climbing Hybrid Tea, 'Marie Nabonnand'. We know this name is correct, even to the extent of having confirmation from members of the Nabonnand family who still grow the original rose, so we are very pleased to report that the Beales Nursery in England is now listing the rose as 'Marie Nabonnand'.

But what of the Tea 'Monsieur Tillier'? Is it correctly named, or should it be called 'Archiduc Joseph', a Tea released a year later? A rose was distributed from the United Kingdom in the 1970s under the name 'Archiduc Joseph' but at the same time it was known and grown in the United States, in Australia and in New Zealand under the name 'Monsieur Tillier'. We lean towards 'Monsieur Tillier' as the correct name, mainly because of the existence of these old, named plants.

But both roses were released within a year of each other and had very similar descriptions, even looked very similar — so we are open to discussion on this one … To add to the mix, 'Monsieur Tillier' aka 'Archiduc Joseph' is also often confused with another two roses, 'General Schablikine' and 'Madame Lambard'. 'Monsieur Tillier', Australia's favourite Tea, is in a class of its own, beautiful, vigorous and free-flowering, with a strong fragrance of both tea and fruit.

3. Incorrectly identified Teas, where we have been able to establish the correct name. A Tea is in commerce around the world today as 'Souvenir d'Elise Vardon', a rose which early colour descriptions tell us was light straw yellow or yellowish white to delicate light pink.

The rose often sold under this name seems too brightly coloured to match these descriptions, but we know that the colours of Teas can vary. So we needed more to go on, and Paquet and Rouillard provided more in the year it was introduced, describing the peduncles of 'Souvenir d'Elise Vardon' as "showing little brownish hairs along their whole length' and the receptacle also as 'sprinkled with little brownish hairs."

Glands or hairs or both, they are *not* present on the shiny, smooth pedicels of the rose sold as 'Souvenir d'Elise Vardon' today, so careful observations from the 1850s gave us proof that this rose was misidentified. But what was it? Fortunately, the same rose is also in commerce under another name, its correct name, 'Mlle Franziska Kruger', 1879 and, as well as early descriptions matching, we have the proof of identity from a colour sport, 'Blumenschmidt', which occurred in Germany and was released in 1905. Like its parent, it can show a hard green centre which occasionally contains many tiny buds. 'Blumenschmidt' is not available in Australia at the present time, so we were delighted to see fine plants at the Antique Rose Emporium in Texas.

4. Teas incorrectly identified, where we have suggested a probable identity. The plate of 'Mme Hoste' from *The Garden*, 1894[7] shows a yellowish-white Tea, but in Australia a very different, bright pink Tea is being sold under that name. How it came to be given such an obviously wrong name is not certain as even on its palest day it does not resemble the plate or early descriptions but it has been growing in the garden of a cottage in South Australia as 'Mme Hoste' for many years. (SEE PLATE 6) It bears likenesses to 'Maman Cochet', although the blooms are usually smaller and there are other differences. The parentage of 'Maman Cochet' is 'Marie Van Houtte' (seed) x 'Mme Lambard' (pollen), and we have suggested this rose is another with the same parentage, 'Auguste Comte', 1895.

Many rosarians use the resources of the Help Me Find website, and here we encountered this rose as a foundling in Sardinia and also, to our surprise, discovered that it could be purchased under four different names in Europe: in Italy as 'Mme Scipion Cochet,' and also as 'Castello della Scala' (a reintroduced rose); as 'Maman Cochet' in the United Kingdom, and in France under the name 'Auguste Comte'. It is also in the United States, as we have seen it as one of the roses under the name 'Niles Cochet'.

We have noticed that the same foundling will be discovered in several places, sometimes several countries, probably indicating that it was once a popular variety and also that it is a an exceptionally good survivor. The rose sold today as 'Princesse de Sagan' is another that we have a tentative identification for. The original Tea was dark red with semi-double blooms. The lighter, double "Not Princesse de Sagan" came to Australia from the Europa-Rosarium Sangerhausen in Germany, undoubtedly wrongly named. The same rose is often found unlabeled in old Australian gardens.

We feel this rose is 'Professeur Ganiviat', a rose our compilation of nursery catalogues[8] tells us was sold widely in Australia in the early 1900s.

Other probabilities are covered in our book, including that the rose known in Australia as "Papillon", seemingly the same rose as "Bermuda's Papa Gontier", is 'Beauté Inconstante'.

Our research has continued since the publication of *Tea Roses,* and a rose not included in the book is a beautiful foundling, one of many unnamed roses rescued by Australia's best known rose rustler, Pat Toolan. Called "Mrs Good's Special Tea" after the owner of the garden in which it was found, this distinctive rose has an unusual colouration and form, has few prickles and a violet-like fragrance. (SEE PLATE 10) Extensive comparisons with early descriptions and portraits led us to the conclusion that this rose is almost certainly 'Marquise de Vivens', 1885. (SEE PLATE 6) We know that 'Marquise de Vivens' was grown in the garden at Anlaby, South Australia, around 1900 as the labels from that garden are still in existence (Appendix V of *Tea Roses*)[9] but unfortunately there are no roses left from that time.

We would love to put this rose in the positively identified category as we are 99% sure we have identified it correctly, but there is one more box to be ticked and if we can find a named plant somewhere we can change the name from "Mrs Good's Special Tea" to 'Marquise de Vivens'.

5. Teas that we have been unable to identify as yet. One of our favourite Teas is known to us as "Octavus Weld", as it was found on the grave of Dr. Octavus Weld in a cemetery in South Australia. This is a rose we have wanted to identify for many years, so imagine our delight when we saw it in Gregg Lowery's garden in Sebastopol, California. Gregg calls it "enchanting" in the *Vintage Gardens Book of Roses*[10] but it is another unidentified rose with a study name, "Angels Camp Tea". Coincidentally, this plant was also found in a cemetery, at Angels Camp, an old gold mining centre east of San Francisco. (SEE PLATE 7)

A Note on the Possibility of Growing Tea Roses
in the American North

Our practice has always been to rely on our own experience and observations, and as we rarely have frosts where we live (Zone 11), let alone prolonged frozen spells, we have no first-hand knowledge of growing Tea roses in colder climates to share.

So we were very interested to hear about the experiences of people in the United States who are growing Teas in colder areas; and what we heard supports what some of the English and American writers were saying a hundred years ago:

> Grow Teas on their own roots. Then, if you do have a particularly bitter winter and roses are severely cut back, they (and not the rootstock) can re-shoot from the base

> Mulch well to provide maximum insulation from temperature extremes

> Do not prune Teas in winter. Teas do not have a natural dormancy, so if they need to be trimmed back or tidied up, wait until ALL danger of frost is over

> Utilise warm walls and more sheltered parts of the garden

> Consider growing Teas in large pots that can be moved inside for the winter

> Be aware that some varieties are much more cold hardy than others

Tea roses are capable of living to a great age once they are well established, but they are most vulnerable during their "childhood" when they may need additional winter care such as mounding with earth or covering with vegetation.

Many of us have seen old, abandoned Teas that have survived the climate extremes of a century or more. These are roses that were probably given care in their early years but have been untended for decades, and they are splendid strong, healthy plants.

Wherever we went during our time in the U.S., we heard stories of how last winter was the most punishing for 80 years, with losses amongst many different classes of rose but that, on the whole, Teas on their own roots fared no worse or no better than Hybrid Teas.

This is most interesting, and we will be watching out for reports from the various test gardens around the U.S. to see whether some varieties are consistently hardier than others.

Because the bloom colour is so variable, the rose is known in the U.S. under several names: "Angels Camp Tea", "Angels Camp White Tea" and "Angels Camp Pink Tea". And in Australia we know and love it as "Octavus Weld" (Renamed Old Rose) which brings us full circle—while we would like to find the original name, the most important thing is that the rose survives and is again in commerce under its study names.

When we embarked on what has been an amazing tour we wanted to spread the message that Tea roses, old and new, are not only beautiful and rewarding but, in the right climate, they are long lived and tough. If you grow Teas we hope we have inspired you to plant more; if you don't, we hope you will try them—and we also hope you will enjoy reading about these wonderful roses.

NOTE: A trial garden of Tea roses, plants provided by Roses Unlimited of South Carolina, has been planted in the Queens Botanical Garden, New York City, as of spring, 2010. Curator Karl Mckoy plans to evaluate the roses for local conditions. With world climate change it will be most interesting to see how these roses perform in what is, for us, the other side of the globe. Good luck, Karl—and we will be watching your results with avid interest.

[1] McFarland, J. Horace, "Colonel Roosevelt's Favorite Rose," The American Rose Annual, 1920, pp. 31–32.

[2] Dickerson, B. Personal Communication, 2009.

[3] Schwartz, J. "Synonymie des Roses," Journal des Roses, January, 1882, pp. 44–46.

[4] Curtis, H. The Beauties of the Rose, 1850–53, London.

[5] Ellwanger, H.B. "American Roses," The Gardener's Monthly and Horticulturist, Vol. XXI, No. 261, September 1880, pp. 258–62.

[6] Chapman, L. et al, Tea Roses: Old Roses for Warm Gardens, 2008, Dural, NSW: Rosenberg Publishing, p. 136.

[7] The Garden: An Illustrated Weekly Journal of Horticulture in All its Branches, 1894, London, plate 952.

[8] Chapman, L. et al, Tea Roses: Old Roses for Warm Gardens, 2008, Dural, NSW: Rosenberg Publishing, p. 216.

[9] Chapman, L. et al, Tea Roses: Old Roses for Warm Gardens, Dural, NSW: Rosenberg Publishing, 2008, p. 221.

[10] Lowery, G. & Robinson, P. Vintage Gardens Book of Roses, 2006, Sebastopol, CA: Vintage Gardens, p. 82.

THE AUTHOR

Roy Hennessey (1897–1968) (*ca.*1942) from *Hennessey on Roses*, Second Edition, 1943 (Portland, Oregon), a slender, self-published volume that went through three editions and firmly established Hennessey's reputation for being both perceptive and opinionated. Roy Hennessey was at the pinnacle of his career as a roseman during the 1940s and early 1950s.

Hennessey Revisited: Sustainability, *or* The Accidental Environmentalist

JAMES DELAHANTY

The golden years of Roy Hennessey's participation in the rose world spanned the middle of the 20th century, from the desperate thirties to the expansionist sixties. If sustainability is considered to be "meeting the needs of the present generation without compromising the ability of future generations to meet their own needs," it is unlikely that Hennessey ever considered at any great length or depth that particular problem in the everyday realities of physical survival in the Depression thirties and the martial forties, or even in the Cold War fifties and early sixties. His answers to the ills of democracy tended to be more democracy with lightning-like responses to public opinion polls as opposed to more careful and preservationist attitudes toward the environment or nature. Nevertheless, the effects of some of his initiatives were to promote a better future without sacrificing the present in the form of the use of beneficial insects, bettering the species, and closely relating the rose to its best location.

USE OF BENEFICIAL INSECTS

In viewing Hennessey in the light of a sustainability meme, it is wise to recall the definition of history as a chronology of the past viewed in terms of the problems of the present. In short, we must not overestimate the weight Hennessey attached to the expression of some of his views that were asides to him but that are fraught with foresight to us. For example, in 1953, an idyll appears under his authorship in *The Rose Annual* of the National Rose Society of Great Britain. In this allegorical tale, Hennessey imagines a world where rose fanciers learn that the fuss and feathers associated with rose growing are totally unnecessary, that weekends devoted to spraying noxious chemicals may be banished, and that a balance of rose predators and natural enemies of predators can be achieved in time through the use of companion plantings and the avoidance of a monoculture that rewards insects by gathering all of their food preferences in one place at one time. Such a statement would seem to be an outlier in the writings of Hennessey, who recommends the use of various chemicals such as ethylene dichloride for thrips in his 1940–1941 columns in the *Oregon Journal,* as well as in various sections of his book, *Hennessey on Roses*. However, in a column in the *Oregon Journal* dated May 18, 1941, Hennessey makes the following assertion:

> I, myself, in my acre and a half of research, experimental and display garden, have long relied on the natural enemies of the aphid, not only from a consideration of the cost of continual and thorough spraying, but also because I had recognized two of the friendly insects and realized that spraying would kill good bugs as well as bad.

He goes on to identify the assassin fly (or one of them) as a more efficient bug killer than the ladybug because it attacks the aphids directly rather than indirectly through its larvae. The other predator he identifies is podabrus, a local beetle that ingests aphids, mealy bugs, and spit bugs with great industry and dispatch. As to the relative weight of economic versus therapeutic values on the decision not to spray, it is probably impossible to separate Hennessey's consideration of economy versus the efficiency of natural predators. As always with Hennessey, the strands of self-interest and beneficial rosarian practice create an impenetrable weave. Hennessey's statement did not go uncontroverted. As often happened with columns in which Hennessey's advice or opinion was controversial or contra the

ROSE PLANTING INSTRUCTIONS

Cut No Roots!   **Leave All Roots On!**   **Cut No Roots!**

Plant your roses as soon as received, providing the ground is not frozen too hard to receive them. Hard frozen ground is the only reason for not planting roses. The bushes do not mind cold or wet.

When you open the bundle see that roots are kept moist. Do not expose them to drying winds or sun for a moment. Keep roots in a bucket of water during planting operations. Should the roses seem to be dried out through shipping delay soak roots and tops in water for 72 hours. They may die if planted when they are dried out.

Put no manure, trash or fertilizer in hole where bush is planted. It may cause root canker or burn the roots. Put only clean soil or subsoil on all sides of roots. This is VERY IMPORTANT. Do not ignore it. Never plant new rose bushes in soil from which old roses have been removed. Always change soil from a bed of annuals or similar source.

A CONE OF SOIL must be made under the center of each plant, where the roots spread downward in all directions, to avoid an air pocket. Do not put your bushes in a flat trench or hole and try to force the center flat against the soil without this support. In planting make the hole or trench large and deep enough to accommodate all roots when spread out and down at an angle of 30 degrees. Plant the union of rose and understock well above soil level. The HIGHER THE UNION the healthier and longer lived your rose will be.

TEN EXTRA MINUTES spent in planting each bush PROPERLY will give you enormously greater results in years to come. The big roots on my plants will work miracles if allowed to.

With your bush placed work soil among roots, gradually firming it down until the hole is nearly full. Then trample firmly over your now well covered roots until you could not possibly pull up the bush with your hands. If you are planting in mud omit the tramping, but tamp soil firmly from time to time.

Now fill the remainder of the hole with water, even though you are planting in mud, to carry earth down into air pockets that may be left and would cause roots in such pockets to decay instead of growing. Finish with a final layer of loose soil.

If you have received bushes having more than four or five canes, thin out the surplus canes, allowing no more than above number on a newly planted bush. Remove with a clean cut at base of the plant, and protect all wounds with tree paint or emulsified asphalt.

HILLING: All canes are to be completely covered with soil after the bush is planted, either in winter or spring. For winter covering in severe climates like Minnesota and Montana a foot of loose material such as peat or anything else of that nature that is handy will do, tho soil should be used if other material is not available this is to be covered when hard frozen in order to prevent early thaws. This may also be used the following summer to protect and keep cool the roots as well as protect the union of the rose and the understock which is the weakest part of the rose.

Be sure and paint the huge wounds on the ends of the canes to prevent drying out and possible dying of these canes—there has been some loss of plants by ignoring this factor as it is impossible to handle a huge plant like mine in the same manner as a small one.

—3—

Rose Planting Instructions, page 3 of Hennessey's 1949–50 catalogue. The flavor of the irascible Hennessey comes through in his provocative prose. Rightly regarded as dogmatic, Hennessey was, nevertheless, honest and invariably based his advice on long and accurate observation.

Even small city lots provide enough garden space in the vast majority of cases to permit of soil being taken from a bed of annuals, etc., for temporary use in the rose garden. Always discard the top layer of trash by skimming it off with a shovel, and HILL YOUR BUSHES WITH THIS CLEAN SOIL. Do not hill with soil contaminated by old rose material.

Uncover your bushes gradually in spring, exposing only a portion of the canes at one time, so the new growth can harden gradually.

ROSES UNIVERSALLY GOOD

ANGELS MATEU, Pat. 174—A translation of this name would be Angels Mantle, and really there is no rose holding this color as well. A big colorful orange coral rose which has the most perfect color stability of any rose of this color to date. These big fully double lovely blooms are produced incessantly. Has very glossy bright green foliage. It has the fragrance of ripe blackberries mingled with that of honey. I have improved the plant of this variety so much that its originator would scarcely believe it.
$1.50 each; $15.00 doz. No further discount.

BETTY UPRICHARD—A striking two-toned rose with backs of petals coppery carmine, inside a soft salmon pink, this vigorous plant is one of the finest garden varieties for cooler gardens although it will do well anywhere with lots of long pointed buds. This variety never sulks in heat.
$1.50

CATHERINE KORDES—Perfectly formed and very long lasting blooms that in the hot east are deep pink but in coastal areas, sometimes is even deep red. This fine rose has almost no bad habits and has the form of its child—Crimson Glory. Crop failure.

CECILE WALTER—This splendid rose grows and develops its bloom in full hot sun, a blessing for hot gardens. It has a remarkably long bud, opening to an informal blossom of soft coral pink, flushed copper, overcast with gold, much the colors that made Los Angeles so beloved in spite of its terrible blackspotting. Cecile Walter, on the contrary, is enormously resistant to blackspot. After going out in the garden and having the huge bloom looking at me from a six-foot plant (that's the way I grow them) I have decided that I want my blooms to bend their neck and look at me. I do not care as much for the pancake on the pencil idea............$1.50

CHRISTOPHER STONE—Nearly the perfect rose. Rich unfading scarlet crimson, with pointed bud of great beauty, and big delicately waved petals on the gorgeous blooms. It grows and opens its buds perfectly in any climate, with absolutely stable color in sun or shade. It is an unbelievably heavy bloomer, is sweetly fragrant, and is low enough in growth to make the finest kind of bedding or border rose. A border of Christopher Stone is a sight not easily forgotten. It is noted among its other virtues for keeping the fresh brilliance of its velvet petals until they drop. I have put an enormous amount of vigor into this variety. Many who have this variety have never been greatly enthused simply because they did not have the Hennessey plants. On my plants it is a wonderful and different variety. In a bed in front of my house I have had many blooms six inches across. Low growing. Around Portland, Oregon, there are driveways bordered with several hundred plants in each one which open the eyes to the results that can be had with Hennessey Plants of this variety..................................$1.50

—4—

Roses Universally Good, page 4 of Hennessey's 1949–50 catalogue. Note how Hennessey claims (in his description of 'Christopher Stone' for instance) to be able to dramatically improve the variety through selection of budwood. This may have been smart marketing, bravado, or—maybe even—the truth. Many people believe, for instance, that historically great varieties—such as 'Peace'—have declined over the years because nurserymen over-propagated and selected any budwood willy-nilly for the next crop of plants.

conventional wisdom, the newspaper ran a column adjacent to his column in which the views of more conventional rosarians were included.

One of Hennessey's many mantras was the notion that the rose was such a wonderful plant that it could and would withstand the most ridiculous treatments devised by well-meaning "eggsperts" and still produce sufficient bloom to encourage the repetition of foolish practices. The idea that roses were tough plants, capable of surviving and thriving despite foul treatment by the well-meaning and the overly educated, permeates Hennessey's writings and catalogs. He honestly believed that the methods he advocated were optimal and geared to providing the best possible environment for roses to fulfill their intermediate destiny of plentiful bloom, color, and fragrance. He acknowledges that there are other methods but regards them as inferior and the result of ignorance of the subject, especially the lack of first-hand experience. According to Hennessey, it isn't that roses cannot or won't survive inferior treatment but rather that optimal treatment yields such rich rewards that there is no real justification for doing otherwise except ignorance or profound cussedness. In his very first column for the *Oregon Journal*, July 28, 1940, Hennessey proclaims that "you can do almost anything with the rose—except grubbing it out and leaving it on top of the ground—and it will grow and bloom." He liked that statement so much that he used it as the heading for his next eight weekly columns. The first chapter in *Hennessey on Roses* attributes the popularity of the Queen of Flowers not to its fragrance or beauty of bloom but to the toughness of a plant that could be "yanked up by its roots, plunked into a shallow hole in the ground, and thereafter practically forgotten, whereas the majority of wild plants so treated cannot."

NEW AND "NOVELTY," MEANING "BETTER"

Another Hennessey notion that ran contrary to developing trends was an idea he expressed repeatedly in his participation in the American Rose Society's Proof of the Pudding—from 1934 until his abrupt departure in 1941. In this process of evaluation of new roses by those in the busi-

ness, Hennessey frequently maintained that any new rose had to be justified by its superiority to a rose already on the market—or there was no
point in introducing it. If a new rose did not exceed others in its class,
it should be summarily dismissed. He evaluates 'Dickson's Red': "there
are so many better that it is not needed." As for the Kordes 'Holstein',
"since we have Karen Poulsen of exactly the same type and color, what
excuse is there for Holstein, as it black-spots far worse?" Or the hapless
'Home Sweet Home', "it is simply an infe-
rior Dame Edith Helen." The Howard and
Smith 'Poinsettia' elicits an outraged "what
excuse is there for this rose. … Southport is
better." 'McGredy's Sunset' gets dismissed
several years in a row as "nothing more
than a sport of Goldenes Mainz."

*Hennessey proclaims that "you
can do almost anything with
the rose—except grubbing it
out and leaving it on top of
the ground—and it will grow
and bloom."*

At times Hennessey lamented the fol-
ly of judges who ignore the standards of
judging in not downgrading the scores of
new roses for "the lack of novelty." Hennessey's notion of "novelty" was
shaded toward the idea of better than the existing cultivars, or introducing something not before seen. In Chapter 25 of *Hennessey on Roses,* he
expounded on the conditions and qualities to be found in an ideal test
garden. In particular he argued that a penalty "of not less than twenty-
five percent must be assessed for lack of novelty, even though the plant
and bloom of any new rose are fully as good as an existing, similar rose."
Hennessey believed this to be essential so as to forestall the appearance of
a substantial number of roses that merely duplicated existing rose varieties at higher prices to the exasperation of the rose-buying public.

Hennessey applied the same standards of superiority in the new to
those roses patented. He could not see the point of patenting an inferior
rose and was dismissive of roses he thought not worth the time or money.
He found 'Mme Cochet-Cochet' so "lacking in vigor and with too few
petals that he could not see the excuse for a patent." 'Token' was reviewed
but once, and he noted that he could "see no excuse for patenting such a
rose as the color was washed out and it had the bad Pernet center."

On the other hand, this desire to preserve and promote a truly fine red rose of the Hybrid Polyantha type by growth characteristics (although classified as a Hybrid Tea) blinded him to other considerations and justified his long contrary and invidious promotion of a rose called 'Nigger Boy', an Australian rose by G. Knight. The name of this rose was putatively chosen to honor the aborigines of that continent. (This flies in the face of dictionary assertions that the term carried negative and prejudicial connotations in the English language since at least 1750.) Nevertheless, Knight refused to change the name of the rose and asserted his intention of honoring the aborigines, and Hennessey supported him in these assertions. Hennessey's support of this rose as the best in its class of a low-growing bedding rose stretched over a 20-year period, from its mention in his test gardens in the spring of 1941 through his fall 1961/spring 1962 catalog, in which he boasted of having supported the rose for 20 years as the best in its class until the next year, when he would introduce a rose created by Hennessey/Jones called 'Flaming Ruby' that would supplant it. Hennessey's support of 'Nigger Boy' was so strong that, when pressured not to sell the rose because of its name in the early 1950s, he took out a half-page advertisement in the October 1951 *American Rose,* advertising Hennessey's Roses as "THE HOME OF NIGGER BOY."

But as an integral part of promoting the rose by presenting it only at its best, he would sell 'Nigger Boy' only in groups of six. In fact, Hennessey would sell the massed border planting roses *"only in groups of six"* or not at all. His contention was that these roses were poor as specimen plants and elicited scorn and derision unless they were sited en masse to give the effect that justified their continued presence on the rose scene. That this position probably cost him customers seemed not to matter any more than his statement that a cost-saving relocation of his nursery would not yield lower prices but a better product. A better rose product also justified the extra effort to dig proper holes for roses with humongous roots that should not be reduced or cut or coiled. Customers reported messages written around the edges and sides of postcards urging "CUT NO ROOTS!!!" or threatening cessation of sales to customers who disobeyed his imperatives.

Hennessey also spent a great deal of time and effort attempting to improve the performance of particular plants whose blooms warranted trying to remove impediments to their greatness. 'Paul's Scarlet Climber' is listed as "mostly a once bloomer," by Vintage Gardens, at the lowest level of repeat by Russian River Rose Company, and as blooming "less so in the fall" by High Country Roses. The other continental company offering this rose is Hortico, and they simply refer to it as a "repeater" without defining the term, although promising to do so at some unspecified date. As early as 1941 Hennessey advertised 'Paul's Scarlet Climber' as "ever-blooming." For the next 20 years, he advertised this rose as ever-blooming and in the 1961–1962 catalog he advertised it thusly:

Hennessey's Ever-Blooming Paul's Scarlet Climber

Now here is a Paul's Scarlet that WILL give steady bloom. ... Now this is guaranteed to rebloom. Also for the benefit of last year's customers, if any do not rebloom, just a word will bring a replacement, for all I had last year were replanted ones that had rebloomed but, mind you BUT, as this rose is product of selection, very definitely, under some conditions it will have the recurring wood damaged, as it is not stabilized nor a sport, it will revert. That is why the guarantee. It is definitely a product of know-how.

Hennessey invested 10 years into introducing vigor into 'Lulu', a mid-century popular corsage rose; he noted that his original introduction from Europe left him skeptical that it would ever be worth anything for it lacked the vigor necessary to sustain it.

With 'The Doctor', Hennessey acknowledged that even his large and strong plants could not withstand afternoon sun, as the wood was susceptible to sunburn and would die back to the bud union. But he noted that the plant was worth all the trouble because "it is the most beautiful of all pink roses in any language." Nor was Hennessey modest about taking credit for the improvement of some plants; he asserted that he had improved 'Angel Mateu' so much that the "originator would scarcely believe it."

Hennessey's catalogs are studded with admonitory cautions; he advises that failure to remove seed pods on 'Schoener's Nutkana' will reduce rebloom. He warns that on cloudy days 'Texas Centennial' displays blood-red buds, but in hot weather it can be pink, and even yellow appears in the fall. 'McGredy's Wonder' can only be planted in coastal areas if magnificent orange blooms nestled in glossy red olive foliage are desired.

But Hennessey's know-how deserted him in the case of 'Doubloons', which he had contemplated coaxing into repeat bloom in the thirties Proof of the Pudding, since by 1961 he had to confess that he was never able to achieve recurrent bloom in Oregon. More contemporary sources indicate that recurrent bloom seems to occur in warmer climates. Hennessey's failure in this regard is unusual, because he was ordinarily so sensitive to the affinities of rose performance and climate.

LOCATION! LOCATION!! LOCATION!!!

In over 20 years of writing—from his first newspaper column in 1940 to his last catalog in the early sixties—Hennessey stressed the importance of knowing the rose and its peculiarities, especially the right region for a particular rose. His concern with the effects of light, humidity, heat, and soil was partially a product of damping down unrealistic expectations and partially to ensure that the rose got a fair chance of displaying its charms where it could perform optimally. Hennessey's discussion of a rose is more likely to stress its idiosyncratic cultural needs as much as its colorful blooms.

Hennessey could attest to the influence of too much sun as well as the baneful effects of too little. And his book is one of the few that contains a chapter on "The Shady Rose Garden." Hennessey's argument is that the emphasis on full sun for roses came from the English experience with roses, where sunlight was in short supply and "full sun" constituted an oxymoron. The very size of America and the variability of its climates mandated a different approach. While conceding that a rose grown in full shade would grow slowly and bloom in a stingy fashion, he argued that full sun in many parts of the country essentially meant that the rose stopped growing and blooming; not only were bloom colors adversely affected, but even daily attempts at watering would be ineffective, preventing transpiration to the detriment of the rose. He believed the main impediment to effective rose growing in shady rose beds are the roots of the trees that provide the shade since they would inevitably steal the water needed by the rose. The selection process for the shady rose garden is to pick those roses that faded in the open garden or sulked in the summer heat. But shady does not mean complete gloom but rather avoidance of the direct mid-afternoon sun.

Hennessey stressed the importance of knowing the rose and its peculiarities, especially the right region for a particular rose.

In discussing the developing class of orange roses in a column of October 20, 1940, Hennessey takes great pains to note that those roses with *foetida* and Tea heritage, such as many Hybrid Teas, could only be grown under conditions featuring less than 4 hours of sun. 'Souvenir de Jean Soupert', for example, has a Tea rose background, which suggests that its blooms can hold their color but not if it receives more than 4 hours of sun. 'Mme Joseph Perraud', a highly touted rose popular on the East Coast, was bred in France, where blackspot was not a problem, and would bloom satisfactorily in comparatively high dry altitudes; "for valley sections of Oregon it blackspots and mildews too badly." At one point Hennessey decried his display garden as "an expensive nuisance" because visitors would fall in love with blooming roses despite the fact that the bloom was atypical because the weather was atypical. No amount of argumentation (or the grower's expertise) could get people to accept that "all roses are not good in all weathers."

Hennessey's comments on fragrance reveal observations that a rose like Dot's 'Girona' has its best fragrance when temperatures are above 80 or 90 degrees, whereas 'Parfum de la Hay' fares better with higher humidity and cooler temperatures. Even the type of scent can vary: 'Etoile de Hollande' has "a musk twang when the temperature is high, otherwise the fragrance is damask."

The 1949–1950 Hennessey catalog listed roses by their geographic affinities, functions, or uses in the garden as well as by classification. Some

50 roses were cataloged under the rubric "Roses Universally Good." But this was a misnomer. Even in these listings, Hennessey was unable to avoid characterizing the rose in terms of its performance under optimal conditions. Thus 'Narzisse', a cream and soft-orange rose, receives the highest of praise as the "finest warm-to-hot-weather rose put on the market in several years"' But he omitted it from his list of "Exhibition Roses" because he oriented that to the Pacific Northwest, where the rose grew poorly in spring and under cool conditions. Even 'Etoile de Hollande' is listed in the "Universally Good" list but faulted for being inferior to 'Christopher Stone' and 'Crimson Glory' as optimal reds in the Pacific Northwest. Specific recommendations are made for Western Oregon and the Puget Sound areas with coolness and humidity, for the Mountain States, where high elevation and dryness prevailed, and for the Deep South or frost-free areas. "Hennessey's Roses" is a compendium of roses in context and climate and location.

THE ACCIDENTAL ENVIRONMENTALIST

Even Hennessey understood that by accurately describing his roses and relating them to particular regions, he was diminishing his chances of sales; nevertheless, he persisted in warning people not to fall in love with a rose without knowing its cultural and climatic needs. Both the notion of promoting "one size fits all" and indifference to the rose once it was sold were simply alien to his personality and his observations. Much of his knowledge was hard-earned in the rose growing fields, and he regarded the size and vigor of his rose bushes and the color and performance of his plants as the justification for his recommendations. However, many of his preferences and beliefs were contrary to those of the evolving rose industry and the imperatives of mass marketing. His catalogs did not feature the latest pictures of the newest varieties in a stage of bloom most gardeners would never see. He was not committed to promoting the latest fad or newest introduction regardless of its excellence as a rose. To the extent that the exhibition rose market moved on to the newest roses available in the same style as its predecessors, he resolutely marched in the opposite direction by focusing on proven performers and what he considered the best in the field. Over time he became less and less concerned with exhibition roses, although in the thirties and forties he boasted of the awards won by his clients.

He regarded 'Peace', the 800-pound gorilla of postwar roses, as a throwback to the performance patterns of Hybrid Perpetuals and not a new development, merely a shift in evanescent rose "styles." His evaluation of the name change to Floribundas from Hybrid Polyanthas was that it was a pure sales gimmick; thus, he missed the huge popularity of the class as it developed in the 1950s. (In fairness, so did the people who were promoting the name "Floribundas," as growers were convinced that Floribundas were a passing fad and were unprepared for the incredible outburst of demand in the early 1950s.) However, 10 years later, after the issue had effectively been settled by market forces, Hennessey still used the terminology "Hybrid Polyanthas" when the rest of the rose world had abandoned Polyanthas completely for all practical purposes and had embraced Floribundas.

Both the notion of promoting "one size fits all" and indifference to the rose once it was sold were simply alien to his personality and his observations.

The basic effect of Roy Hennessey's attitudes and advice promotes the notion of sustainability—of growing roses in such as way as to ensure that the resources are not wasted and that future generations will have the means of sustaining themselves. But that was not his intent. His intent was to promote the growing of roses by methods that would permit the rose to be its optimal self so that the growing public could enjoy the glorious bounty that the rose could offer. So, he deserves the credit for offering advice that is useful today and necessary to achieve a world of roses that does no harm to the future. But as an accidental environmentalist, he is less a seer than a source of sensible advice, a starting point for a sustainable future.

NOTE: For the most part, the sources of quotes and Hennessey opinions are indicated in the main part of the text. I have drawn upon earlier writings on Roy Hennessey, such as the foreword to the forthcoming *Hennessey on Roses* reprint. Any errors of fact or interpretation are my own.

'Buff Beauty', a Bentall Hybrid Musk from 1939, is a prolific repeat bloomer that can be grown in partial shade. The fragrant flowers have an ethereal quality that has helped keep 'Buff Beauty' a favorite for decades.

Rose Poems by Emily Dickinson

A ROSE

A SEPAL, petal, and a thorn
    Upon a common summer's morn,
A flash of dew, a bee or two,
A breeze
A caper in the trees, —
    And I'm a rose!

SHE SPED AS PETALS OF A ROSE

She sped as Petals of a Rose
Offended by the Wind —
A frail Aristocrat of Time
Indemnity to find —
Leaving on nature — a Default
As Cricket or as Bee —
But Andes in the Bosoms where
She had begun to lie —

IF I COULD BRIBE THEM BY A ROSE

If I could bribe them by a Rose
I'd bring them every flower that grows
From Amherst to Cashmere!
I would not stop for night, or storm —
Or frost, or death, or anyone —
My business were so dear!

If they would linger for a Bird
My Tambourin were soonest heard
Among the April Woods!
Unwearied, all the summer long,
Only to break in wilder song
When Winter shook the boughs!

What if they hear me!
Who shall say
That such an importunity
May not at last avail?

That, weary of this Beggar's face —
They may not finally say, Yes —
To drive her from the Hall?

WHERE ROSES WOULD NOT GO

Where Roses would not dare to go,
What Heart would risk the way —
And so I send my Crimson Scouts
To sound the Enemy —

THE ROSE DID CAPER ON HER CHEEK

The Rose did caper on her cheek —
Her Bodice rose and fell —
Her pretty speech — like drunken men —
Did stagger pitiful —

Her fingers fumbled at her work —
Her needle would not go —
What ailed so smart a little Maid —
It puzzled me to know —

Till opposite — I spied a cheek
That bore another Rose —
Just opposite — Another speech
That like the Drunkard goes —

A Vest that like her Bodice, danced —
To the immortal tune —
Till those two troubled — little Clocks
Ticked softly into one.

A FULL FED ROSE ON MEALS OF TINT

A full fed Rose on meals of Tint
A Dinner for a Bee
In process of the Noon became -
Each bright Mortality
The Forfeit is of Creature fair
Itself, adored before
Submitting for our unknown sake
To be esteemed no more

WHEN ROSES CEASE TO BLOOM, SIR

When Roses cease to bloom, Sir,
And Violets are done —
When Bumblebees in solemn flight
Have passed beyond the Sun —
The hand that paused to gather
Upon this Summer's day
Will idle lie — in Auburn —
Then take my flowers — pray!

NOBODY KNOWS THIS LITTLE ROSE

Nobody knows this little Rose—
It might a pilgrim be
Did I not take it from the ways
And lift it up to thee.
Only a Bee will miss it—
Only a Butterfly,
Hastening from far journey—
On its breast to lie—
Only a Bird will wonder—
Only a Breeze will sigh—
Ah Little Rose— how easy
For such as thee to die!

IF I SHOULD CEASE TO BRING A ROSE

If I should cease to bring a Rose
Upon a festal day,
'Twill be because beyond the Rose
I have been called away—

If I should cease to take the names
My buds commemorate—
'Twill be because Death's finger
Claps my murmuring lip!

A pointed bud   A tapering bud   An urn-shaped bud   An ovoid bud

A globular bud   High-centered bloom   Globular bloom

Informal cactus type of bloom   Cupped bloom   Flat bloom

Single bloom   Imbricated bloom   Old-fashioned bloom

Floral variety among roses. The 1929 Bobbink & Atkins catalogue, in common with other catalogues of the period, sought to instruct gardeners. Other drawings illustrated rose diseases and points about proper planting and pruning.

Historic Disease and Pest Control among Roses

ALICE FLORES

In one of my Internet rose groups there seems to be a perpetual discussion/argument going on between rose growers who spray with the array of chemical "helpers" available today and those who eschew such problematic substances in favor of an "organic" approach to gardening. The subject can elicit surprisingly emotional stances from the generally rational members. This fact may not be so surprising when one considers that the decisions made to spray (usually presented by proponents as "individual choice") have, without doubt, an impact on nonspraying neighbors and entire communities. Often, irrationally and somewhat romantically, people hark back to a "simpler" era with the presumption that historic cultivation methods were somewhat more "pure" and nontoxic than those employed by so many gardeners today. One person mentioned that he was curious about researching some of the methods of pest and disease control that had been used by rosarians in the past, so I spent a few hours browsing through old books, marking pages with advice on cultivation techniques with this goal in mind.

This person noted that Dr. J. Horace McFarland's beautiful tome *Roses of the World in Color* (1936) has merely a passing mention of cultivation; however, McFarland and Robert Pyle in 1930 compiled *How to Grow Roses*, which offered more detail. Perhaps McFarland figured he'd

J. HORACE MCFARLAND
(1859–1948), KNOWN
AS "DR. MCFARLAND"
(HIS DOCTORATE WAS
THE HONORIFIC L.H.D.) AND
AS "MR. ROSE" DURING MOST
OF THE FIRST HALF OF THE
20TH CENTURY, DOMINATED
AMERICAN ROSE CULTURE
THROUGH FORCE OF CHARACTER.
A LEADING PROGRESSIVE FROM
PENNSYLVANIA, HE SHAPED
THE AMERICAN ROSE SOCIETY
AS A SOCIETY FOR GARDENERS
AS WELL AS NURSERYMEN. *THE
AMERICAN ROSE ANNUAL* AND
THE *MODERN ROSES* SERIES,
CREATED AND EDITED BY HIM
DURING HIS MANY YEARS OF
ACTIVITY, CONTINUE TO BE
IMPORTANT INFLUENCES IN
AMERICAN ROSE CULTURE TO
THE PRESENT TIME.   —EDITORS

covered the territory in the earlier book and chose to focus on descriptions of varieties and his feelings about them in the later edition. What was interesting to me was that these books from the 1930s offered very little more in the way of suggestions for fighting rose pests than books that were written a century or more before! Since my focus was on the historic methods, I didn't do any reading past 1936, so I don't know when the miracle of modern chemistry began inspiring gardeners with promises of more control over their efforts. I will report on my findings by following a chronological trail through my rose library.

In 1846 Thomas Rivers wrote *The Rose Amateur's Guide*, a book that is fascinating and still informative today. He didn't include a chapter on cultivation per se, but in his discussions of the various classes and varieties known to him he usually spends a page or two on "culture." From what I gather out of this and other books of the era, much more time was spent on finding the correct site for a "fussy" rose than in trying to overcome its natural predisposition to disease in a less-suitable location. He often mentions that one rose or another prefers sun, partial shade, protection from wind, etc. What he does offer in the way of "chemical intervention" is simple and along the lines of one-size-fits-all. He recommends this sort of care only for potted or greenhouse-grown roses, offering no advice on garden roses. His main suggestion for controlling aphis (which he calls green fly) is tobacco smoke. That's it. The houses, apparently, could be smoked overnight with a smoldering heap of tobacco and moss. He also advises weekly watering with "guano water" and top-dressing with manure. For outdoor roses he mentions that manure not only helps the growth of the rose but also protects the roots from the heat of the sun—he piled it on thick. Both he and William Paul speak about using night-soil on roses. He applied it in the winter time and seemed to use some care in handling it.

Rivers also offers an interesting method of winter protection; he describes it thus: "Placing to each plant three stakes triangularly, sticking them firmly in the ground, and over these stretch a piece of calico, prepared as follows: 3 pints of old pale linseed oil, 1.5 oz. sugar of lead, 5 oz. pale resin: the oil must be heated, and the sugar of lead and resin pounded and added to it, while hot, and laid on the calico, while hot, with a brush. This should be tacked to the stakes with small tacks, and brought down within two inches of the ground, leaving a small aperture at top, at the apex of the triangle: this will admit of a moderate circulation of air from the bottom to the top, and will keep the plant in perfect health during the winter." Hmmm, hold the lead, please.

> *"The enemies of the rose are many. They are of two classes; the insect foes, and diseases caused by Fungi. And their prevention and destruction are tasks, as every rose-grower knows only too well, which call for ceaseless vigilance and constant work."*
>
> —ROSE KINGSLEY (1908)

William Paul, who wrote *The Rose Garden* in 1848, offers more specific instruction on cultivation than Rivers, but again, there are only a few sources of intervention available to him and his contemporaries, and he relies heavily on hand-picking pests and general garden cleanliness. He is a great advocate of manure and has a lengthy discussion of various types, mostly delineated by age and degree of composting. As with Rivers, it is with his potted and indoor roses that he employs the most pro-active techniques of protection. In his greenhouses mildew presented a problem, and he dealt with it by dusting with sulphur. He advises sprinkling or "syringing" the plants first with water so that the sulphur will stick and warns that "this is not a preventive, but a temporary cure." He mentions mice giving him problems with his seeds and seedlings and gives directions for covering seed beds with wire to exclude them. His solution for dealing with "rose grubs" is hand-picking, and he gives advice about how to find the larvae in curled leaves. He states, "I had a lot of plants remarkably free from these pests one season, which I could only account for by the fact that they were closely sought and destroyed the year before."

Paul goes on:

> The aphis, or green-fly, may be destroyed by removing the plants to a pit or house and smoking them: it may be kept away by dipping the ends of the shoots in, or syringing with, tobacco water, or by laying the shoot in the palm of the hand, and brushing the fly off.
>
> There is a very small canary-coloured fly, which did great mischief among Roses last season. They are generally found on the back of the leaf, close to the midrib, eating the leaf, working from the under side, and not only disfiguring, but injuring the plants. They are remarkably active. By giving the plant a tap, they will rise instantly in the air, fly round, and settle again on the leaves. As they were too nimble to be dealt with as their more sluggish compeers in mischief, I applied sulphur and snuff in equal portions, dusting the mixture on the back of the leaves when wet, and found it prove an excellent remedy.
>
> A long thin caterpillar, the larva of a saw-fly, committed great havoc among Roses in many places last year. They came in such myriads upon a Rose Garden in this county that the plants were almost stripped of their leaves before their course could be arrested. Hand-picking was resorted to, by which means they were ultimately got rid of.
>
> The red fungus [rust], which often attacks Roses out of doors late in autumn, may visit the pot-plants; and should it do so, the leaves where it appears should be carefully rubbed between the finger and thumb, using a little sulphur in the operation.
>
> Mildew is sometimes a source of great annoyance. Watering with a solution of nitre [saltpeter] is said to destroy it. If the situation is airy and sunny, there is little to fear on this account.

Even Paul is concerned about the possible effects of inhaling some of the substances he is using! In his greenhouses he advises sulphur for mildew, fumigation of the entire house for aphids, and for spider mites: "The red spider is sometimes productive of sad results, for which moisture is the best remedy. Syringe the plants abundantly and daily with tepid soot water, perfectly clear, driving the water with some force against the young leaves through a fine rose-syringe, so as not to bruise or injure them." He

also suggests treating outdoor plants by tenting them and applying tobacco smoke with a "fumigating bellows."

In 1902 Gertrude Jekyll, in *Roses,* includes a chapter titled "Enemies of
the Rose," which begins, "There is scarcely any other plant which is attacked by so many or such persistent enemies as the Rose. Strange to say,
writers on Rose culture, in enumerating these, invariably omit to mention the most potent enemy of all, and that is, adverse weather. It is not
only that these adverse weather conditions often inflict more serious and
lasting injuries than all the other enemies of the Rose put together, but
they are also indirectly responsible for the worst attacks from insect and
other pests." Having said that, she goes on to state, "Against the foregoing
and other adverse weather influences the Rose grower is to a great extent
powerless, whereas insect pests, if attacked with promptness and perse-
verance, can, as a rule, be readily subdued. The great thing is to watch
for their appearance and at once proceed to destroy the first comers, and
when this is done to continue to harass the enemy until the attack has
entirely ceased." She goes on to emphasize that good culture is essential, noting that healthy plants suffer less than weak ones from insect and
other attacks. She says that the only remedy against all the larger insects
like caterpillars, grubs, beetles, sawflies, etc. is hand-picking, whereas the
smaller ones like greenfly, thrips, red spider, etc. are kept in check by
syringing. She describes the larger insects in detail and how to hand-pick
and destroy them—for "boring grubs" she stuck a piece of copper wire
into their holes to kill the invader "in situ" and pruned off damaged wood
back to firm, unblemished portions of the cane.

For aphids she mentions that "most exhibitors keep greenfly under entirely by the skillful use of thumb and finger" and adds that "occasional
sharp syringing with a garden-engine with clean water will be found in
most cases sufficient." If this doesn't work, she gives a recipe of two oz.
of quassia chips, boiled in a gallon of water, and with a tablespoonful of
soft soap added. She also mentions that there are products "in the market" but doesn't list them—apparently, she didn't use them. She advises
water spraying for thrips, even though it might spoil some of the existing
blooms. For mites—water again. She sprinkled plants with "flowers of

sulphur" for mildew or made a mixture of potassium sulphide to use as a spray. She had no remedy for rust.

A few years later, in 1908, Rose Kingsley produced her wonderful *Roses and Rose Growing*. Her chapter on "Rose Pests" begins, "The enemies of the rose are many. They are of two classes; the insect foes, and diseases caused by Fungi. And their prevention and destruction are tasks, as every rose-grower knows only too well, which call for ceaseless vigilance and constant work." Mildew, she refers to as "this odious disease" and fights with flowers of sulphur, blown over the plants with bellows. She also mentions syringing with Potassium sulphide, she calls it "liver of sulphur"—with egg-whites used as a spreader. The same solution is used for blackspot and rust. She pooh-poohs the washing of aphids from roses but warns about people becoming desperate enough to spray with paraffin(!), as it destroys the rose. She found that ladybugs and lace-wings were effective and helpful in eliminating them. But she also offers a recipe for a quassia and soap solution to use as a spray. Tobacco juice, 1 part to 15 parts water, is suggested for aphids and "cuckoo spit." Beetles, chafers, and grubs are all hand-picked and tossed into boiling water. She spends some time discussing sawflies and their larvae and advises hand-picking, careful cleaning of the ground around the roses in winter, and a wash made of hellebore, flour, and water. For moth caterpillars and "rose maggots," she resorted to "arsenate of lead" which came in an "arsenate paste" and was mixed with water [shudder]. She warns that it is poisonous. Beyond that, she hand-picked. She included recipes for her arsenal.

In 1930 Robert Pyle began his chapter on "How to Fight Pests" with the information that "vigorous, strong-growing bushes are almost always able to defend themselves. Proper cultivation and fertilization win half the battle by keeping the roses in condition to repel attacks." For mildew, blackspot, and canker he recommends sulphur. He dealt with insects using arsenate of lead (warning of its toxicity) and nicotine. He advised keeping plants dusted with sulphur as a preventive, but renewing it after rains. He also mentioned using a solution of bicarbonate of soda for mildew. He is the first in my research to mention Bordeaux mixture, a combination of copper sulphate and lime, for fungal attacks. He mentions, however, that it stains the leaves. He used Bordeaux as a protection for canker, applied in the fall. He mentions a combination of sulphur and arsenate of lead, called Massey Dust, with which he dusted plants regularly. For beetles and chafers (he includes Japanese beetles), he hand-picks and drops them into kerosene. He does mention one commercial product by name, Black-Leaf 40, a solution of nicotine sulphate. He also mentions tobacco dust but says it is unpleasant to handle, as well as a mulch of tobacco stems. Nicotine sulphate for mites.

In 1936, McFarland, in a very brief couple of paragraphs in his book *Roses of the World in Color,* presents Massey Dust, powdered tobacco dust, and Bordeaux mixture as the basic weaponry for rosarians. He also notes the staining that comes from the Bordeaux mixture.

So—there you have it. And I suspect that's about "it." The advice is consistent and fairly unchanged from 1846 to 1936. I suspect that most modern gardeners wouldn't feel comfortable handling some of the substances that were employed at that time. I also suspect that some of the substances we do handle with varying degrees of precaution today will, in 100 years, produce horrified reactions from readers of garden history—"You mean, they actually used Sevin?!?" The choices, as always, remain individual—all we can do is make them as educated as possible.

'Mutabilis', in common with other China Roses, blooms repeatedly. As its flowers fade, they take on deeper and deeper coloration, beginning light yellow, changing to pink, and finally aging to red—unlike the flowers of most roses, which fade lighter.

Rose Studies:
Watercolors and Drawings
Documenting the Genus *Rosa*

MARIA CECILIA FREEMAN

The project I call "Rose Studies" grew out of a convergence of interests. Some years ago, I had been producing pen-and-ink scientific illustrations for a botanist at the Jepson Herbarium of the University of California at Berkeley, while independently pursuing watercolor botanical art. At the same time, I was increasingly interested in growing and learning about roses, especially wild species and old garden varieties. It was a natural step to begin using art to study and enjoy the roses. I sat down to draw the 'Altissimo' by my front door, and the project—to document members of the genus *Rosa* through art—was launched.

Cover of "Rose Studies," a catalogue for the artist's one-person exhibition of rose watercolors at The New York Horticultural Society, June 9–30, 2010.

Rose Studies
Watercolors and Drawings

Maria Cecilia Freeman

These "studies" emphasize species that have played an important role in the cultivation of garden roses. Many of the wild roses documented in this project are by their nature tough and undemanding plants in their native habitats or similar environments. Others, including "found" roses and some modern hybrids, demand little care in a sustainable rose garden. All of them have a story of social history attached to them. I hope to contribute to efforts to collect and preserve the old roses that might otherwise be lost to development and neglect. Through art I can make salient the characteristics that help us recognize a rose, connect it with other roses, and appreciate its particularities. Many of these roses are not showy but offer a subtle beauty—and can play an important role in sustainable gardens.

The artist at work in her Santa Cruz, California, studio.

I find that the intrigue and beauty of a rose lies in the small details at least as much as in the flower and foliage. I want to portray a rose's beauty in form, color, and detail with botanical accuracy—merging traditions of fine art and scientific illustration. Many artists see these separate traditions as representing a bifurcation in the world of botanical art. The goal of one is primarily aesthetic, while the primary concern of the other is to

I sat down to draw the 'Altissimo' by my front door, and the project—to document members of the genus Rosa *through art—was launched.*

inform, in a clear and pleasing way. But despite their different emphases, both traditions rely on accuracy and beauty in presentation, and can complement each other.

Most of the roses in this project are portrayed in a synthesis of complementary presentations: a watercolor composition that represents botanical characteristics in an aesthetic but accurate manner, accompanied by an informal collage of annotated graphite pencil drawings, documenting my observations of the rose as well as my process of making the art.

Both of the presentations are intended to be informative and aesthetically pleasing, and to work symbiotically to achieve these goals. For example, the colors of the plant are captured in the collage and also accurately represented in the painting. Important details that are annotated in the drawings tend to be salient in the painting. I always work directly from live plants, and revisit the rose at different times of the year as much as possible, to capture its development through the seasonal cycle. I conduct my research in public and private rose collections, botanical gardens, and in the wild, and I consult with expert rosarians in an effort to be accurate in my observations.

Many of the wild roses documented in this project are by their nature tough and undemanding plants in their native habitats or similar environments. Others, including "found" roses and some modern hybrids, demand little care in a sustainable rose garden.

The example of *Rosa roxburghii* var. *normalis* in this book (SEE PLATES 11 AND 12) demonstrates the portrayals of roses in these studies. The annotated drawings document distinctive botanical characteristics of this variety of the 'Chestnut Rose', while its appearance at different times of the year is painted in watercolor. Each piece reflects and informs the other. For example, the precise colors in the painting are documented in annotated watercolor patches among the drawings, and the watercolor composition draws attention to the bristly sepals and receptacles, emphasized in the collage, that give the rose its common name.

Many of the roses I've studied, drawn and painted have been included in exhibitions at the Horticultural Society of New York in 2008 and in 2010, and the San Francisco Botanical Garden in 2011. More images can be seen in the catalogue from those exhibits, and at my website *mcf-art.com*.

Dr. J. Horace McFarland (1859–1948) in the U.S. (above) and hybridizer Alister Clark (1864–1949) in Australia (right) maintained a lively correspondence, some published in the American Rose Annuals that Dr. McFarland edited for twenty-eight years. Both were visionaries. Alister Clark was perhaps the first hybridizer to place sustainability above floral factors in the creation of his roses; Dr. McFarland advocated the need for *rosariums* as early as the 1930s, where the genetic variety of roses could be maintained, a dream that is only partly realized today. The U.S.–Australian connection at the intellectual level, largely broken following the passing of these leaders, is again a significant feature of world rose culture as of recent years. (Images from the 1948 and 1930 American Rose Annuals courtesy American Rose Society)

Tea and Roses

BILL GRANT

At the end of the nineteenth century in England, the snobs grew Tea roses and the rest grew a wide range of roses, most of them once-bloomers. The Hybrid Tea was slowly making its way into the nurseries and public gardens and would replace almost all the other types in popularity because they rebloomed — most of the time.

From the beginning, the species roses offered a short bloom season and generally were not sought by gardeners. By a variety of means (bees, birds, wind) these roses formed hybrids. Later, from the time of the Albas, Bourbons, Centifolias (the alphabetical list is long), there was a hope that someday a reblooming rose would appear. It did.

What sets Teas apart from other roses? Their fragrance is mixed; their color range is far wider; their high-centered flower shape predates the Hybrid Tea.

The China rose that came to Europe was a cultivated form that had reblooming genes. When it was crossed with other roses, the spectrum of garden-worthy plants increased enormously — and still does. The Tea is a close relative.

The China rose, as it is still called today, established itself, as it is fairly hardy and has a long bloom season. In Peter Beales' latest catalog, he offers 44 varieties. Even those who are not rosarians would recognize a popular China like 'Mlle Cécile Brunner' or 'Irène Watts', as they have been on the market since they were introduced.

The Tea name became that because the clipper ships that brought tea from China also carried the first plants. For myself, a tea drinker for years, they always have a tea scent. Not so for many of my gardening friends.

They are different from their cousins in a number of ways, which I will describe in detail a bit later. But there was no doubt about their early success in England. Jack Harkness' grandfather John said of them: "If the Rose be the queen of flowers, the Tea-scented Rose may be regarded the queen of queens, for undoubtedly the 'Teas', as they are familiarly called, are in refinement and delicate beauty superior to their robust and more highly coloured relatives."

Although Tea Roses *comes from Australia … much of the information is about the form, color, and cultivation which will serve anyone, anywhere, who wants to grow Teas.*

Jack, in his book *Roses* in 1978, said something quite different: "They must have been beautiful. But where has all the beauty gone? The Teas which survived for my eyes to see had little in the way of growth or flower to compel one to take up a spade and go planting." Jack devoted most of his life to the Hybrid Tea, so that may explain some of his dislike. But they do best outdoors in southern England.

Those snobs I mentioned at the start were often people who had property where they could build greenhouses and grow the Teas without fear of their enemy—the cold. Teas do best in warm climates.

Which leads me to a wonderful new book called *Tea Roses – Old Roses for Warm Gardens,* written by six Western Australian ladies who spent 10 years growing and researching these roses. They are fondly referred to as the "Tea Bags." This is only the second book ever devoted to the Teas; the other was by Rudolf Geschwind in 1884 (in German). Western Australia is one of the richest horticultural areas of the world, and their native plants have found homes in many gardens overseas. The climate is excellent for most of the Teas.

What sets Teas apart from other roses? Their fragrance is mixed; their color range is far wider; their high-centered flower shape predates the Hybrid Tea. Some do not like their nodding heads. They are usually bushy, twiggy. I have two climbing forms. And the ones in my garden really do bloom, on and off, all year, even at Christmas.

English nurseryman Peter Beales offers 57 shrub and climbing Teas, which is a larger collection than the Chinas. He says, "The early Teas were not fully hardy and were more often grown in greenhouses and conservatories than as garden plants." He cautions that they should be grown in sheltered warm positions or in pots. Because I could not find Teas in the U.S. when I started my big garden, I imported them from Beales, and they all have remained happy and healthy here.

The first import to England, and still a popular one, was 'Hume's Blush Tea-scented China', but the one sold by nurseries today is not the same rose. Which illustrates one of the more difficult things about Teas, as they are hard to identify. The book *Tea Roses* details the chore the ladies had in separating their closeness: Tea-China hybrids, Noisettes, Dijon Teas, *Rosa gigantea* hybrids, and the impostors. During all the years that I have grown all kinds of roses, the battle has never stopped about what is the real 'Sombreuil'. I saw what I think is the original at Tete d'Or, the Lyon rose garden, and it does not look at all like mine, which is a treasure regardless of the name.

Although *Tea Roses* comes from Australia and restricts much of the detailed history to the Teas that have been grown there, much of the information is about the form, color, and cultivation which will serve anyone, anywhere, who wants to grow Teas.

Each rose is given a close-up photo and often there are shots of large plants. Old prints do not always help with identification, but they do show color and form.

These details of each rose I found to be most helpful. As the authors grew almost all of the roses themselves, one can count on their accuracy. We find details of inflorescence and pedicel, bud shape and color, sepals, flower size and shape, flower color, petal shape and texture, stamens and carpels, receptacle and hips, fragrance, leaves, and bush. Such exhaustive information will serve any gardener who wishes to choose new plants or identify ones already in the garden.

The roll call of Teas begins with, appropriately, 'Adam' (1833/1838), which illustrates one of the serious problems about identification. I imported mine from Beales back in the 1970s, thinking it was the real thing. However, a number of experts say that it does not closely resemble the one described at its introduction. So what is one to do? I have kept it because it is beautiful and looks very much like the real thing. As the authors say, "In the case of the rose known as 'Adam' in Australia today, we feel the jury is still out!"

There is no problem with the next rose—'Alexander Hill Gray' (1911)—as everyone agrees it is the real thing. As each rose is given its full space, it convinces the reader that a great deal of work has been done with identification, bringing up a great deal of history that is often fascinating in its own right.

From here to the end, 'William R. Smith' (1908), there are the confirmed names and those that are still questionable. But the popularity and hardiness of all won't bother those who want to grow lovely roses.

There is a section called "Mystery Roses," four popular ones that are still under investigation. No doubt, with the publication of this book and its wide distribution, the true names might be found.

One of the appendices is a color chart, from light yellow to blood red, which may help with identification. A rather humorous section is devoted to a "What Not to Grow" list—compiled in 1921 for the catalog of a nursery in New South Wales. There were an enormous number of Teas introduced before that time, and the list may warn buyers that these are not doing well or not selling well.

The last sections of the book offer a variety of lists, sports, bibliography (which is excellent) as well as a first-rate index.

EARTH-KIND® ROSE TRIALS
Identifying the World's Strongest, Most Beautiful Landscape Roses

DERALD A. HARP, DAVID ZLESAK, GAYE HAMMOND,
STEVE GEORGE, AND WAYNE MACKAY

ABSTRACT

"Earth-Kind®" is the most prestigious horticulture designation bestowed by the Texas AgriLife Extension Service (part of the Texas A&M System). This designation is awarded based on multiyear scientific research studies, combined with extensive regional field trials, conducted by or in collaboration with Texas A&M horticulturists. Only rose cultivars possessing an extremely high level of landscape performance, coupled with outstanding disease and insect tolerance and/or resistance, may receive the designation. The Earth-Kind® philosophy is based on the premise that it is possible to identify beautiful plants that tolerate harsh, low-maintenance environments without fertilizers, pesticides, and other agricultural chemicals along with a significant reduction in irrigation. This cutting-edge, environmental effort is the most popular and fastest-growing, research-based environmental university program of its kind in the United States and directly benefits all sectors of horticulture: growers, retailers, landscapers, and consumers. Earth-Kind® rose research is under way in 25 states and four foreign countries, including Bermuda, Canada, India and New Zealand.

Keywords: disease resistance, Diplocarpon rosae, drought tolerance, environmental research, Rosa, soil management

INTRODUCTION

The rose is the most popular garden plant in the world as well as one of the most important commercial cut flowers (Horst 1995). Over 200 million roses are planted annually with a value of approximately $720 million in retail sales (Short et al. 1991). No other group of plants provides as wide a range of plant, flowering, and blossom traits (Buck 1964a). They combine the best characteristics of annual bedding plants and perennials, but with a wealth of flower forms, colors and scents, and plant forms and habits that few other plants can provide (Buck 1978). The public's demand for low-maintenance "environmentally-friendly" roses is growing as (1) more gardeners are becoming less willing to expose themselves and their families to pesticides, (2) city governments restrict landscape irrigation, (3) legislation restricts pesticide usage, and (4) the costs associated with commercial fertilizers and rose care products skyrocket (Zlesak 2006).

The Earth-Kind® environmental landscape management system applies to the entire landscape and was created by horticultural specialists in the Texas AgriLife Extension Service. It addresses, in a beautiful way, the four major horticultural challenges facing today's American homeowners and landscape professionals:

- Stewardship of precious water resources
- The abuse and/or misuse of commercial fertilizers
- The abuse and/or misuse of pesticides, and
- The need to keep natural resources (tree leaves and branches) in our landscapes and out of landfills, thereby making room for more non-recyclable waste.

DEMAND FOR IMPROVED CULTIVAR PERFORMANCE

Today's gardeners face many new horticultural challenges and, as a result, have become more demanding of the plants they choose for inclusion in their landscapes. Drought and above normal temperatures have forced communities to limit irrigation during periods of severe plant stress. In response, homeowners in several states have proven to be mindful of water resource challenges and are prepared to make changes in their landscapes to accommodate limited water supplies (Israel et al. 1999; Spinti et al. 2004; Hurd et al. 2006). The term "xeriscape" (landscaping in ways that do not require supplemental irrigation) was first coined in Colorado in 1978 and is an important landscape movement in Texas (Welsh et al. 2000). Additionally in many areas salt levels have increased due to a decrease in available groundwater supplies, further limiting plant available water (PAW) (Brady et al. 2001). In addition to direct results of difficult environmental conditions, these stressors also increase susceptibility of rose cultivars to insect and disease pressure.

Horticulturists typically recommend supplemental irrigation, application of fertilizers, and spraying of the appropriate pesticide to im-

Earth-Kind® roses must be tolerant of the three primary soil textures (sands, loams, and clays), tolerant of high alkalinity and, once established, capable of surviving on the limited moisture and fertility provided by the native soil initially amended with compost and covered with organic mulch.

prove plant performance or to correct inherent landscape problems. In the past, horticulturists and pathologists have routinely directed their research programs toward the development of control methods rather than resistance mechanisms (Hagan et al. 1988). Unfortunately, when supplemental irrigation is not always available, and in the face of increased costs for commercial synthetic fertilizers, consumers are showing a preference for more environmentally friendly landscape management techniques, eschewing the use of synthetic fungicides and pesticides.

For example, blackspot is a serious and often devastating disease of outdoor roses, caused by the fungus *Diplocarpon rosae* (Horne et al. 1988). It is the most serious disease problem of roses worldwide (Horst 1995; Rajapaska et al. 2001; Whitaker et al. 2007). Roses vary widely in their susceptibility, with popularly cultivated Hybrid Tea cultivars typically being the most susceptible (Jenkins 1955; Palmer et al. 1966). Control measures require repeated sprays with fungicides, often as frequently as once each week from the first flush of growth in the spring until the first hard frost in the fall (University of Illinois 1987; Reddy et al. 1992; Hagan et al. 2005). The repeated and prolific use of fungicides at this level not only increases the cost to the consumer but can also be potentially hazardous to the environment. It also places selection pressure on the pathogen and can lead to the development of acquired resistance to different chemistries and dynamic pathogen populations.

There has been a strong movement away from the use of roses as general garden plants in the United States during the past 80 years. In part, this can be attributed to the general level of culture required to keep roses healthy (Buck 1979). That consumers are making the shift to low maintenance roses and more environmentally responsible landscapes is illustrated in sales of the Knock Out® series of roses (the original cultivar in the series was introduced in 2000). "To date, Knock Out® and its siblings have sold between 10 million and 12 million plants in the states," says Steve Hutton, President of Conard-Pyle. "No other rose, not even 'Peace' which took the world by storm 60 years ago, has sold like that" (Virag 2007) (SEE PLATE 15).

The use of synthetic and organic fertilizers is strictly forbidden in Earth-Kind® trials. Candidate cultivars must have the ability to develop a healthy and aggressive root system with effective nutrient uptake and use efficiency for consistent, superior performance.

Consumers have demonstrated a willingness to pay premium prices for cultivars that are resistant to common diseases. For instance, the University of Tennessee developed a powdery mildew (*Microsphaera pulchra* Cook & Peck) resistant flowering dogwood tree (*Cornus florida* L.) that created a potential net nursery financial gain of $800,000 (Gardner et al. 2004). Another important example is the work done identifying cultivars of American and non-American elm species that show resistance to Dutch elm disease (Santamore et al. 1995; Townsend et al. 2004). Current environmental and economic concerns behoove horticulture researchers to identify disease-resistant and tolerant species and cultivars.

The Earth-Kind® program requires the support of researchers in biotechnology, molecular genetics, plant breeding, plant pathology, and entomology. In a typical breeding program, individual plants or genotypes are identified that exhibit a particular trait, such as drought tolerance, and pest or disease resistance. These unique individuals would be utilized in breeding and biotechnology programs as a genetic resource. Through the Earth-Kind® program, the universities and communities involved provide this initial research and make available to plant breeders and others a long list of successful cultivars that possess adaptive traits across multiple environments. Also, once successful varieties are identified, basic research can be performed on these varieties to identify the specific morphological, physiological, or biochemical character that imparts these desired characteristics. As we broadly work across the various fields of science, the ultimate goal of identifying effective landscape plants can be realized. Once known at the basic level, the traits identified that make Earth-Kind® roses successful could also be transferred or utilized in other species, including ornamental, food, and fiber crops.

LOW-MAINTENANCE LANDSCAPES
MUST BE AESTHETICALLY PLEASING

Over the past several years, virtually every state has developed programs that promote the use of native species adapted to local environmental conditions (Nelson 2003; Stack 2008). While many attractive native species have been identified, native species tolerant of local environmental conditions often lack the aesthetic qualities of their widely commercialized brethren. Unfortunately, the supposed hardiness and pest resistance of native species may not necessarily hold true, as that knowledge is often based on anecdotal and not scientific evidence. Scheiber et al. (2008) found that canopy size in nonirrigated plots declined similarly for eight introduced and eight native species in Florida. Similar results have been replicated in other states and across numerous other species (Glenn et al. 1998; Stabler et al. 2000; Garcia-Navarro et al. 2004; Zollinger et al. 2006).

Many landscape professionals feel that the solution to today's landscape challenges with roses lies in the development of more disease-resistant, drought- and heat-tolerant, winter-hardy roses. However, the development of new rose cultivars can take 10 to 20 years to complete. Additionally, rose breeding is mainly carried out by amateurs or commercially by highly competitive companies whose genetic knowledge is often proprietary and unpublished (Gudin 1998, 2000; Australian Government 2005). For these reasons, researchers throughout the world now have a tremendous opportunity to develop or identify rose cultivars that are beautiful and highly adapted to regional environmental conditions. The goal of the Earth-Kind® program is not to recreate the breeding programs of hybridizers around the world, but rather to identify those truly special cultivars that combine beauty with proven durability in the landscape.

EARTH-KIND® OVERVIEW

The Earth-Kind® philosophy is based on the premise that it is possible to identify beautiful plants that tolerate harsh, low-maintenance environments without fertilizers, pesticides, and other agricultural chemicals and with a significant reduction in irrigation. This cutting-edge environmental effort is the most popular and fastest-growing, research-based environmental university program of its kind in the United States, with testing of Earth-Kind® roses currently underway in 25 states (from Alaska to Florida) and four foreign countries (Bermuda, Canada, India, and New Zealand). Six universities (Colorado State University, Iowa State University, Kansas State University, Louisiana State University, University of Minnesota, and the University of Nebraska) have joined Texas A&M in conducting peer-reviewed Earth-Kind® rose research.

Earth-Kind® systems are a revolutionary approach to landscape management suitable for almost any geographic region, climate zone, and soil type. Traditionally, gardeners have used peat moss and synthetic fertilizers to grow plants in areas where they are not adapted, protecting stressed plants from insects and disease through an arsenal of agricultural chemicals and from drought with an abundance of irrigation. These plantings suffer greatly when cities restrict landscape irrigation. While native landscapes may survive on limited irrigation, they often lack the aesthetic appeal of traditional gardens. Organic landscapes limit the use of synthetic pesticides but force gardeners to use expensive organic fertilizers and depend on often dubious concoctions for fertility and pest control. Organic management approaches are often supported only by anecdotal observations and frequently do not hold up to validation in controlled experiments (Grabowski et al. 2007). The Earth-Kind® approach identifies aesthetically pleasing plants that combine the toughness and durability of well-adapted natives, environmentally friendly aspects of organic gardening, and techniques and recommendations based on university-based peer-reviewed research.

Since Earth-Kind® rose trials last multiple years, each site has a minimum of 15 plants, and pesticides are not used, regional pests that affect roses tend to quickly invade Earth-Kind® plantings and allow differences in tolerance impacting performance to become quickly evident.

EARTH-KIND® ENVIRONMENTAL SOIL MANAGEMENT

Success in any gardening program is dependent on proper soil management, as improvements in the soil directly impact and enhance water and nutrient availability, as well as overall plant health and growth. The Earth-Kind® principles of environmental soil management emulate natural environments for nutrient cycling. Leaves, branches, and other forms of organic matter fall to the ground and slowly decompose into humus, providing the required plant nutrients and improving soil tilth. In this natural environment, soil microflora flourish, increasing populations of beneficial fungi and mycorrhizae and improving conditions in the root zone. In an Earth-Kind® program, compost is incorporated only one time into the native soil to provide the essential elements needed for plant growth. An organic mulch is applied to the soil surface and replenished once or twice yearly to maintain a 3-inch-thick layer. This mulch decomposes into humus and acts as a slow-release fertilizer. Harp et al. (2008) demonstrated this relationship, illustrating how separating the soil/mulch interface with synthetic weed barriers can decrease the transfer of nutrients from decomposing mulch into the root zone. Likewise, McBee et al. (2004) demonstrated how organic matter also contributes to improvements in soil porosity, drainage, aeration, and plant available water.

EARTH-KIND® ROSES

No landscape species is better suited to serve as the flagship model crop for the Earth-Kind® system than roses. The beauty of the species and its tremendous genetic diversity makes it an ideal candidate for refocused research. The genus *Rosa* is represented by over 100 species across four continents (Hortus 1976). Until recently, roses have been selected primarily on the basis of flower size, form, color, and, less frequently, fragrance. While the rose's popularity is exemplified by the number of products specifically developed for rose care in the landscape, many gardeners have shied away from roses, choosing to buy species with lower maintenance requirements (Buck 1979). Roses whose minimal maintenance requirements have been validated by peer-reviewed scientific research provide individuals with reliable alternatives for successful and productive landscapes.

EARTH-KIND® ROSE EVALUATION CRITERIA

"Earth-Kind" is the most prestigious horticulture designation bestowed by the Texas AgriLife Extension Service. This designation is awarded based on multiyear scientific research studies, combined with extensive, regional field trials conducted by or in collaboration with Texas A&M horticultural experts. Only rose cultivars possessing an extremely high level of landscape performance, coupled with outstanding disease and insect tolerance and/or resistance, may receive the designation.

Furthermore, roses will only be designated Earth-Kind® if they meet several additional criteria. First, the rose must be attractive in both plant form and flower characteristics throughout the growing season. This beauty must be natural and not the result of manipulation, excessive fertilization, or heavy pruning. The Earth-Kind® program recognizes, but does not evaluate differently between the various classes of roses, except for the evaluation of climbing roses. Climbers are not penalized for asymmetric plant habit because it is part of their nature as they mature in size. Besides this exception for plant habit, all roses, regardless of class, are evaluated by identical standards (see Table 1).

Second, Earth-Kind® roses must be durable, well-adapted plants capable of withstanding the local and regional environmental conditions. They must be growing on their own roots and not a product of grafting.

TABLE 1.
Monthly rating scale used to evaluate Earth-Kind® trial roses during the growing season in years 2–4.

Rating	5	4	3	2	1	0
Foliage cover	100% coverage	90% coverage or more	75 to 90% coverage	25 to 50% coverage	<25% leaf coverage	Plant dead
Foliage color	Dark green	Green, no chlorosis	Green, up to 25% of leaves chlorotic	Lt. green, 25 to 50% chlorotic	Yellow, >50% chlorotic	Plant dead
Blossom coverage*	90% or more	75–90% coverage	50–75% coverage	25–50% coverage	<25% coverage	Plant dead
Growth habit	Symmetrical in all directions, branches consistent in size	Symmetrical in most directions, branches consistent in size	Symmetrical in one direction only, one branch w/irregular growth	Asymmetrical growth, two or more branches w/irregular growth	Inconsistent and irregular growth over entire plant	Plant dead
Disease	No disease	<10% of leaves or blossoms infected	10 to 25% of leaves or blossoms infected	25 to 50% of leaves or blossoms infected	<50% of leaves or blossoms infected	Plant dead
Pest	No pest	<10% of leaves or blossoms w/ insect damage	10 – 25% of leaves or blossoms w/ insect damage	25 to 50% of leaves or blossoms w/ insect damage	<50% of leaves or blossoms w/ insect damage	Plant dead

One point is added to blossom coverage for those cultivars with fragrant blooms.

Rootstock–scion interactions can affect vigor and other traits as well as plant longevity (Lindstrom and Kiplinger 1955; Buck 1964b; Mackay et al. 2008). Earth-Kind® roses must be tolerant of the three primary soil textures (sands, loams, and clays), tolerant of high alkalinity and, once established, capable of surviving on the limited moisture and fertility provided by the native soil initially amended with compost and covered with organic mulch. In several trials across the state of Texas, many specimens in heavy clay soils have survived severe and prolonged drought with little or no supplemental irrigation. The use of synthetic and organic fertilizers is strictly forbidden in Earth-Kind® trials. Candidate cultivars must have the ability to develop a healthy and aggressive root system with effective nutrient uptake and use efficiency for consistent, superior performance.

It is important to use the term tolerant, as minimal pest and disease incidence can be expected in virtually any landscape plant during periods of heavy pressure. … Earth-Kind® roses range from being only tolerant to being fully resistant, with the disease or pest damage being extremely limited in scope.

Finally, Earth-Kind® roses must be tolerant of insects and disease. Since Earth-Kind® rose trials last multiple years, each site has a minimum of 15 plants, and pesticides are not used, regional pests that affect roses tend to quickly invade Earth-Kind® plantings and allow differences in tolerance impacting performance to become quickly evident. Varieties selected as Earth-Kind® are tolerant of common rose insects, such as Western Flower Thrips (*Frankliniella occidentalis* Pergande), spider mites (*Tetranychus* spp.), and aphids (numerous species), and common rose diseases, such as blackspot and powdery mildew. It is important to use the term *tolerant,* as minimal pest and disease incidence can be expected in virtually any landscape plant during periods of heavy pressure. However, depending on the cultivar, Earth-Kind® roses range from being only tolerant to being fully resistant, with the disease or pest damage being extremely limited in scope. One of the best known roses in the Earth-Kind® program, Knock Out® (*Rosa* 'RADrazz'), has variations in the lipid component of the cuticle layer that account for its resistance to blackspot (*Diplocarpon rosae*) (Goodwin et al. 2007). Similarly resistant roses may share this characteristic or have morphological variations in the leaflet surface (Reddy et al. 1992). It is understood that vigorous, healthy plants are less susceptible to insect and disease damage, so a good deal of the insect and disease tolerance and resistance can be attributed to prudent soil management under the Earth-Kind® program that greatly reduces soil-related plant stress. As of 2008, there were 19 cultivars that had earned Earth-Kind® status in the Southern U.S. region out of over 115 evaluated (Mackay et al. 2008; Table 2) representing diverse flower and plant characteristics. (SEE PLATE 17)

It should be understood that, as currently implemented, the Earth-Kind® designation recognizes tolerance of regional environmental and soil conditions only. For example, a trial evaluating 20 rose cultivars is currently under way in Minnesota, Iowa, Nebraska, Kansas, Colorado,

TABLE 2.

The 19 Earth-Kind® roses designated for the Southern region of the United States.

CULTIVAR[a]	HORTICULTURAL CLASS	YEAR OF INTRODUCTION
Souvenir de St. Anne's	Bourbon	1950
Ducher	China	1869
Mutabilis	China	<1894
Spice	China	unknown
Climbing Pinkie	Climbing polyantha	1952
Else Poulsen	Floribunda	1924
New Dawn	Large flowered climber	1930
Caldwell Pink	Polyantha	unknown
La Marne	Polyantha	1915
Marie Daly	Polyantha	unknown
Perle d'Or	Polyantha	1884
The Fairy	Polyantha	1932
Belinda's Dream	Shrub	1992
BUCbi (Carefree Beauty™)	Shrub	1977
RADrazz (Knock Out®)	Shrub	1999
Sea Foam	Shrub	1964
Duchesse de Brabant	Tea	1857
Georgetown Tea	Tea	unknown
Mme. Antoine Mari	Tea	1901

[a]*Trademark or exhibition name, if different from cultivar name, is listed in parenthesis.*

and Texas (Table 3). It would be perfectly reasonable to believe that cultivars recognized as Earth-Kind® in Minnesota and Iowa may not be recognized in Texas or Kansas, as these states have very different climatic conditions. However, the researchers may be able to identify a cultivar that thrives across all the environments presented and merit Earth-Kind® designation in multiple regions. This single rose variety could then be used as a source of genetic material for the improvement and development of current and new rose cultivars that will hopefully also have wide climatic adaptation.

Ultimately, the goal of Earth-Kind® is to identify those cultivars that have the genetic potential to thrive in landscapes under normal cultural conditions. Extreme climatic events (heat wave, extreme cold, drought, etc.) and/or exposure to elevated disease and insect pressure is likely to

TABLE 3.

The 20 rose cultivars included in the current Northern Earth-Kind® rose trials.

CULTIVAR[a]	HORTICULTURAL CLASS	YEAR OF INTRODUCTION
Radbrite (Brite Eyes)	Large flowered climber	2006
RADramblin (Ramblin' Red)	Large flowered climber	2001
John Cabot	Hybrid kordesii	1978
John Davis	Hybrid kordesii	1986
Quadra	Hybrid kordesii	1994
William Baffin	Hybrid kordesii	1983
Alexander Mackenzie	Shrub	1985
BAIine (Yellow Submarine)	Shrub	2004
BAIlena (Lena)	Shrub	2007
BAIole (Ole)	Shrub	2007
BAIore (Polar Joy)	Shrub	2004
BAIset (Sunrise Sunset)	Shrub	2004
BAIsven (Sven)	Shrub	2007
BUCbi (Carefree Beauty)	Shrub	1977
Frontenac	Shrub	1992
George Vancouver	Shrub	1994
Morden Blush	Shrub	1988
Prairie Joy	Shrub	1990
Seafoam	Shrub	1964
Summer Wind	Shrub	1975

[a]*Trademark or exhibition name, if different from cultivar name, is listed in parenthesis.*

overwhelm any genetic advantage these plants may possess. However, the identification of these traits through Earth-Kind® protocols can provide plant breeders a focal point from which tolerance and resistance traits may be obtained. For example, chilli thrips (*Scirtothrips dorsalis* Hood) are becoming a serious threat to numerous ornamental, orchard, and field crops in the Southern United States. Chilli thrips are known to attack roses in India; therefore, a program, like Earth-Kind®, that was able to identify tolerance in India could provide valuable information to biotechnologists, plant breeders, and pest control operators in the United States. This program would be further enhanced through international cooperators, as tolerant genotype(s) could be identified in areas known to be infested with the pest in question as it becomes established in other parts of the world.

OVERVIEW OF EVALUATION PROTOCOL

Cultivar Selection

Candidate cultivars must undergo an extensive preliminary evaluation process before being entered into a regional Earth-Kind® rose trial. Researchers consult numerous studies that have been conducted across the United States and Canada that evaluate roses according to their winter hardiness, disease incidence, and/or susceptibility to insect damage. Earth-Kind® researchers also consult noted rosarians, looking to identify cultivar limitations prior to inclusion in an Earth-Kind® trial. Roses that flower only in the spring and are not everblooming or recurrent and those that are Hybrid Rugosas at this point are being omitted from consideration. The public demands roses that have an extended season of flowering and Hybrid Rugosas are omitted due to their extreme sensitivity to iron chlorosis in alkaline soils. With the large quantities of cultivars being introduced annually, this preliminary screen of available knowledge helps to direct limited resources more efficiently toward roses that have a greater likelihood of being worthy of the Earth-Kind® designation. Consulting various cultivar performance studies to pinpoint cultivars that merit inclusion provides further validation for the Earth-Kind® program, supporting the recommendation of Earth-Kind® varieties, even in other climatic regions.

Evolving Evaluation Models

The original and primary Earth-Kind® model consists of two phases of rigorous testing: (1) a 4-year university-based research study used to screen a large collection of cultivars and (2) 3-year multiple-site field trials over a wide geographic area to confirm cultivar performance of the best-performing cultivars in phase one evaluation. A new model is being implemented for the Northern Earth-Kind Rose Trials (initiated in 2007 for landscape roses targeted for USDA Plant Cold Hardiness Zones 3 and 4). Due to the relatively limited number of cultivars with demonstrated cold hardiness in the far North, a smaller number of cultivars (20) were selected for this trial, which is being accommodated simultaneously at several locations initially across the region (see Table 3). This approach can help identify Earth-Kind® worthy roses more quickly and is reasonable for this region, with fewer cultivars with reputations as being cold-hardy and pest-tolerant in a typical landscape.

One of the best known roses in the Earth-Kind® program, Knock Out®, ...has variations in the lipid component of the cuticle layer that account for its resistance to blackspot ... Similarly resistant roses may share this characteristic or have morphological variations in the leaflet surface.

Earth-Kind® research programs are not based on anecdotal evidence, but rather on randomized replicated studies conducted with scientific rigor and honest evaluations. Care is taken to make them as free as possible of personal and commercial biases. Selection bias is avoided by excluding individuals and/or entities with a financial interest in any rose cultivar(s) as direct funding sources for the research studies. It is important to note that, while individuals and entities (i.e., nurseries) are excluded as direct funding sources, cultivars produced or promoted by these individuals are commonly included for evaluation purposes and donation of plant material is permissible. To date, primary funding for Earth-Kind® rose research has been provided through research grants from the Houston Rose Society and the Texas Nursery and Landscape Association. As other universities joined Earth-Kind® research efforts, additional organizations within those states and regions are also contributing funding to support Earth-Kind® research.

Earth-Kind® rose studies are under way as of 2008 at seven universities in the United States. To ensure consistency, these trials are conducted according to a strict set of protocols. Site development begins with bed layout and must include sufficient space for four replicates of each cultivar with at least 2.5 m (8 feet) between plants in Southern and mid-America trials and at least 1.9 m (6 feet) in Northern trials. (SEE PLATE 13) A minimum of 15 cultivars are included in these initial studies. Experimental design is a randomized complete block design, with one specimen of each cultivar per block. There is flexibility in how the blocks are designed in order to best account for environmental variability across a site and to make the gardens accessible and aesthetically pleasing. (SEE PLATE 14) Soil preparation begins by killing and removing existing vegetation. Clean beds are tilled to a depth of 30 cm (12 inches). A layer of fully finished, plant-derived compost, 7.5 cm (3 inches) deep, is tilled into the native soil. The Earth-Kind® protocol does not distinguish between forms of compost, although compost from local sources is recommended, and manure is discouraged due to the greater potential for burn if not fully composted. Following planting, a minimum of 7.5 cm (3 inches) of organic mulch is applied to the soil surface. Again, a preference for mulch from local sources is noted and typically is chipped wood and bark mulch. (SEE PLATE 13) Water is supplied via drip irrigation as drip irrigation is a very efficient way to get water to the root zone. Compared to overhead irrigation for instance, drip irrigation can provide the same amount of moisture to plants with up to a 50% reduction in the water applied (Berstein and Francois 1973). Irrigation is provided freely during the first year of establishment, but only as needed to prevent wilt during year 2. During the final 2 years of the trial, irrigation should be applied only in the case of extreme and abnormal drought. Earth-Kind® site coordinators recognize that evaluations taken during weather that is atypical and unlikely to occur on a regular basis are not realistic and likely discriminate against selections that would survive normal conditions. No fertilizers or pesticides, including those labeled organic, are applied during the course of the 4-year study. Roses are not pruned or deadheaded during the duration of the study, with the exception of the removal of dead wood.

The evaluation process, other than survival, begins at bud break and continues through the first killing frost and occurs in year 2 through the duration of the study. The first-year data are not taken, to allow for variations in starting plant material (i.e., initial plant size and logistics when plants can be acquired and planted) and to allow residual pesticides that may have been used during production to dissipate. For most of Texas, evaluations begin in April and end in November. These dates vary according the growing season of the evaluation site. Data collected include quantitative measures such as plant height, width (averaged across two measurements, perpendicular to each other), number and size of blossoms, and chlorophyll content using a SPAD 502 meter (Konica Minolta Sensing, Inc., Osaka, Japan). Leaf tissue analysis should be used to confirm plant nutrient status. Pressure bomb readings and gravimetric measures are used to quantify plant moisture status. Tensiometer readings, or other appropriate measures of soil water tension, should be used to quantify soil water tension at each recording interval. Qualitative measures include visual assessment of foliage coverage, foliage color, blossom coverage, growth form, disease incidence, and pest activity, including notation of diseases or pests present (see Table 1). Disease and pest data are collected by individuals trained in insect identification and plant pathology. Unidentifiable diseases and pests are sent to state plant pathologists and entomologists for identification purposes. Data are analyzed using SAS. Because of the repeated-measures nature of the study, quantitative measures should be analyzed using Proc MIXED (Littell et al. 1998). For analysis of qualitative data, the Kruskal–Wallis statistic should be used. At the end of year 4, the Earth-Kind® research team meets to evaluate the performance of the cultivars tested. High-performing cultivars are selected for inclusion in regional field trials.

The purpose of regional field trials is to determine whether the trends observed in the university study also apply across a wider region, and differ from phase 1 trials only in the number of cultivars and replications, the duration of study, and posttrial data analysis. Field trials are conducted through multi-disciplinary partnerships between Extension Service agents, master gardener groups, rose societies, public gardens, and city governments. They tend to be located in publicly visible spaces such as city parks and public gardens providing publicity for the program. Regional field trials feature those cultivars that have already proven to be successful performers in phase 1. Cultivar selection is carefully monitored so that every cultivar is included in a similar number of field trials within the respective climatic zones. With the on-going and dynamic evaluation process, not all cultivars being evaluated are in each site. However, the Earth-Kind winning rose in the South, Carefree Beauty™

It should be understood that, as currently implemented, the Earth-Kind® designation recognizes tolerance of regional environmental and soil conditions only. … Ultimately, the goal of Earth-Kind® is to identify those cultivars that have the genetic potential to thrive in landscapes under normal cultural conditions.

('BUCbi'), is planted at all sites as a control because of its widespread zone adaptability (USDA Cold Hardiness Zone 4) and consistent performance in past trials. The minimum number of plants in a regional trial is 15, three plants of each of five cultivars. Soil preparation and plant maintenance in field trials are the same as for phase 1 studies. Cultivars in field trials receive supplemental irrigation as needed for the first year of plant development, once per month during the summer of the second year, and then only in extreme drought in the final year. Likewise, field trial coordinators agree to never apply fertilizers or pesticides to the plants for the duration of the study. As of 2008, regional field trials were under way at more than 40 sites across the United States encompassing USDA Plant Cold Hardiness Zones 4 through 10.

Through field trials in Odessa, Texas, we have demonstrated that several roses designated Earth-Kind® are tolerant of receiving drip irrigation water with high salinity. These saline-tolerant roses tend not to exhibit symptoms of chlorotic tissue normally found on other rose cultivars growing under these less-than-optimal conditions.

EARTH-KIND® OUTREACH

One of the most important aspects of the Earth-Kind® program is outreach and education geared toward the general public. For over a decade, Earth-Kind® field trials have demonstrated the ability to produce high-quality landscape roses while reducing irrigation by potentially 70% or more (with the benefit of drip irrigation versus overhead irrigation and the use of mulch), eliminating fertilizers and pesticides, and reducing pruning, including the complete elimination of deadheading. Implementation of Earth-Kind® principles with Earth-Kind® plant materials allows for a very significant and measurable reduction of the introduction of pollutants into the environment, as well as a measurable reduction in maintenance costs to public gardens and city park departments. Gardeners and landscapers are enthusiastically receptive to these new techniques and plant materials that make their gardens more productive and much easier to maintain. The Earth-Kind® program truly benefits all segments of the horticulture industry chain, from the grower to the final consumer (Rodda 2008).

Earth-Kind® is publicized through:

- The Earth-Kind® website (EarthKindRoses.tamu.edu);
- Aggie-Horticulture (haggie-horticulture.tamu.edu), Texas's repository for horticulture information; and
- Texas AgriLife Extension and other state Extension publications, field days, and public events

Additionally, Earth-Kind educational publications are being distributed by more than 80 horticultural organizations across the United States. One of the strongest recent partnerships for dissemination of Earth-Kind®

rose research is the American Rose Society. They have featured articles on the progress of the Earth-Kind® program in their bimonthly magazine *(American Rose)* distributed to their members and many libraries. Beginning in 2008 local rose society chapters could request regionally tailored Earth-Kind® brochures designed to be distributed internally and externally to promote rose growing using Earth-Kind® cultivars and methods. Preliminary reports from local societies indicate that there is a strong positive public response to Earth-Kind®. The American Rose Society calendar for 2009 (used to promote rose growing and as a fundraiser for the society) was devoted to Earth-Kind® and featured Earth-Kind®-winning rose cultivars. In addition, commercial nurseries that are promoting Earth-Kind®-winning cultivars as such and in the context of education on Earth-Kind® methodology are finding exponential increases in sales of those cultivars (Mark Chamblee, personal communication).

Earth-Kind® research programs are not based on anecdotal evidence, but rather on randomized replicated studies conducted with scientific rigor and honest evaluations. Care is taken to make them as free as possible of personal and commercial biases.

As the Earth-Kind® message continues to grow, it is important to recognize that Earth-Kind®, and its accompanying logo, is a legal trademark of the Texas A&M University System. While no royalties are involved in use of the term and our goal is to expand the Earth-Kind® system worldwide; the Texas A&M University System and the Earth-Kind® team retain control over the trademark. People wishing to use the term must comply with the strict guidelines to maintain the purity of official Earth-Kind® approved information.

FUTURE PROSPECTS FOR EARTH-KIND®

The current goal of the Earth-Kind® program is to see its expansion worldwide. In many communities, organic and traditional gardeners share different values and goals, frequently even becoming antagonistic toward one another. The Earth-Kind® program provides horticulturists, scientists, gardeners, and landscapers a cohesive message that is easily recognized, understood, and implemented. By adopting the Earth-Kind® program and operating under the Earth-Kind® banner, researchers and rosarians need not develop and refine new testing methods, as the basic Earth-Kind® protocols have proven to be successful regardless of climate, soil type, and other local variables. Regional variations can be incorporated as necessary. Earth-Kind® provides a uniform testing procedure for university and regional field trials at a global level.

Defining what should constitute the extent of a region as more regions in the United States and beyond are developed within the Earth-Kind® program will be an important and ongoing consideration. Taking into account ranges in temperature, moisture, soil, and other critical factors impacting plant growth and performance will be imperative. United States Environmental Protection Agency (U.S. EPA) Ecoregions could provide the framework for regional distinctions. However, this illustrates the challenge for this program. As of 2008, the U.S. EPA recognizes 84 Level III Ecoregions in the United States (Griffith et al. 2004, Commission for Environmental Cooperation 1997). Texas alone has 13 ranging from the Chihuahuan Desert in far west Texas to the coastal plain in southeast Texas. (SEE PLATE 17) Average annual rainfall may range from 200 mm or less in El Paso, while Beaumont may receive in excess of 1200 mm per year (Arnold 2008). At the same time, pan evaporation rates in El Paso may exceed precipitation rates by 1500 mm (Arnold 2008). Nonetheless, since 1998 the program has identified 19 roses that may be successfully grown using Earth-Kind® recommendations throughout these varied regions.

As Earth-Kind® moves worldwide, it is hoped that each participating country would use the Earth-Kind® approach to identify and honor the strongest, most attractive roses from their own country. In so doing, each country would be developing its own national collection of beautiful Earth-Kind® roses. These high-performance selections could be shared with other Earth-Kind® researchers around the world to see how wide a region such cultivars are adapted. As the number of Earth-

Kind® researchers increase, a natural progression would be to convene a World Earth-Kind® Conference to assemble a truly "World Collection of Earth-Kind® Roses," where representatives from each country could report on roses and share propagation material of the top cultivars from their own trials. Through this uniform research mechanism, the hardiest specimens of *Rosa* germplasm could be identified, shared, and perpetually preserved.

The purpose of the Earth-Kind® program is not one of exclusivity but rather a single organizing entity that can provide a basic framework for individual research and creativity in the development of the hardiest and most beautiful landscape plants around the world. As additional researchers contribute their expertise and trial data, the overall program will benefit. Unique expertise and resources can greatly benefit the growing research base. Although landscape performance in regional trials with local pest and climatic pressures is the key method by which regionally adapted cultivars are identified, laboratory or other assays to screen plants for tolerance or resistance to a particular pest or environmental stressor common to a region or across regions can be very useful. With the high volume of cultivars available to consider, challenging candidate cultivars with the most problematic factors for successful landscape performance in a region can help objectively pinpoint which to include in extensive field trials. In addition, if for some reason natural pest pressure or environmental extremes are atypical for a region during the trial, controlled resistance screens can help provide essential information that may not otherwise be possible.

For instance, blackspot is one of the most universal and devastating diseases of roses in the landscape. Three races of the pathogen (*Diplocarpon rosae*) causing blackspot collected from Eastern North America and characterized and preserved by the University of Minnesota Woody Plant Breeding Program are available to challenge roses and characterize their resistance (Whitaker et al. 2007). A grant provided by the University of Minnesota Garden Calendar Fund has allowed the 30 roses in the Earth-Kind® National Brigade (phase 2 of trialing) (see Table 4), the 20 Northern Earth-Kind® trial roses (see Table 3), and 17 Earth-Kind® winners

TABLE 4.

Earth-Kind® Brigade roses being trialed in the Mid-United States.

CULTIVAR[a]	HORTICULTURAL CLASS	YEAR OF INTRODUCTION
MACdub (Dublin Bay)	Climbing floribunda	1975
Chuckles	Floribunda	1958
Penelope	Hybrid musk	1924
KORtersen (Rosarium Uetersen)	Large flowered climber	1977
New Dawn	Large flowered climber	1930
The Fairy	Polyantha	1932
Amiga Mia	Shrub	1978
April Moon	Shrub	1984
Barn Dance	Shrub	1975
Belinda's Dream	Shrub	1992
BUCbi (Carefree BeautyTM)	Shrub	1977
Country Dancer	Shrub	1973
Earth Song	Shrub	1975
Flora Dora	Shrub	unknown
Folksinger	Shrub	1985
MEIpitac (Carefree WonderTM)	Shrub	1990
Pearlie Mae	Shrub	1981
Polonaise	Shrub	1984
Prairie Breeze	Shrub	1978
Prairie Harvest	Shrub	1985
Prairie Princess	Shrub	1972
Princess Verona	Shrub	1984
Quietness	Shrub	2003
Radcon (Pink Knock Out®)	Shrub	2005
RADrazz (Knock Out®)	Shrub	1999
Radyod (Blushing Knock Out®)	Shrub	2004
Sea Foam	Shrub	1964
Square Dancer	Shrub	1972
Summer Wind	Shrub	1975
Winter Sunset	Shrub	1997

[a] *Trademark or exhibition name, if different from cultivar name, is listed in parenthesis.*

in the South (omitting 'La Marne' and 'Souvenir de St. Anne's' because they were designated Earth-Kind® after the experiment started (see Table 2) to be surveyed for their resistance. Race-specific and nonrace-specific resistance using detached leaf assays and these three races will be compared to a growing body of field data. If the lab tests prove predictive of field results, future Earth-Kind® candidates can then be characterized for resistance to these and potentially additionally identified and preserved races. University of Minnesota Earth-Kind® collaborators have the expertise and resources to provide this service to the greater Earth-Kind® team. Blackspot resistance/tolerance data can be coupled with other available performance data to help better pinpoint roses with Earth-Kind® potential for inclusion in future trials.

There are multiple assays available to screen roses for resistance or tolerance to pathogens and abiotic factors and more that can be developed. Some assays that have been developed that may be useful in some regions include assessing the maximum cold tolerance of acclimated rose canes (Rajashekar et al. 1982) and screening for resistance to downy mildew (Peronospora sparsa Berk) using detached leaf assays (Schulz and Debener 2007). Additional areas of expertise and resources that support regional research under the broad Earth-Kind® umbrella mission are most welcome to be proposed and considered.

Reprinted with permission from Global Science Books © 2009. The manuscript appears within the 2009 special issue of *Floriculture and Ornamental Biotechnology* dedicated to roses (www.globalsciencebooks.info/JournalsSup/09FOB_3_SI1.html).

Full citation: Harp, D. A., Zlesak, D. C., Hammond, G., George, S., and W. Mackay, 2009. "Earth-Kind® Rose Trials—Identifying the World's Strongest, Most Beautiful Landscape Roses," in: Zlesak D.C. (Ed), Roses. *Floriculture and Ornamental Biotechnology*. 3 (Special Issue 1):166–175.

Corresponding author: Dr. Derald Harp, Derald_Harp@tamu-commerce.edu

"Earth-Kind®" is a registered proprietary trademark of the Texas AgriLife Extension Service, on file with the U.S. Patent and Trademark Office since 1991, and no person, entity, or organization may use the term "Earth-Kind" or its accompanying logo in any form or media without the express written permission of the owner. The Texas AgriLife Extension Service is an agency of the Texas A&M University System. Inquiries should be directed to Dr. Steve George, Texas A&M University, Dept. of Horticultural Sciences, Texas AgriLife, Extension, 17360 Coit Road, Dallas, TX 75252.

REFERENCES

Arnold, M (2008) Landscape Plants for Texas and Environs (3rd ed.), Stipes Publishing, 1334 pp

Australian Government, Office of the Gene Technology Regulator (2005) The biology and econology of Rosa x hybrida (rose). p 6

Berstein L, Francois LE (1973) Comparisons of drip, furrow, and sprinkler irrigation. Soil Science 115, 73–86

Brady NC, Weil RR (2001) The Nature and Properties of Soils (13th Edn), Prentice Hall, 960 pp

Buck GJ (1964a) Roses: Divide and conquer. American Rose Magazine May, pp 6–8, 26

Buck GJ (1964b) Stock-scion relationships in roses. American Rose Annual 49, 159–164

Buck GJ (1978) Of all flowers, methinks a rose is best. Horticulture January, 40–47

Buck GJ (1979) Roses, Ltd. American Rose Annual 64, 124–132

Commission for Environmental Cooperation (1997) Ecological Regions of North America, Toward a Common Perspective. Bibliotechque nationale du Quebec, 60 pp

Garcia-Navarro MC, Evans RY, Montserrat RS (2004) Estimation of relative water use among ornamental landscape species. Scientia Horticulturae 99, 163–174

Gardner JG, Eastwood DB, Hall CR, Brooker JR (2004) Pricing powdery-mildew resistant dogwoods: Simulated impact on the nursery-industry supply chain. HortTechnology 14 (1), 114–119

Glenn E, Tanner R, Mendez S, Kehret T, Moore D, Garcia J, Valdes C (1998) Growth rates, salt tolerance and water use characteristics of native and invasive riparian plants from the delta of the Colorado River, Mexico. Journal of Arid Environments 40, 281–294

Goodwin SM, Edwards CJ, Jenks MA (2007) Leaf cutin monomers, cuticular waxes, and blackspot resistance in rose. HortScience 42 (7), 1631–1635

Grabowski MA, Zlesak DC, Gillman JH (2007) Control of blackspot on rose, 2007. Plant Disease Management Reports 2, OT005

Griffith GE, Bryce SA, Omernik JM, Comstock JA, Rogers AC, Harrison B, Hatch SL, Bezanson D (2004) Ecoregions of Texas (color poster with map, descriptive text, and photographs): Reston VA, US Geological Society (map scale 1:2,500,000)

Gudin S (2000) Rose: Genetics and breeding. In: Janick J (Ed) Plant Breeding Reviews (Vol 17), John Wiley & Sons, Inc., pp 159–189

Gudin S (1998) Improvement of rose varietal creation in the world. Acta Horticulturae (ISHS) 495:283–292

Hagan AK, Gilliam CH, Fare DC (1988) Evaluation of new fungicides for control of rose blackspot. Journal of Environmental Horticulture 6, 67–69

Hagan AK, Rivas-Davila ME, Akridge JR, Olive JW (2005) Disease resistance and response of shrub and ground cover roses to fungicides. Auburn University, Auburn, AL, 22 pp

Harp DA, Colbert D, Gopffarth H (2008) Variation in organic matter and macronutrient availability in landscape soils under landscape fabric. HortScience 43 (3), 626

Horne CW, Amador JM, Johnson JD, McCoy NL, Philley GL, Lee TA Jr., Kaufman HW, Jones RK, Barnes LW, Black MC (1988) Texas Plant Diseases Handbook, Texas Agricultural Extension Service, College Station, TX. 321 pp

Horst RK (1995) Compendium of Rose Diseases, The American Phytopathological Society, APS Press, St. Paul, MN, 50 pp

Hortus (1976) Liberty Hyde Bailey Hortorium, Ed. MacMillan Publishing Co., Inc., 1312 pp

Hurd BH, Hilaire RS, White JM (2006) Residential landscapes, homeowner attitudes, and water-wise choices in New Mexico. HortTechnology 16 (2), 241–246

Israel GD, Easton JO, Knox GW (1999) Adoption of landscape management practices by Florida residents. HortTechnology 9 (2), 262–266

Jenkins WR (1955) Variability of pathogenecity and physiology of Diplocarpon rosae Wolf, the rose blackspot fungus. American Rose Annual 40, 92–97

Lindstrom R, Kiplinger DC (1955) Blindwood of 'Better Times' roses as affected by selection of stock and nitrogen and potassium nutrition. Proceedings of the American Society for Horticultural Science 66, 374–377

Littell RC, Henry PR, Ammerman CB (1998) Statistical analysis of repeated measures data using SAS procedures. Journal of Animal Science 76, 1216–1231

Mackay WA, George SW, McKenney C, Sloan JJ, Cabrera RI, Reinert JA, Colbaugh O, Lockett L, Crow W (2008) Performance of garden roses in north-central Texas under minimal input conditions. HortTechnology 18, 417–422

McBee O, Smalley TJ, Radcliffe DE (2004) Soil water in amended landscape soils. HortScience 39 (4), 883

Nelson G (2003) Florida's Best Native Landscape Plants: 200 Readily Available Species for Homeowners and Professionals. University Press of Florida, 432 pp

Palmer JG, Semeniuk P, Stewart RN (1966) Roses and blackspot. I. Pathogenecity to excised leaflets of Diplocarpon rosae from seven geographic locations. Phytopathology 56, 1277–1282

Rajapaska S, Byrne D (2001) Gene map speeds selection of commercial traits. FlowerTECH 4 (4), 1–4

Rajashekar C, Pellett HM, Burke MJ (1982) Deep supercooling in roses. HortScience 17, 609–611

Reddy S, Spencer JA, Newman SE (1992) Leaflet surfaces of blackspot-resistant and susceptible roses and their reactions to fungal invasion. HortScience 27 (2), 133–135

Rodda K (2008) EarthKindTM rose program finds national audience. Nursery Management and Production 25 (5), 12–14

Santamore FS, Bentz SE (1995) Updated checklist of elm (Ulmus) cultivars for use in North America. Journal of Arboriculture 21(3), 122–131

Scheiber SM, Gilman EF, Sandrock DR, Paz M, Wiese C, Brennan MM (2008) Postestablishment landscape performance of Florida native and exotic shrubs under irrigated and unirrigated conditions. HortTechnology 18 (1), 59–67

Schulz DF, Debener T (2007) Screening for resistance to downy milidew and its early detection in roses. Acta Horticulturae 751, 189–198

Short KC, Roberts AV (1991) Rosa ssp. (roses). In vitro culture, micropropagation, and the production of secondary products. In: Bajaj YPS (Ed) Biotechnology in Agriculture, Forestry, (Vol 15) Medicinal and Aromatic Plants III, Springer-Verlag, Berlin, pp 377–397

Spinti JE, Hilaire RS, van Leeuwen D (2004) Balancing landscape preferences and water conservation in a desert community. HortTechnology 14 (1), 72–77

Stabler LB, Martin CA (2000) Irrigation regimes differentially affect growth and water use efficiency of two southwest landscape plants. Journal of Environmental Horticulture 18, 66–70

Stack LB (2008) Gardening to Conserve Maine's Landscape: Plants to Use and Plants to Avoid, University of Maine Cooperative Extension Bulletin #2500, 2 pp

Townsend AM, Douglass LW (2004) Evaluation of elm clones for tolerance to Dutch Elm Disease. Journal of Arboriculture 30 (3), 179–184

University of Illinois (1987) Report on Plant Disease, Blackspot of Rose, RPD N. 610, October 1987, pp 4

Virag I (2007) A man outstanding in his field (of roses). Newsday, April 18, 2007

Welsh DF, Welch WC, Duble RL (2000) Landscape water conservation… Xeriscape. Available online: aggie-horticulture.tamu.edu/extension/xeriscape/xeriscape.html

Whitaker VM, Zuzek K, Hokanson SC (2007) Resistance of 12 rose genotypes to 14 isolates of Diplocarpon rosae Wolf (rose blackspot) collected from eastern North America. Plant Breeding 126, 83–88

Zlesak DC (2006) Rosa x hybrida L. In: Anderson NO (Ed) Flower Breeding and Genetics: Issues, Challenges, and Opportunities for the 21st Century, Springer, The Netherlands, pp 695–738

Zollinger N, Kjelgren R, Cerny-Koening T, Kopp K, Koenig R (2006) Drought responses of six ornamental herbaceous perennials. Scientia Horticulturae 109, 267–274

From THE FAERIE QUEENE

She bathed with roses red,
And violets blew
And all the sweetest flowres
That in the forrest grew

— EDMUND SPENSER

THE MYSTERY

He came and took me by the hand
   Up to a red rose tree;
He kept His meaning to Himself
   But gave a rose to me.

I did not pray Him to lay bare
   The mystery to me,
Enough the rose was Heaven to smell
   And His own face to see.

—RALPH HODGSON

Faith Whittlesey™, a Viru™ Tea, heralds the introduction of a new line of disease-resistant, moderately sized roses for sustainable warm-weather gardens in the U.S.

Charmed by the "Thereness" of My Roses

PAT HENRY

There is never a day so dreary that roses in some form cannot lighten my way. Whether from an old rose book, the garden or a call from a friend in roses, I find beauty and excitement always *there*!

As long as I can remember, roses were always *there*. Perfection for me did not come into being until the late 1960s, when I wanted to achieve a Queen of the Show. (Not a bad thing, even in the age of the Sustainable Rose Garden.) It was a learning experience that is still a map for me today.

Fast-forwarding to the late 1970s, I was given a small rooted plant of 'Carefree Beauty' by Noah Wilson, who was installing me as President of the Tri-State Rose Society. This was the spark that led the way to my wanting more of Dr. Buck's roses—Griffith Buck was a man far ahead of his time.

A move in the early 1980s to South Carolina with a separate truck just for roses; and *there* I began my special garden that continues to this day. In the late 1980s, Roses Unlimited also began. A collection of Griffith Buck roses was a quest I could not set aside. "The Sustainable Garden" was an expression not yet spoken—but it was in the wind.

It was not until the morning after 9/11 that 'Quietness' came on the scene. Dr. Buck had not released this rose at the time he passed away, but a group of cuttings sent to me by Mary Buck, his daughter, to evaluate became a plant. This plant bloomed for me on that morning, September 11, 2001. So beautiful, so carefree, so fragrant; 'Quietness' had all the qualities we want for roses in the Sustainable Rose Garden. Today, this variety has bloomed and is testing out well all over the United States, and I take great pride in my introduction of a truly great rose.

In the late 1980s ... "The Sustainable Garden" was an expression not yet spoken — but it was in the wind.

My love in a garden is directed toward roses with many faces, not structured but flowing. The small flowers, the exploding flowers, the nodding ones; the singles, the upright, the climbing; roses to look down on, others to look up toward, ones to walk under—*there,* among these roses, is my playhouse of beauty.

I cannot let go this revery without thinking further, of a smaller garden within my garden—and in that nook my thoughts drift to 'Quietness', 'Mystic Beauty', 'Bloomfield Abundance', 'Champney's Pink Cluster', "Secret Garden Musk Climber": roses to love and roses that are easy to maintain, too. This space will not permit all my loves—but leafing through a Roses Unlimited catalogue will permit me to touch on a few more!

A most exciting wave is sweeping our country from Germany. These are the new Kordes Roses. As I walk around the garden today (in February), I find the leaves are still attached and healthy among 'Cinderella Fairy Tale', 'Elegant Fairy Tale', 'Floral Fairy Tale', 'Lion's Fairy Tale', 'Petticoat Fairy Tale'. Many other Kordes Roses will be added for 2010/11 in a new garden, which I will call metaphorically "My Potted

'Quietness', a Griffith Buck seedling introduced by Roses Unlimited, is getting high marks for "sustainability" wherever it is being tested.
PHOTO: STAN HENRY

'Mystic Beauty'™, similar in every respect to 'Souvenir de la Malmaison' excepting that its larger bloom almost always opens in soggy weather, is a sport of 'Kronprincessin Victoria' that was discovered at and introduced by Roses Unlimited. PHOTO: STAN HENRY

Garden," because so many of these can be container grown.

Other special loves are the Romantica Roses from Conard-Pyle: 'Michelangelo', 'Tchaikovski', 'Traviata'. 'Easter Basket' is indeed a lovely basket of roses.

Alister Clark was Australia's counterpart to our Dr. Griffith Buck. He was a hybridizer who was far ahead of his time in breeding tough roses designed to be trouble free. 'Borderer', a low-growing, quick-repeating Polyantha is a treasure. His pink climber 'Amy Johnson' is another beauty.

A wonderful personal reward of Roses Unlimited is the friends you come to know but might never have met otherwise. You get to glimpse into their exciting world. Many customers become friends, even good friends. "Friends in roses" is the motto of the nursery.

When I think further of lovely roses and lovely people I have come to know through roses, Viru and Girija Viraraghavan from India come to mind—and the roses they have created. Faith Whittlesey™, named for another most lovely person, the former U.S. Ambassador to Switzer-

My love in a garden is directed toward roses with many faces, not structured but flowing. The small flowers, the exploding flowers, the nodding ones; the singles ... there, among these roses, is my playhouse of beauty.

land, is the first of these. My garden will never be without this blush-white beauty, which is one of the 5 modest-growing (to 4 feet) Viru™ Teas that are beginning to grace Southern and warm-weather gardens. Others include: Krishna's Peach™ (rare apricot Tea), now growing up and so very lovely, Garnet Crest™ (white with red edging), Aussie Sixer™ (another apricot—named in honor of the 6 co-authors of *Tea Roses: Old Roses for Warm Gardens),* and Dixie Beauty™ (light yellow and very fragrant). These round out the new Viru™ Teas, with more anticipated.

I am reminded by the *thereness* of my roses and friends in roses that the world should never be crowded with the woes of the day but should also have room for the promise, beauty, and excitement that can come from and through the roses of yesterday and today.

A BOWL OF ROSES

There is no woman who can place
  A bowl of roses on a shelf
Without an inward upward urge
  To be more beautiful herself.

There is no woman who can keep
  Disorder reigning in a room
Whose chastely fresh-cut roses shed
  The light and fragrance of their bloom.

Something there is of sun and wind—
  Of rain—and clean bright summer air
Held captive, when a bowl is filled
  With roses—and placed anywhere—

That works a charm on ugliness,
  And lightens all dark-cornered gloom;
A bowl of roses can perform
  A miracle in any room.

—GRACE NOLL CROWELL

Rosa moyesii from the 1920 American Rose Annual is known for its hips as well as vibrant flowers. Species roses are often relatively sustainable, and many are known for their beautiful or decorative foliage, or other special features that make them desirable landscape plants.

Beautiful Foliage,
an Important Design Element

JANET INADA

The foliage of roses is certainly not what we think of first, or second, for that matter, when we contemplate the way roses have insinuated themselves into our memories. And yet, if we pause to think of it, the wide world of roses—the thousands of varieties of the fifty or so classes of roses—offers diverse examples of beautiful, memorable foliage. From the stunning fall color ranges of roses like 'Corylus', *R. nitida,* 'Inermis Morletii', or *R. foliolosa* to the subtle way that the tiny glossy foliage of 'Snow Carpet' flows over a wall or around a boulder, there are many varieties from diverse groups that are quite worthy of being selected for their foliage "interest."

What's more, most roses with beautiful foliage rarely, if ever, need spraying, even in demanding climates. Among climbers in his "no-spray" Jacksonville, Florida, garden, Gene Waering, for instance, cites *R. gigantea*, 'Marechal Niel', 'Lady Hillingdon', 'Amber Cloud'™, 'Evergreen Gene'™, *R. chinensis spontanea, R. laevigata* and the glossy foliaged 'Cooper's Burmese' as some examples of roses with interesting foliage qualities that almost never get blackspot.

And who has not noted the quietly dazzling, dark green foliage of the Wichurana Ramblers that give that extra bit of elegance to the entire clan? From 'Albertine' to a rose I treasure, 'Mme. Alice Garnier', also known

GRAHAM STUART THOMAS WOULD HAVE SHARED JANET INADA'S APPRECIATION FOR BEAUTIFUL AND INTERESTING FOLIAGE. HE WROTE OF ONE FAVORITE ROSE, "IN LATE SUMMER THE BOURBON ROSE 'MME. ERNST CALVET' PRODUCES WHAT IS PROBABLY THE MOST GORGEOUS OF ALL ROSE FOLIAGE, HANDSOME AND LARGE AND OF RICH DARK PLUM AND MAROON. FOR ADDING DEPTH AND RICHNESS TO AN ARRANGEMENT OF CRIMSON AND MAROON AND PURPLE ROSES, MODERN OR OLD-FASHIONED, THIS FOLIAGE IS UNRIVALLED, WHILE AGAINST ITS OWN COLOUR, SOFT PINK OR WITH YELLOW OR WHITE ROSES, THE CONTRAST IS STRIKING." (FROM "DECORATIVE FOLIAGE," *THE ROSE*, VOL. 1, NO. 1, AUTUMN, 1952, PP. 39–41) —EDITORS

as 'The Brownlow Rambler', to the little known but wonderful 'La Perle', these roses, the Wichuranas, so under-planted in gardens today, provide drama and spectacle.

Then there is the uniquely beautiful apple-green, veined wine-red, spring foliage of the Boursault, 'Amadis', offering a perfect complement to the purple blooms. In comparison, the blooms of *R. glauca*, which is grown almost entirely for its foliage, are insignificant.

"That's a rose?!" is sure to be evoked by oddities such as the variegated Japanese maple-cut leaves of *R. watsoniana*. The pink blooms of 'Centifolia Bullata' are lovely though unremarkable. It's the crinkled "lettuce" leaves that distinguish it among the other antique pinks. *R. sericea pteracantha*, also known as 'Dragon Wings' or the 'Firethorn', is a plant noteworthy in all aspects from its tiny, lacy leaves, to its signature vertically elongated red thorns and unique four-petaled blooms (arrayed like a dusting of snow atop the branches), to its jewel-like juicy, delicious tiny hips.

One friend, Conrad Johnson, a premier garden designer, suggests that there are basically two types of rose foliage to consider when contemplating the play of light on foliage in the garden. Light dances from the glossy leaves of some species such as *R. Bhutan*, the Teas, and many of the modern roses and these may be said to form a "reflective foliage" group. Back- or side-lighting plays through the thinner, more delicate leaves of other classes like the Albas and Spinosissimas and many of the Species, or near Species, and these can be said to make up the "transparent foliage" group. It is common for leaves of the latter group to have a slightly silky quality as well, which sometimes creates just a hint of reflectivity.

Often we see glossy, reflective foliage in the work of modern breeders highly concerned with disease resistance. In my opinion, there is all too often a repetitive, almost plastic, quality to the large, similarly shaped foliage of so many modern roses, however disease resistant or shiny they may be.

Ralph Moore, however, who frequently worked with varieties from underused classes, has given us a wide variety of modern roses with love-ly glossy foliage that varies from the exquisite micro-mini, 'Baby Austin', to the peach-leafed Climbing Poly-antha, 'Renae', and the beautiful quilted red tinged foliage of two Ru-gosa hybrids, 'Linda Campbell' and 'Moore's Striped Rugosa'.

Paul Barden is another breeder working with many classes of roses who is aware of the importance of fo-liage visual interest even as he strives for disease resistance and healthy fo-liage. I find that the foliages of Barden's roses have distinctive touches that maintain our interest—here a toothed leaf with the finest of red edges, and there the darkest green set off by red canes. Barden's spectacular Gal-lica, 'Marianne', and his Miniature, 'Unconditional Love', are examples of the success Barden has had in working to produce healthy, vigorous foliage that provides both a lovely background for blooms and is also ef-fective in the garden visually for its leaves alone.

Surely a bit of thought given to the design potential and the extremely varied range of roses with beautiful foliage will result in a more interest-ing garden, both in and out of bloom.

And who has not noted the quietly dazzling, dark green foliage of the Wichurana Ramblers that give that extra bit of elegance to the entire clan? ... these roses, the Wichuranas, so under-planted in gardens today, provide drama and spectacle.

"Secret Garden Musk Climber" attests to the importance of "Found Roses" and the heritage rose movement. Discovered on a neglected property in California, its name of origin is unknown. It is among the most fragrant and free-blooming roses of all time.

Secret Garden Musk Climber

JERI JENNINGS

My nose led me to "Secret Garden Musk Climber".

On a warm spring morning in Descanso Gardens' vast International Rosarium, I followed the scent of honey and spice to its source: brilliant golden stamens centering simple ragged, single white blooms, on a vigorous climbing rose. From the big clusters of bloom, fragrance filled the air for a distance of several feet from a rustic wooden arbor.

An identification tag read simply: SECRET GARDEN.

No date of introduction was indicated. No hybridizer. No country of origin. "Secret Garden", it seemed, was a mystery.

The Rosarium more or less eschews Found Roses. This garden wants its roses clearly defined and of known pedigree. Roses collected in old gardens and deserted cemeteries that have not been matched to a historic identity are well represented in some other public gardens but not in this one. Despite California's rich treasure of such Found Roses, and their excellent adaptation to California conditions, they are for the most part unrecognized in the Descanso collection.

Nonetheless, there it was. Bursting with vigor, covered with blooms, wantonly wafting its honey-spice fragrance on the warm spring breeze, it was, undeniably, NOT listed in any compendium of officially recognized roses. Careless of its illegitimate status, it tumbled happily over an arbor at the entrance to a child-sized hidden Secret Rose Garden.

THE HERITAGE ROSES
GROUP MOVEMENT,
A FELLOWSHIP OF
ROSARIANS WITHOUT A
CENTRAL FORMAL ORGANIZATION
AND HEADQUARTERS, WAS
ESTABLISHED IN 1975. *THE
ROSE LETTER*, OF WHICH JERI
JENNINGS IS THE CURRENT,
MUCH ADMIRED EDITOR, IS ITS
QUARTERLY JOURNAL, SEE WWW.
theheritagerosesgroup.org FOR
OTHER INFORMATION, OTHER
RESPECTED *ROSE LETTER* EDITORS
OVER THE LAST DECADE INCLUDE
MARLEA GRAHAM AND THE LATE
RAE CHAMBERS. FOR MORE ABOUT
RAE CHAMBERS, GOOGLE SEARCH
SEIDEL REMEMBERING RAE
CHAMBERS.   —EDITORS

I took cuttings. They failed.

Much later, I learned that this isn't the easiest cultivar to propagate from cuttings.

I had, however, an ace in the hole. Subsequent purloined cuttings were shared with a friend whose access to a state-of-the-art misting house gave him an advantage. He succeeded handily, keeping one plant for his own garden and returning six to me.

The 6-acre International Rosarium is part of the 150-acre Descanso Garden, located in Flintridge/La Canada, southern California. The property, once the home of newspaper publisher E. Manchester Boddy, is best known for its vast camellia forest.

"SECRET GARDEN MUSK CLIMBER" IN THE AUTHOR'S GARDEN

I was thrilled to have the rose in my garden and happy to share it with a few discerning friends. The lack of documentation didn't bother me (or my friends), but it *did* tickle my curiosity. Seeking enlightenment, I turned, of course, to the Internet.

The late Colonel Mel Hulse of the San Jose Heritage Rose Garden held the key. From Mel, I learned that the Descanso label should have read, not SECRET GARDEN, but SECRET GARDEN MUSK CLIMBER.

A classic example of California's Found Roses, SGMC is one of many cultivars discovered, rescued, propagated, and introduced (or re-introduced) by northern California rosarian Joyce Demits. Having donated it to the Rosarium and the San Jose Heritage Rose Garden, Joyce offered the rose for a time through her Tanglewood Farms rose nursery. With the closing of that wonderful nursery, the rose disappeared from commerce.

Mel loved this fragrant mystery as much as I did. We became its cheer-leaders, complaining, proclaiming, cajoling, and enabling, until we succeeded in pushing the rose back into commerce, where it now clings to a tenuous foothold.

"Secret Garden Musk Climber" and its companion "Secret Garden Noisette" are said to have come from a garden in the Sierra foothills. That's California's historic, romantic Gold Rush country.

The area was settled from the mid-19th century onward. For a time, it was said—not always in jest—that fully half of the population of the United States, it seemed, could be found in California, drawn by stories of gold in California's rivers and mountains. The flood of gold seekers included people from every part of the globe. And when people came, many of them brought roses.

"Secret Garden Musk Climber" is at its best when it is given enough space to let it reach out and arch gracefully and naturally. It tolerates fairly firm pruning … if that is required.

Today the area of small towns is linked by 230-or-so miles of California Highway 49—the Golden Chain. It remains a mother lode of roses. Teas, Noisettes, Chinas, and Polyanthas are common there, in a mix that includes a little of everything. Roses have been found in old cemeteries; in deserted gardens and carefully tended ones; in parking lots and cow pastures.

Some roses found here are easily identified, and many of those have been returned to commerce under their verified historic identities. Many cannot and may never be matched to a known verifiable historic name. With or without that desired "historic identity," their ability to survive and bloom even when left untended proclaims their value as garden roses.

"Secret Garden Musk Climber" and "Secret Garden Noisette" are said to have come from a privately owned garden. The ownership and exact location of that garden remain (and may always remain) a closely held secret. It's probable that both the garden and its roses are now gone, and this is hardly surprising. Time, climate change, and the inexorable Path of Progress combine to kill more heirloom plants every year, erasing history, along with old homes, gardens, and crumbling mines.

HOW DOES IT GROW?

In my mild-climate coastal southern California garden, "Secret Garden Musk Climber" makes a large, vigorous, continuously blooming climber. It can grow massively enough to overfill the average garden arch but can be accommodated nicely if the arch is large and sturdy.

From personal experience, I believe that "Secret Garden Musk Climber" is at its best when it is given enough space to let it reach out and arch gracefully and naturally. It tolerates fairly firm pruning, however, if that is required. Descanso Gardens prunes their pair hard enough to place me in annual danger of heart failure. The reason for this virtual butchery is spatial rather than cultural, and the roses would be better served (and lovelier by far) with less draconian handling. There is simply not enough room where they are placed. SGMC appears to accept this very rough treatment with good grace and bountiful bloom, but it is not an approach I would recommend.

In our garden, forewarned of the mature size of the plants, we augmented a commercially made metal arbor by adding upright side trellises. Thus encouraged, the rose has formed a 10-ft.-wide wall of bloom and foliage, interrupted by a central gate. A species fuchsia *(F. hatschii)* climbs through the rose, blooming in contrasting clusters of small, vivid red trumpets. The plants flourish on half-day (afternoon) sun and bloom, for the most part, on the sunny side of the floral wall. A few blooms stray into a deeply shaded garden room, a secret shade garden hidden and protected by the rose.

In our conditions, bloom production is heaviest in spring but continues right through our typically mild winters. Unless pruned into a period of inactivity, few roses go dormant here. "Secret Garden

"Secret Garden Musk Climber" at the Jennings home in Camarilla, California, is almost never out of bloom.

Musk Climber" drops petals cleanly. Hips form, but they are few and far between. Deadheading speeds repeat bloom and curtails the size of the plant a bit.

The rose seems well adapted to our increasingly warm and dry summers. In our land of little rain, of course, regular irrigation is a requirement for the survival of any garden plant, including most cacti. In our cool, humid, coastal conditions, we may see occasional mild signs of powdery mildew. These vanish with the onset of warm weather.

We have never seen "Secret Garden Musk Climber" touched by rust. In our garden, it requires no spraying. Hummingbirds and other visiting birds scoop up aphids and most other insect pests. Blackspot is a very rare visitor to our area, but imperfect resistance to that fungal disease has been reported in areas where it is a common problem.

Reports indicate that, without heroic protective measures, "Secret Garden Musk Climber" may fail to survive colder than- average winters in zones colder than 6. With heroic protection, it has been successfully grown in Zone 4a Minnesota, but it is clear that such conditions do not favor long-range survival or the achievement of great size.

WHAT IS IT?

I have little or no scientific training, and none at all in the plant sciences. My professional background is in commercial art, copywriting, and photography. My response to roses is visual rather than analytical, and my appreciation of a good Found Rose generates only secondary interest in its origin or real name. If a rose is beautiful, vigorous, disease-free, and blooms well, I am content. In my garden, roses are not asked to provide documentation of their birth and baptism. Study names work for me. Call it what you wish, with my blessing, so long as we all know what rose we're discussing.

This philosophy sets me in opposition to the American Rose Society, which has historically required verifiable historic identification as the price of recognition.

If, however, a real identity is sought for "Secret Garden Musk Climber", a relationship of some sort to *R. moschata* must be considered. Mel Hulse, after years of observation, was convinced that the rose was a hybrid (chance or man-made) between *R. moschata* and SOMETHING. Field Guide reports and personal observation of both "Secret Garden Musk Climber" and The Old Musk Rose indicate points of similarity. But there are differences.

The fragrance of "Secret Garden Musk Climber" seems to match that of *R. moschata*. The identification of fragrance is surely subjective, but to my nose the fragrances are indistinguishable.

Both SGMC and *R. moschata* bloom in both large and small panicles of white single blooms. Both roses open blooms sequentially, extending the range of time-fresh blooms within an inflorescence that are available to pollinators.

Pollinators are strongly attracted to "Secret Garden Musk Climber". In a time when the honeybee population is dropping, it's heartening to see them dancing around those masses of fragrant white bloom. In both *R. moschata* and "Secret Garden Musk Climber", fragrance resides in the stamens rather than the petals.

Individual blooms are similar in size (perhaps 2 inches in diameter). *R. moschata*'s blooms open somewhat cupped but, in my observation, seem to reflex back fairly rapidly, presenting the stamens with an almost embarrassing boldness. Blooms of "Secret Garden Musk Climber" open slightly cupped and remain so.

The leaves of "Secret Garden Musk Climber" differ markedly from those of *R. moschata*. They are longer, more acutely pointed, and have a soft peach-leaf texture that contrasts with leaves I have seen of *R. moschata*.

Hips of *R. moschata* and "Secret Garden Musk Climber" differ greatly in size, shape, and even numbers. SGMC hips, moreover, are of variable form. Hips of *R. moschata* are described as hispid, small, and subglobose, or (in the specific case of Graham Stuart Thomas's Musk) ovoid. Most plants of *R. moschata* surveyed appeared to set hips profusely.

"Secret Garden Musk Climber", by contrast, produces much larger hips. These vary widely in shape, with some being urn-shaped in form while others are subglobose. Though pollinators work busily among its blooms, "Secret Garden Musk Climber" sets surprisingly few hips, but they are consistently larger than those of *R. moschata*.

I lack the expertise to even begin to sort all this out or make a guess at the historic or "true" identity of "Secret Garden Musk Climber" (assuming that there is one to be discovered). It seems to me that its changeable nature may indicate a particularly complex pedigree. It might be argued that a rose of such complexity must have been the product of a deliberate and complex breeding program. If so, whose?

Where enough roses are grown, plant sex sometimes happens, and wonderful things can be produced. One friend calls these chance-created cultivars God Roses, giving credit to the Greatest Hybridizer of all.

Pollinators are strongly attracted to "Secret Garden Musk Climber". In a time when the honeybee population is dropping, it's heartening to see them dancing around those masses of fragrant white bloom.

I thank Brent Dickerson for the following lines from Vibert: ("Essay on Roses," *Second Cahier* [1826], Chapter 3.)

> There is one important observation that we get from examining seed-grown roses. It is that, along with all the natural pollinations that have taken place—particularly in the gardens which combine a great number of species and varieties in a space confined by walls—the characteristics can join and change in a very obvious way, lacking which, nevertheless, all the sorts which could contribute to the birth of whatever hybrid could give it as far as growth goes some qualities no others would have.

It is possible that "Secret Garden Musk Climber" is one of these gifts of chance, but ... Years of study might or might not uncover a true name for this stunning rose. Whether that eventually happens or not, I am happy to accept "Secret Garden Musk Climber" for what it is. As Mr. Shakespeare notes, it will smell as sweet—and bloom as generously—under any name we choose to give it.

Through my kitchen window, I've watched bees and hummingbirds visit "Secret Garden Musk Climber". I have rested in its shade on hot days and added its delicate blooms to my Christmas bouquets. I don't have to know where it came from. I am content. The What Is It question won't go away, of course, but others are welcome to take on that quest.

Please keep me posted. You'll find me sitting here with a cool drink and a good book, in the shade of my rose.

Rodents versus Roses

Keeping Roses Alive in Gopher Country

JERI JENNINGS

Every place man tries to garden probably has its own sort of burrowing rodent. The problem might be rats, field mice or voles, ground squirrels, gophers. Herbivorous rodents that eat the roots of plants are destructive garden pests, but the damage they cause can go far beyond the garden. Colonies of burrowing rodents can even destabilize the land they infest. (If your house is sitting on that land, or is protected by a burrow-ridden levee, this is a problem.)

In our part of southern California, the burrowing rodent du jour is the western pocket gopher, genera Geomys and Thomomys, sometimes called "pouched rats." With powerful forequarters, large front claws, small beady eyes, and huge teeth that grow constantly, they're perfectly designed for their lifestyle. They can chew through water or information cable lines.

I once read that gophers were not attracted to rose roots. That is SO wrong! They LOVE the roots of roses. There's plenty of information about them online, so learning about gophers isn't hard. Getting rid of them, however, can be virtually impossible. Traps are inefficient. Poison threatens domestic pets and raptors. The gophers seem to know this, for

RODENT DEFENSE

Own-root rose – no roots left.

Nursery squat pot ready for use.

A squat long in the ground. A gopher
has dug here, but could not reach the
roots of the rose in the pot.

Salvaged plants, growing new roots,
This time, protected in squat pots.

periodically they will stick their heads out of their holes and look right at you.

If you cannot remove the gophers, you must protect your roses against them.

One of our young roses caught my eye recently. It had been growing well. Now it was dying, and I figured I knew why. I grasped a still-green cane, and pulled, gently. She popped right out of the ground. NO ROOTS. Days later, a second plant, three-feet away, suffered the same fate.

@#$%^%$##@ GOPHERS!!!

It was in part our fault. In an area where there had been no gopher activity in several years, we had taken a chance. Two promising own-root plants had gone directly into the ground. Now, we saw the result. In a short time, the gopher or gophers ate all the roots of both young plants.

I once read that gophers were not attracted to rose roots. That is SO wrong! They LOVE the roots of roses.

Chicken wire or metal mesh baskets are often recommended for gopher protection. They're a huge hassle, though, if you ever have to move a rose to a different location, and we do sometimes move roses. Moreover, chicken wire can deteriorate, making a doorway for the first gopher that happens along.

Chew THAT, you @#$%^%$##@ GOPHERS!!!

Our chosen solution was borrowed from our friends Una and Jim Lopez. Their Santa Ynez, California, garden rivaled ours for gopher population. In their garden, we were intrigued to see the rims of large nursery pots rising 2–3 inches above ground level, around each rose bush. Their roses were planted in individual pots that were sunk into the ground. Irrigation water went directly into each pot; so, the roses were watered, but nearby weeds were not. Plant losses to gophers had dropped to zero.

That was all we needed to hear! We immediately placed an order for an initial 100 black plastic nursery "squats."*

---

* *Nursery supply companies have been our best source for nursery pots of all sizes and shapes.*

Lower and wider than the average nursery pot, our squats have sturdy, molded handles. In our sole departure from the Lopez method, we drill MANY extra .75-inch to 1-inch holes in each pot. The holes, distributed across the bottom, and several inches up the side of the squats, allow anchor roots an egress from their plastic prison.

This planting method requires a jumbo-sized planting hole. It must be dug large enough to accommodate a 15-gal. squat[*], with the rim remaining above the ground. The rose is planted in the squat, as if it were a hole rather than a pot. If it's more convenient, a rose can be planted in its squat, and wait above ground for a move to its eventual location. Filled pots are HEAVY, if the pots must be moved. Handles on the squat pots are invaluable.

In the garden, the rim of the squat is left slightly above ground level. We believe that the rim aids in water retention. It also facilitates removal if that's needed later. A good coating of mulch renders the pots invisible to the casual visitor.

The method is not without its downside. A rose planted in a squat, for example, is slower to mature than a rose planted directly in the ground. Maturity may be delayed a year or more—until substantial roots have reached the outer soil. Plant growth and performance increase noticeably when this has been achieved. Because of that slowed development, we are occasionally tempted to put roses directly into the ground. The fate of our two young bushes demonstrated (again) why we cannot take that chance.

Our poor rootless roses, after a long soak in water and root stimulant, were replanted—in 15-gal. squats. Own-root plants to begin with, they appear to be generating new roots, and we believe they will live. Maturity, however, will be GREATLY delayed. (Had they been budded plants, I believe their survival would have been less likely.)

We've found one other downside to the use of pots in the ground, and it is a troubling one. We live in Bermuda grass territory *(Cynodon dactylon)*, often called "devil grass." We didn't plant it. We don't know who did. It is feral here and virtually indestructible.

---

[*] *We have made use of a few 20-gal. squats.*

Bermuda grass has in some cases invaded pots from the bottom, growing up through the drain holes in the pot. Once inside the pot, the grass sends its roots around and around, eventually filling up the pot to the exclusion of soil. When this occurs, we've found no recourse but to dig up the rose, pull up the pot, bare-root the plant, and remove all vestiges of the invasive grass. (If you are fortunate enough to live where Bermuda grass is unknown, celebrate your good fortune!)

This planting method requires a jumbo-sized planting hole. It must be dug large enough to accommodate a 15-gal. squat, with the rim remaining above the ground.

THE GOOD NEWS

The good news is that the "devil grass" problem is not widespread. Through most of our garden, roses are growing happily in buried nursery squat pots. Some roses have been in their squats for close to 15 years, and have grown to 10 feet or more in height. The size and vigor of these first experiments testify to the success of the method. When mature roses have been removed and replaced, we have found the squat pots to be in perfect condition and ready for reuse for a new rose.

Take THAT, Gopher!

Rose hips are highly variable. At center, Golden Threshold™. Clockwise from upper left: "Grandmother's Hat", 'Francis E. Lester', 'Carefree Beauty', "Secret Garden Musk Climber", *Rosa canina, Rosa californica.*

The Peggy Rockefeller Rose Garden's Dual Mission of Disease Resistance and Protecting 'Eva'

Expanded and Revised

PETER E. KUKIELSKI

THE ROSE: A NATIONAL AND STATE EMBLEM

If public gardens represent the culmination of advanced horticultural practices—as they should—then the public rose garden is the application of those practices to the flower most would agree is the most evolved flower—the veritable "Queen of Flowers," as it has become known throughout most of the world. In America and New York, the rose has an extra-special place. It is officially our National Floral Emblem (designated so by Act of Congress and Presidential Proclamation in 1986) and also the State Flower of New York (1955), as well as the State Flower of several other states.

Because of the rose's popularity and practically unique stature, for me it is not only a joy but also an honor and a privilege to work in the Peggy

Rockefeller Rose Garden at The New York Botanical Garden to preserve the enjoyment of this flower by identifying and applying hopefully proactive, consistent, yet constantly evolving horticultural practices to its cultivation.

The solemn nature of this responsibility in part derives from President Ronald Reagan's Presidential Document 5574, which states:

> Americans have always loved the flowers with which God decorates our land. More often than any other flower, we hold the rose dear as the symbol of life and love and devotion, of beauty and eternity. For the love of man and woman, for the love of mankind and God, for the love of country, Americans who would speak the language of the heart do so with a rose.
>
> We see proofs of this everywhere. The study of fossils reveals that the rose has existed in America for age upon age. We have always cultivated roses in our gardens. Our first President, George Washington, bred roses, and a variety he named after his mother is still grown today. The White House itself boasts a beautiful Rose Garden. We grow roses in all our fifty States. We find roses throughout our art, music, and literature. We decorate our celebrations and parades with roses. Most of all, we present roses to those we love, and we lavish them on our altars, our civil shrines, and the final resting places of our honored dead.
>
> The American people have long held a special place in their hearts for roses. Let us continue to cherish them, to honor the love and devotion they represent, and to bestow them on all we love just as God has bestowed them on us.
>
> The Congress, by Senate Joint Resolution 159, has designated the rose as the National Floral Emblem of the United States and authorized and requested the President to issue a proclamation declaring this fact.

Doesn't this make the public rose garden almost a sacred place? I imagine myself standing on the edge of a steep cliff, looking out into vastness and declaring emphatically to the universe, "I accept this responsibility with great pride and joy ... I pledge to protect this symbol of floral joy and of our nation." WOW, how is that for a statement?! Some people would say, "Get serious! Cut him off!" But humor me! Hyperbole aside, the public rose garden is a great responsibility as well as a pleasure, and I believe many people share this view that the rose has a special place and sometimes an even more personal connection with themselves.

THE PEGGY ROCKEFELLER ROSE GARDEN AND 'EVA'

To give the reader a little background, I am the Peggy Rockefeller Rose Garden Curator. The Peggy Rockefeller Rose Garden at The New York Botanical Garden is a significant living display of 3,700 rose plants of 600 different varieties. The eminent American landscape architect Beatrix Jones Farrand laid out the historic design in 1916. With a generous gift from David Rockefeller in honor of his wife, Peggy, the garden was completed and named for her in 1988. With continuing support from Mr. Rockefeller, it was renovated in 2007. Nestled among beautiful, established trees, the site offers some of the most breathtaking vistas available at The New York Botanical Garden. The Rose Garden comprises a triangular shape of just over an acre, with 83 beds of roses radiating out from a central circle and a planting area of over 19,000 square feet.

> *"The Congress ... has designated the rose as the National Floral Emblem of the United States and authorized and requested the President to issue a proclamation declaring this fact."*
>
> —PRESIDENT RONALD REAGAN (1986)

Here is an interesting anecdote:

In June 2007, after the extensive renovation of the Peggy Rockefeller Rose Garden was completed, we reopened the garden. The spectacular first bloom was under way. I was in the garden talking with some visitors when I was approached, somewhat abruptly and sharply, by a young lady.

"Good afternoon!" I greeted her.

"Where is 'Eva'?" she asked with firmness and little patience.

"I bet your name is Eva," I replied.

"Yes," she said, still waiting for an answer.

"I guess you are here to see your rose then ... it is right over there."

Without hesitation, she walked briskly to the area of the garden for the Hybrid Musks, where *Rosa* 'Eva' was blooming beautifully with its red-blend clusters in what seemed like never-ending splendor. (SEE PLATE 23)

'Eva' in the Peggy Rockefeller Rose Garden blooms repeatedly if deadheaded, producing panicles that can contain 75 or more red flowers.

Eva (the visitor) then proceeded back in my direction as quickly as she had left and said, "Thank you. She looks good! I'll be back again next year and ..." — pointing her finger toward me — "make sure you take good care of her!"

"Oh, I will!" I said, almost fearing for my life and pledging to protect this lady's personal symbol of floral joy.

Having received direct orders from the one, all-knowing, little dynamo Eva, I was stopped, literally in my tracks, to think how this conversation would change me for the rest of my days. It became completely clear at that moment that this was not only *my* garden to care for and curate ... but it was absolutely *everyone else's* — every Eva's — garden as well. I watched visitor after visitor come into the garden and take ownership, stake their special claim to a favorite rose or two (or three or more), and derive immense joy from this public space that they saw as their own. A lesson learned for this curator: 'Eva', and the other 600-plus varieties, must be well taken care of for the enjoyment of one and all.

EXCELLENT ROSE CULTURE AND SUSTAINABILITY

Here is a humorous story — relevant, I believe — found on the Internet:

Four Worms and a Lesson ...

A minister decided that a visual demonstration would add emphasis to his Sunday sermon.

Four worms were placed into four separate jars. The first worm was put into a container of alcohol. The second worm was put into a container of cigarette smoke. The third worm was put into a container of chocolate syrup. The fourth worm was put into a container of good clean soil.

At the conclusion of the sermon, the minister reported the following results: The first worm in alcohol: dead. The second worm in cigarette smoke: dead. The third worm in chocolate syrup: dead. The fourth worm in good clean soil: alive!

Lifting the jars slowly, one by one, the minister stared long and hard at the congregation, paused, then asked boldly, "What message can ye learn from this demonstration?"

Maxine, sitting in the back, quietly raised her hand and whispered softly, "As long as you drink, smoke, and eat chocolate, you won't have worms?"

Thus endeth the sermon ...

When we talk about excellent rose culture and the sustainable rose garden we must talk about healthy soils, which in turn give us healthy plants. Period. Well-cared-for soils reward us with roses that are healthy and naturally disease-resistant.

Consider the following: If you and I didn't eat or drink, except minimally, for a month, we would probably be very weak, susceptible to disease, and not very productive. Would you agree? Using the minister's sermon as a further example, if all we did for a month was drink alcohol, smoke cigarettes, and eat chocolate, again, we would probably be very weak, susceptible to disease, and not very productive (or dead!). Still agree?

Thinking of roses in the same way, the more we proactively feed, water, and nurture the soil *in the right way* ... the more vigorous, disease-resistant, and productive our plants should be. When we can feed and bring our soils into a natural balance, then our roses should thrive, but if we starve them or put them on the wrong diet, we can expect to see weak, sick, and unproductive plants.

A curator's internal mantra: "Spraying the entire garden eliminates all opportunity to understand the pest and disease resistance that naturally exists in the garden."

Visitors will ask, for example, "How does that Kordes variety hold up without spray?" My answer these days is "really great." Yet I also tell our visitors that we monitor the garden proactively on a weekly (sometimes daily) basis and do spray for any concerns or hot spots that we feel are getting out of control. Here at The New York Botanical Garden, we have the great luxury of a trained and attentive staff of gardeners and an Integrated Pest Management team who are on the constant lookout for problems and able to address them as soon as they are discovered and before they become catastrophic.

I tell the questioner, "You should try a Kordes rose," and I explain all the known great characteristics of Kordes roses and engage in dialogue about good rose culture. However, it really comes down to a common, increasingly unpopular declaration—in this public rose garden, yes, we do still spray when we need to and with the allowed chemical assistance that is given to us.

So … one puts time, money, and faith into a planting or collection that has been hybridized to be truly disease-resistant and the challenge is to "let go" and see what the plant can do. But in the reality of the public display garden, the question becomes for curators such as myself, "Will the public applaud the attempt to forego chemicals by tolerating some evidence of blemish and disease?" Can you imagine what Eva would say? "MY ROSE HAS BLACK SPOTS ALL OVER IT and I saw a bug on one of the leaves! This is unacceptable. I feel ill … get me a cold towel!"

In today's public rose garden, we are following what I would call Plan A. While we increasingly select and grow rose varieties that are more disease-resistant, we require the roses in the garden to be picture perfect, which means we continue to spray some of the varieties that are known to be prone to disease to ensure that an otherwise unrealistic public expectation of perfection is maintained. However, Plan A is in jeopardy and becoming increasingly subject to limitations.

We can consider an alternative—let's call it Plan B—which would be to apply spot spraying on any "hot spots." Plan B would contain a proactive spray program minimally based on "ripe" weather conditions—conditions that we know favor the development of diseases. With Plan B, perhaps the right spray at the right time could accomplish the goal expected by the public—perfect roses—while greatly reducing the amount of spraying on the whole.

This is based on the premise that the right spray at the right time can greatly reduce the need for spraying. Unfortunately, sprays are in general harsh chemicals which, while achieving their intended purpose, also achieve an unintended purpose: the destruction, for instance, of beneficial organisms as well as pathogens. Counterbalancing the negative effects of sprays represents a challenging dilemma, especially for a public rose garden striving to become more organic and to find that ever-delicate balance.

Why? Visitors to the Peggy Rockefeller Rose Garden expect to see beautifully blooming roses for 6 months of the year. The garden's initial bloom in June (or late May, depending on weather) is breathtaking to say the least. Thousands of people come to see our extravaganza of brilliant color and intoxicating fragrance! Modern varieties give us bloom from June (late May) until first frost. This is the longest bloom season of any perennial plant. Our visitors receive an education on what the rose's growth habit is like, its variety of floral form, a dozen distinctive fragrances … or just the sheer joy of experiencing such a beautiful place. Being proactive with the Plan B program of good horticultural practices and regimens might allow for us to attain our goals.

In June 2010, the Great Rosarians of the World presented the Peggy Rockefeller Rose Garden with the International Rose Garden Hall of Fame Award "in recognition of the Creation of a Sustainable Public Garden Representing an Outstanding Collection of Historic Roses."

Plan B would offer practical garden application/education that cannot be found in any advertisement as a real-time experience. Maybe such a plan would also introduce the discussion of having plant trial areas versus a public display area that would permit us to explore the limits of sustainability, while still maintaining the need to always look perfect.

As of this writing, with the introduction/addition of known disease-resistant varieties, and constant attention to the health of our soils, we have been able to reduce the amount of fungicide sprays by 53 percent. Who knows what the next year will bring … our goal is that we can raise this percentage each and every year! We are starting to tell a different story … one that perhaps foretells a no-spray future!

Moving beyond Plans A and B, we might consider Plan C: creating a public rose garden based on organics and natural products and principles. The question is: Would the public tolerate Plan C if it entailed accepting a degree of blemish and imperfection in the public rose garden? And what would the costs be — maybe very high?

We would need to establish a soil lab sophisticated enough to take all the guesswork out of analyzing soils so we could modify soils naturally to bring them into and keep them in "balance." In Plan C, the public rose garden would be a place to provide the public with an education in organic and natural practices and all that entails. We could talk about the health of soils and what that means in terms of results to rose plants, and encourage people to try these practices at home in their own gardens.

However, Plan C may, for us in New York City at least, be mandated! As societies have limited or even banished the use of chemicals in countries worldwide, new laws limit the application of pesticides in any property leased or owned right here in New York City. There probably isn't any argument that New York and California are leading the way in enacting environmental laws. This legislative trend is bound to continue, and we must continue to evolve our gardens to anticipate it. These laws encourage us to engage in a healthy dialogue about creating healthy soils, the betterment of our environment and the limited exceptions we might need to make in the interest of horticulture. As the title of my article reads — "disease resistance" has now become the issue. And in the public rose garden, what in the world do we do about Eva (the person)? As of this writing, the answer to Eva is, "We have to figure it out."

ESTABLISHING A ROSE COLLECTION AT THE PEGGY ROCKEFELLER ROSE GARDEN WITH "GREEN THINKING" IN MIND

When we embark on a public rose garden display representing a historical and educational perspective, we choose plants that are significant on a multitude of levels. The rose's history, medicinal contributions, or genealogical status as it has evolved through 34 million years may all be points of interest. This type of collection, spanning so much of historical and evolutionary history, must be allowed to be protected in a safe, reasonable fashion for everyone to learn from as well as enjoy.

That being said, it is probably correct to mention that some roses are "better" to display than others. And I always like to keep in mind when considering individual varieties that the only way to know what a rose can do is to grow it. With literally thousands of varieties to choose from, which ones should be selected? After considering the historical perspective, if you are going to invest time, garden space, energy, and financial resources in a particular variety for a public garden area, it is desirable that the variety perform for as long a time as possible.

When we can feed and bring our soils into a natural balance, then our roses should thrive, but if we starve them or put them on the wrong diet, we can expect to see weak, sick, and unproductive plants.

With a monoculture environment, such as we have in the Peggy Rockefeller Rose Garden, special challenges will exist. We continue to scrutinize our collection for "better" performing varieties with our new mission of disease resistance.

A side note: The vast majority of new plants brought into the garden are on their own roots. Own-root roses take a little more time to build up and become established than grafted roses, but they are always true to their variety, are more likely to survive hard winters and temperature fluctuations, and tend overall to be healthier garden plants. It is this curator's opinion that own-root roses are to be preferred over grafted plants and are less prone to pathogens.

Although the main goal of the 2007 renovation was to increase diversity and make better use of the planting space, 2009 presented a new mission. As we go through the 2010 growing season, we must look at ways of preserving our efforts while incorporating the goal/mission of disease resistance.

With this in mind, the new modern collections we have been adding may represent in large measure a "green" way of thinking and are in many cases the result of many years of hybridizing efforts to produce "no-spray" rose varieties. Some of these collections we have added or expanded upon are as follows: David Austin English Roses, French Delbard Roses, Texas Pioneer Roses, Griffith Buck Roses, Easy Elegance Roses, and Earth-Kind® Roses.

Hybridization efforts from Kordes of Germany, Meilland of France, and Bill Radler's family of roses are also extensively used throughout the garden along with several of the winners from the ADR trials in Germany. It is also fun for me to constantly hear of new "backyard" hybridizing efforts that are producing some really great plants.

COLLECTION SUMMARY

The above groups of new roses have been added to existing rose collections, including many additions to the heritage classes, to reflect our effort, in part, to modify our collection to better represent the diversity of roses and yet have "great garden plants" for the public to learn about and enjoy.

Within our new stated mission, as new plants are hybridized, trialed, and introduced from around the world, we feel we should be supportive, in particular by bringing to the forefront roses that are highly disease-resistant and easy to grow.

Incorporating these plants into the Peggy Rockefeller Rose Garden and moving forward toward a nonchemical approach are continuing goals and responsibilities. However, the question arises, "If we keep moving forward with the 'latest and greatest,' how do we preserve important historical rose varieties of the past for educational purposes?" We have to really define or re-define the stated purpose of the garden if we are to protect these varieties, which we must endeavor to do.

Returning to my dramatic metaphor that has me "standing on the edge of a steep cliff," let me say that more than ever, it is a very exciting time to be talking about roses. In terms of desired characteristics, many of our fondest dreams are close to bearing fruit. The thought of the chemically dependent rose—so much with us for more than 50 years—may soon be a thing of the past, as disease-free, tough new landscape roses for all purposes emerge from the brilliant work of today's hybridizers. We have some more work to do before this is achieved, but we are moving forward rapidly.

Blackspot is a serious and often devastating disease of outdoor roses, caused by the fungus *Diplocarpon rosae.* It is the most serious disease problem of roses worldwide. Roses vary widely in their susceptibility, with popularly cultivated Hybrid Tea cultivars typically being the most susceptible. Control measures require repeated sprays with fungicides, often as frequently as once each week from the first flush of growth in the spring until the first hard frost in the fall. The repeated and profuse use of fungicides at this level not only increases the cost to the consumer, but can be potentially hazardous to the environment. It also places selection pressure on the fungus and can lead to the development of acquired resistance to different chemistries and pathogen populations.

There has been a strong movement away from the use of roses as general garden plants in the United States during the last 80 years. In part, this can be attributed to the general level of culture required to keep roses healthy. That consumers are making the shift to low-maintenance roses and more environmentally responsible landscapes is illustrated in sales of the Knock Out® series of roses developed by American amateur hybridizer Bill Radler (the original cultivar in the series was introduced in 2000). To date, Knock Out® and its siblings are among the largest selling plants in rose history. Consumers have demonstrated a willingness to pay premium prices for cultivars that are resistant to common diseases, easy to maintain, and ever-blooming.

Bill Radler has revolutionized the concept of what great garden roses should be: hardy, disease-free and ever-blooming. Many say that he single-handedly has brought rose genetics from the 20th century into the 21st century.

The level of disease resistance coming from the Kordes and Meilland hybridization efforts continues to impress me and persistently score at the highest levels within the Peggy Rockefeller Rose Garden.

I can say with great enthusiasm that (shouting from the cliff again): "modern hybridizing efforts are really putting the rose in the stature of a great garden plant again! This is very exciting indeed!"

I remember walking through the rose garden with David Rockefeller on one of his visits. At one particular moment, this kind and gentle man turned to me and whispered, "Peggy would have loved this." It was then that I had a sense of "mission accomplished." But, as gardens go, we must continue to evolve our mission. We will continue to make this garden as beautiful and sustainable as we possibly can, so that everyone will have the same experience of loving this garden year after year.

A LOOK TO THE FUTURE

Ours is a continuing dialogue in a process to reach a better solution that is foreseeable in the near future. Whatever we think about and desire can work. As rosarians and human beings we are involved in the weightier issues of our time, such as climate change and making Mother Earth a better place for all. Let's continue to work toward common goals so that our beloved flower, the rose, will be enjoyed by generations to come.

I believe that within the public rose garden arena the attention we are giving to going "back to the basics" of understanding, creating, nurturing, and maintaining healthy soils (becoming "organically minded") will help educate gardeners of the future in creating a viable rose culture.

The Peggy Rockefeller Rose Garden is under the watchful eye and care of a team of horticultural professionals with many years of very specific rose experience. It is with proactive, consistent care—the use, for instance, of compost, compost teas, fish emulsions, and other organic methods—that the health of this garden can be kept at its highest.

Visitors can enter the garden through three entry points—the main gate, and gates to the north and south. Reds and apricots decorate the main gate to accentuate the 'Peggy Rockefeller' Hybrid Tea bed that is prominently planted near the entrance. Displays of Earth-Kind® varieties enhance the north and south gates. With the mission of disease resistance in the forefront, the Rose Garden showcases all different classes, shapes, and sizes of roses, allowing visitors to look at the palette and attempt to duplicate the designs in their own home gardens.

The borders of the Rockefeller Rose Garden have been redefined to diversify and reorganize the rose classes in the existing collection. The Heritage Rose Border by the southeast fence is a "sampling platter" of the history of roses, planted chronologically, showing the lineage of roses as they were hybridized over the centuries. It begins with Species Roses and their cultivars, wild plants which natural selection has given us, and continues down the timeline of rose history. The border features a broad diversity of roses, from Gallicas and Damasks, to Albas, Centifolias, and China Roses, from Spinossisima shrubs to Moss Roses, Portlands, Bourbons, and finally Hybrid Perpetuals. New signage tells the story of the evolution of the rose, from the heritage plants to the modern varieties. Modern roses dominate the other two borders. As always, the Peggy Rockefeller Rose Garden boasts some truly outstanding rose collections.

> *With a monoculture environment ... special challenges will exist. We continue to scrutinize our collection for "better" performing varieties with our new mission of disease resistance.*

In June 2010, The Great Rosarians of the World presented the Peggy Rockefeller Rose Garden with the International Rose Garden Hall of Fame Award "in recognition of the Creation of a Sustainable Public Garden Representing an Outstanding Collection of Historic Roses."

ROSE TRIALS IN NEW YORK

Perhaps it might be possible for the New York area to have its own trials and certificates of merit for roses? Imagine how we could be a leader in setting our own "chemical free" standard. As stated before, this is being mandated.

In the spring of 2010 we planted the Northeast Earth-Kind® rose trials site at The New York Botanical Garden. It is very exciting to be part of the Earth-Kind® team! It is a particularly exciting accomplishment as we will truly be able to certify some of the best possible roses for our particular region. To date, 32 varieties are planted in the Northeast trials. So often the case, I will be lecturing or giving a tour talking about the Earth-Kind® movement, and yet I will have to clarify that this started as a Texas trial and that our New York winters are just a little different. It is exciting that the Earth-Kind® movement is growing nationwide and in four different countries!

The Earth-Kind® program requires the support of researchers in biotechnology, molecular genetics, plant breeding, plant pathology, and entomology. In a typical breeding program, individual plants or genotypes are identified that exhibit a particular trait, such as drought tolerance, and pest or disease resistance. These unique individuals would be utilized in breeding. However, the development of new rose cultivars can take 10 to 20 years to complete. Additionally, rose breeding is mainly carried out by amateurs or commercially by highly competitive companies whose genetic knowledge is often proprietary and unpublished. For these reasons, researchers throughout the world now have a tremendous opportunity to develop or identify rose cultivars that are beautiful and highly adapted to regional environmental conditions. The goal of the Earth-Kind® program is not to recreate the breeding programs of hybridizers around the world, but rather to identify those truly special cultivars that combine beauty with proven durability in the landscape.

The Earth-Kind® philosophy is based on the premise that it is possible to identify beautiful plants that tolerate harsh, low-maintenance environments without fertilizers, pesticides, and other agricultural chemicals and with a significant reduction in irrigation.

Future Earth-Kind® trials around the world are proposed to include herbaceous perennials as well as shrubs.

Please come and visit the Peggy Rockefeller Rose Garden and our new Earth-Kind® rose trials, stake your claim to favorite roses, become vested in the shared joy of this space… and don't ever forget to take time to stop and smell the roses.

You will likely spot me in the garden or at the top of the hill … watching all of the visitors come and go with their senses filled … looking out for Eva … waiting for her in-eva-table return "next year"!

The Great Rosarians of the World (GROW™) International Friend of the Rose Award was presented for the first time in 2010 by GROW™ Chairman Clair Martin. The Award recognizes Americans who have made unique contributions in support of the GROW™ program and also singular contributions to reach out to the rest of the world. The 2010 honorees were William A. "Bill" Grant and Ambassador Faith Whittlesey (former U.S. Ambassador to Switzerland). Bill Grant was cited for his decades-long work to improve understanding between U.S.–European and U.S.–Australian rose communities; Ambassador Whittlesey was cited for her work in helping revive the U.S.–Chinese connection in rose culture at the highest level. East and West, Ambassador Whittlesey and Bill Grant have helped to enrich American and world rose culture.

PLATES 1 AND 2. Above—Presentation of *R. chinensis* var. spontanea for the Washington, D.C., Chinese embassy garden at a dinner in New York, June 11, 2009. Ambassador Faith Whittlesey (center) with Minister Kuang Weilin of China (left), Jeff Wyckoff (far left), and Pat Shanley. At right—Ambassador Whittlesey in her Winter Haven, Florida, garden, in 2010, demonstrating pruning to her 4-year-old grandson, Joseph Ryan Whittlesey.

PLATE 3. Bill Grant in his garden in Aptos, California, in 2010. In the words of Australian hybridizer Lilia Weatherly, "Bill Grant is the complete gentleman." On his 85th birthday in 2010, Bill writes, "Roses have been a great part of my world for over the past sixty years. Roses not only charm us and feed our souls, but are passports to friendships."

Tea Roses

Old Roses for Warm Gardens

Lynne Chapman, Noelene Drage,
Di Durston, Jenny Jones,
Hillary Merrifield, Billy West

PLATE 4. The subtle colors of Tea Roses.

PLATE 6. 'Marquise de Vivens', illustrated in *The Garden*, 1889.

PLATE 5. The unmistakeable 'Devoniensis', from Henry Curtis, *The Beauties of the Rose*, 1850.

PLATE 7. The found rose known as "Angels Camp Tea" and "Octavus Weld".

PLATE 8. 'Safrano' is an early Tea rose that was well documented, including this plate from the *Journal des Roses* of July 1882.

PLATE 9. Possibly 'Auguste Comte', this rose is known under several other names.

PLATE 10. "Mrs Good's Special Tea".

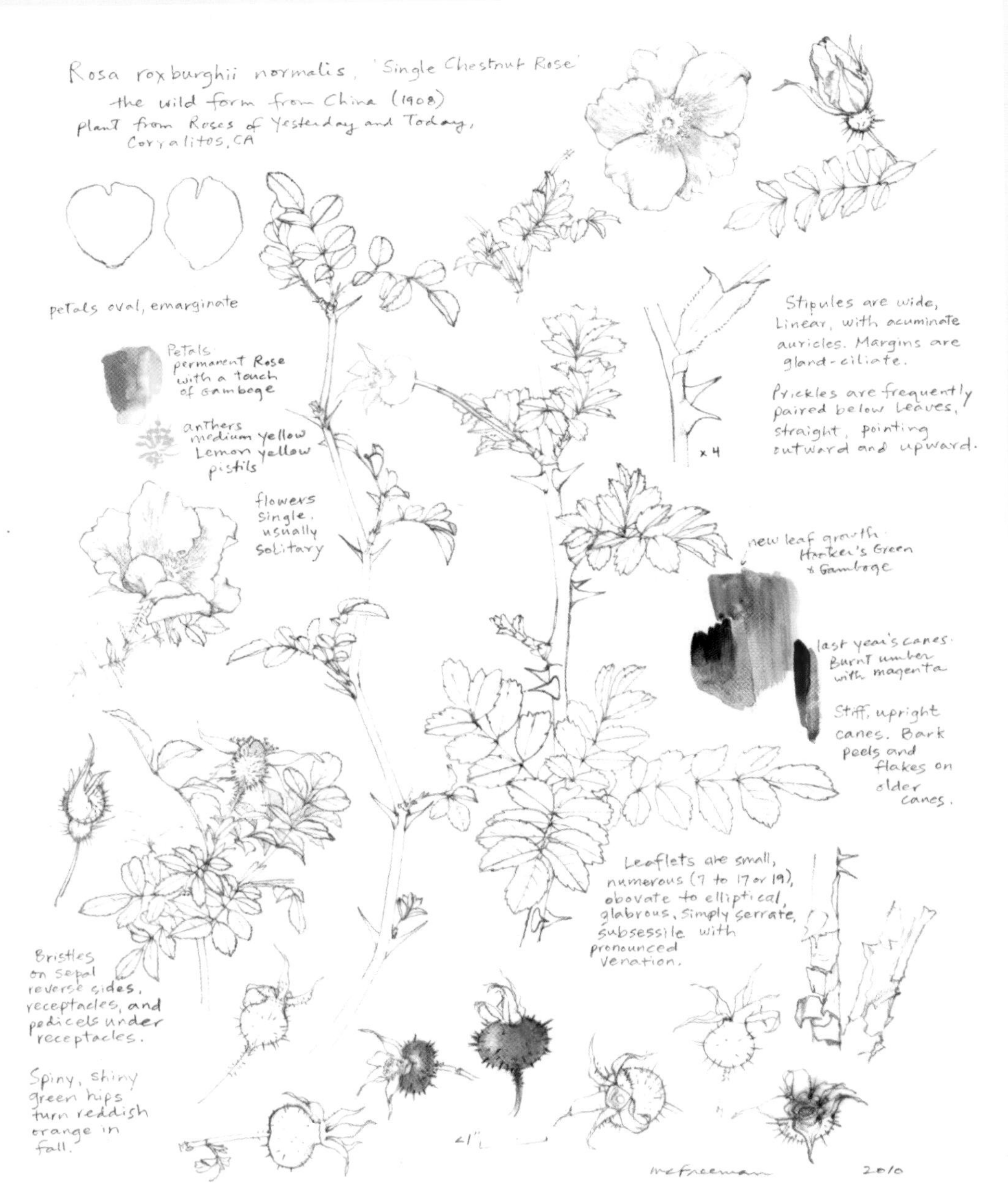
Rosa roxburghii normalis, 'Single Chestnut Rose'
the wild form from China (1908)
Plant from Roses of Yesterday and Today, Corralitos, CA
petals oval, emarginate
Petals permanent Rose with a touch of Gamboge
anthers medium yellow
Lemon yellow pistils
flowers single, usually solitary
Stipules are wide, Linear, with acuminate auricles. Margins are gland-ciliate.
Prickles are frequently paired below leaves, straight, pointing outward and upward.
x 4
new leaf growth Hooker's Green & Gamboge
last year's canes. Burnt umber with magenta
Stiff, upright canes. Bark peels and flakes on older canes.
Leaflets are small, numerous (7 to 17 or 19), obovate to elliptical, glabrous, simply serrate, subsessile with pronounced venation.
Bristles on sepal reverse sides, receptacles, and pedicels under receptacles.
Spiny, shiny green hips turn reddish orange in fall.
<1"
mcFreeman
2010

PLATES 11 AND 12. Typical of Maria Cecilia Freeman's work, subjects are done as pairings. The study for *Rosa roxburghii* (left) and finished watercolor (right), for instance, serve to inform each other.

PLATE 13. Planting of the first Northern Earth-Kind® rose trial at the University of Minnesota Outreach, Research, and Education (UMore) Park in Rosemount, Minnesota. Grass was removed from beds (A) and plant derived compost was obtained (B) and incorporated. The four beds served as blocks with one of each of the 20 cultivars randomized and planted (June 2007) per block (C) and mulched with a 7.6cm layer of wood chips. Well-established plants are blooming during the second growing season (July 2008) (D); the growing season when monthly performance data is first taken

PLATE 14. Layout of blocks is flexible to provide sites the necessary freedom to arrange them to best account for environmental variability and to be aesthetically pleasing. In 2008 a new phase 1 trial in the Southern U.S. region was planted at Gussie Field, Watterworth Park, in Farmers Branch, Texas in concentric arches large enough to accommodate 100 cultivars (A). Also in 2008, a Northern Earth-Kind® trial site was planted using cross- and square-shaped beds (crosses contain the test roses and squares contain additional roses not part of the trial) at the Horticultural Research Station in Ames, Iowa (B). A minimum-sized phase 2 trial site consists of five cultivars replicated three times, and this site (collaboratively sponsored by the Dallas County Master Gardeners and Farmers Branch Parks and Recreation in Farmers Branch, Texas) consists of three blocks arranged in a serpentine design (C).

PLATE 15. The Earth-Kind®-winning rose for the Southern U.S. region, 'RADrazz' (=Knock Out®; foreground), has demonstrated consistently superior resistance to blackspot and other diseases and contributes to the reason it is one of the most widely sold rose cultivars in history

PLATE 16. Earth-Kind®-winning roses in the Southern U.S. region: 'Belinda's Dream' (A), 'Bucbi' (=Carefree Beauty™) (B), 'Caldwell Pink' (C), 'Climbing Pinkie' (D), 'Ducher' (E), 'Else Poulsen' (F), 'Duchesse de Brabant' (G), 'Georgetown Tea' (H), 'La Marne' (I), 'Mme. Antoine Marie' (J), 'RADrazz' (=Knock Out®) (K), 'Marie Daly' (L), 'Mutabilis' (M), 'New Dawn' (N), 'Perle d'Or' (O), 'Seafoam' (P), 'Souvenir de St. Anne's' (Q), 'Spice' (R), and 'The Fairy' (S).

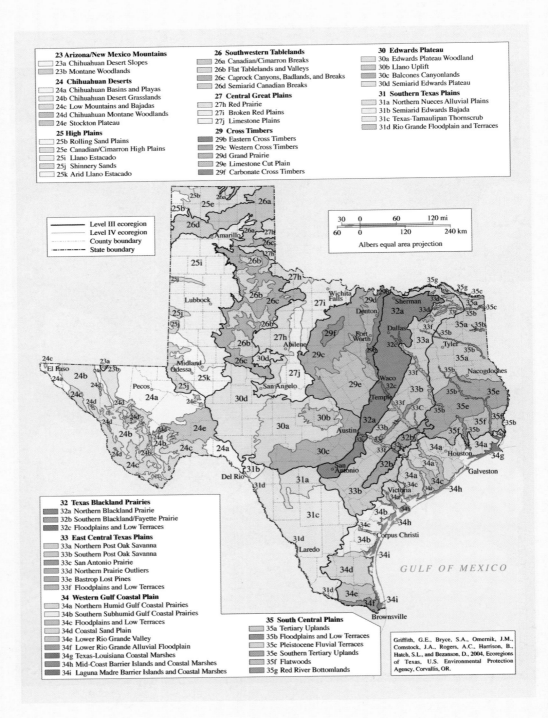

23 Arizona/New Mexico Mountains
23a Chihuahuan Desert Slopes
23b Montane Woodlands

24 Chihuahuan Deserts
24a Chihuahuan Basins and Playas
24b Chihuahuan Desert Grasslands
24c Low Mountains and Bajadas
24d Chihuahuan Montane Woodlands
24e Stockton Plateau

25 High Plains
25b Rolling Sand Plains
25e Canadian/Cimarron High Plains
25i Llano Estacado
25j Shinnery Sands
25k Arid Llano Estacado

26 Southwestern Tablelands
26a Canadian/Cimarron Breaks
26b Flat Tablelands and Valleys
26c Caprock Canyons, Badlands, and Breaks
26d Semiarid Canadian Breaks

27 Central Great Plains
27h Red Prairie
27i Broken Red Plains
27j Limestone Plains

29 Cross Timbers
29b Eastern Cross Timbers
29c Western Cross Timbers
29d Grand Prairie
29e Limestone Cut Plain
29f Carbonate Cross Timbers

30 Edwards Plateau
30a Edwards Plateau Woodland
30b Llano Uplift
30c Balcones Canyonlands
30d Semiarid Edwards Plateau

31 Southern Texas Plains
31a Northern Nueces Alluvial Plains
31b Semiarid Edwards Bajada
31c Texas-Tamaulipan Thornscrub
31d Rio Grande Floodplain and Terraces

Level III ecoregion
Level IV ecoregion
County boundary
State boundary

30   0   60   120 mi
60   0   120   240 km
Albers equal area projection

32 Texas Blackland Prairies
32a Northern Blackland Prairie
32b Southern Blackland/Fayette Prairie
32c Floodplains and Low Terraces

33 East Central Texas Plains
33a Northern Post Oak Savanna
33b Southern Post Oak Savanna
33c San Antonio Prairie
33d Northern Prairie Outliers
33e Bastrop Lost Pines
33f Floodplains and Low Terraces

34 Western Gulf Coastal Plain
34a Northern Humid Gulf Coastal Prairies
34b Southern Subhumid Gulf Coastal Prairies
34c Floodplains and Low Terraces
34d Coastal Sand Plain
34e Lower Rio Grande Valley
34f Lower Rio Grande Alluvial Floodplain
34g Texas-Louisiana Coastal Marshes
34h Mid-Coast Barrier Islands and Coastal Marshes
34i Laguna Madre Barrier Islands and Coastal Marshes

35 South Central Plains
35a Tertiary Uplands
35b Floodplains and Low Terraces
35c Pleistocene Fluvial Terraces
35e Southern Tertiary Uplands
35f Flatwoods
35g Red River Bottomlands

Griffith, G.E., Bryce, S.A., Omernik, J.M., Comstock, J.A., Rogers, A.C., Harrison, B., Hatch, S.L., and Bezanson, D., 2004, Ecoregions of Texas, U.S. Environmental Protection Agency, Corvallis, OR.

PLATE 17. The Ecoregions of Texas.

PLATE 18.
Detached leaves from two rose seedlings inoculated with *Diplocarpon rosae* Race A exhibit resistant and susceptible reactions. The seedlings were from a cross between 'George Vancouver' (Race A resistant) and 'Morden Blush' (susceptible); the seedling population from this cross segregated approximately half resistant and half susceptible.

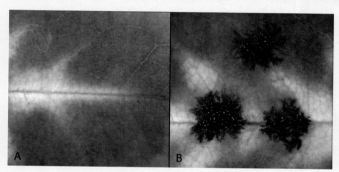

PLATE 19.
(A) A leaf from a rose containing a race-specific resistance gene shows no symptoms when inoculated with an isolate of *Diplocarpon rosae*.
(B) A leaf from a rose lacking the resistance gene forms blackspot lesions with characteristic feathery margins and whitish masses of asexual spores (conidia).

Roosevelt Island Rose Garden

PLATE 20.
The Roosevelt Island Rose Garden is all organic and natural and part of a "community garden." 'Darlow's Enigma' (at center on trellis) is a sight to behold in the spring!

PLATE 21. Chocolate and roses are two of my favorite things. Take any dessert, homemade or from a bakery, and add fabulous touches like chocolate rose leaves and colorful edible flowers and herbs. Growing roses organically, I have materials at my fingertips from May to November. We decorated a cake for Annabelle Platt's eighth birthday. She and her 5-year-old sister Lucy made the chocolate leaves and placed all the flowers on the cake. I picked the materials to make sure I chose only edibles.

In addition to the chocolate leaves we used roses and rose petals, calendula petals, pansies, lavender, and mint leaves. They proclaimed it the most beautiful cake they had ever seen.

WHAT YOU NEED

— 4 ounces semisweet or milk chocolate
— 15 leaves from a rose bush or other nonpoisonous shrub. The leaves should be dark-green older leaves, not the lighter-green new leaves
— Look for medium-sized leaves with nice thick veins. Keep a little stem on the leaf. This will be your handle
— Very clean paint brush or butter knife
— Wax paper and paper towels
— Tray
— Dinner knife

WHAT YOU DO

Rinse the leaves quickly, and pat them totally dry with a paper towel. Unwrap the chocolate, break it or chop it into pieces, and melt it in a microwaveable bowl on high for 1 minute. Stir and, if not fully melted, return for 30 seconds more. Let the chocolate cool off for 1 minute. Never get water drops anywhere near melting chocolate.

Put a piece of wax paper on the bottom of the tray.

Turn the leaves bottom side up, so the veins of the leaves stand out more. Hold the leaf at the stem end.

Dip the brush or knife in the melted chocolate and cover the bottom side only with chocolate. Don't cover the sides or the stem at all. When you finish coating each leaf, put it on the tray, chocolate side up.

IMPORTANT TIP: *Make the coat of chocolate about ⅛ of an inch thick or more. If it's too thin, the chocolate will crack when you try to peel back the leaf. If you use a paintbrush, dab on the chocolate to make a thick coat. If you use a butter knife, spread a thick coat.*

When all of the leaves are coated or when you run out of chocolate, put the whole tray in the refrigerator for an hour or more. When the chocolate is hard, the leaves are ready to peel.

Now take a leaf and put the chocolate side down on a clean plate, hold the stem, and peel the leaf away from the chocolate. Use the dinner knife as a tool to hold the chocolate in place while you peel.

Of course, you could hold it in place with your finger, but

CHOCOLATE MELTS as you touch it. Discard the greenery.

Soon you'll have a whole plate of chocolate rose leaves that have the shape and pattern of the real thing. You can keep them in the refrigerator until you use them to decorate. When you're ready, slide a dinner knife under each leaf, and place it on the cake or other dessert just where you want it.

When you peel the leaves, there might be a hole or two where the chocolate was too thin. Well, nature isn't perfect, either.

Hide any holes by overlapping the leaves when placing on the cake, or cover imperfections with other flowers and petals.

Vanity

Ballerina

Kathleen

Cornelia

Moonlight

Buff Beauty

PLATES 22 AND 23. Hybrid Musks (above and page right) are tough and generally care-free and are widely considered to be among the best varieties to grow in sustainable rose gardens.

Eva

Danae

Wind Chime

Prosperity

Nur Mahal

Francis Lester

PLATE 24. *Rosa Mundi*, the quarterly journal of the Heritage Rose Foundation.

PLATE 25. The American Rose Society has published its Annual since 1916. It also publishes a bimonthly magazine, *American Rose*, and the annual "Handbook for Selecting Roses." All of these publications are benefits of membership.

PLATE 26. *The Rose Letter* is the quarterly publication of the Heritage Roses Groups. Other journals such as *The Yellow Rose of Texas* and *Gold Coast Roses* are examples of local rose society publications. Most local rose societies offer a monthly or bimonthly newsletter.

PLATE 27. Foreign rose society publications abound. *The Rose* and *Heritage Rose Journal* are from the United Kingdom. *Journal of Heritage Roses* in Australia is from the other side of the world.

PLATE 28. The Australian rose community has been active in the publications area in recent years. *The Women Behind the Roses* is a 2010 book about the roses of Australia's famed hybridizer Alister Clark.

PLATE 29. *The Combined Rose List* is issued annually, offering listings on the availability of rose varieties worldwide. *Modern Roses 12*, *The Vintage Gardens Book of Roses*, and the various volumes of Brent Dickerson's work documenting roses are also important resources for rose collectors, "rustlers," and historians.

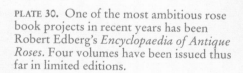

PLATE 30. One of the most ambitious rose book projects in recent years has been Robert Edberg's *Encyclopaedia of Antique Roses*. Four volumes have been issued thus far in limited editions.

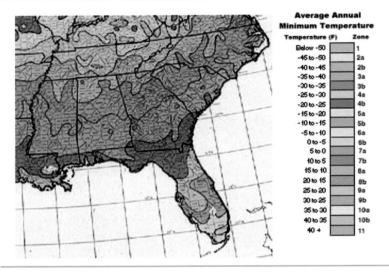

USDA Hardiness Zones and Average Annual Minimum Temperature Range

Zone	Fahrenheit	Celsius	Example Cities
1	Below -50 F	Below -45.6 C	Fairbanks, Alaska; Resolute, Northwest Territories (Canada)
2a	-50 to -45 F	-42.8 to -45.5 C	Prudhoe Bay, Alaska; Flin Flon, Manitoba (Canada)
2b	-45 to -40 F	-40.0 to -42.7 C	Unalakleet, Alaska; Pinecreek, Minnesota
3a	-40 to -35 F	-37.3 to -39.9 C	International Falls, Minnesota; St. Michael, Alaska
3b	-35 to -30 F	-34.5 to -37.2 C	Tomahawk, Wisconsin; Sidney, Montana
4a	-30 to -25 F	-31.7 to -34.4 C	Minneapolis/St.Paul, Minnesota; Lewistown, Montana
4b	-25 to -20 F	-28.9 to -31.6 C	Northwood, Iowa; Nebraska
5a	-20 to -15 F	-26.2 to -28.8 C	Des Moines, Iowa; Illinois
5b	-15 to -10 F	-23.4 to -26.1 C	Columbia, Missouri; Mansfield, Pennsylvania
6a	-10 to -5 F	-20.6 to -23.3 C	St. Louis, Missouri; Lebanon, Pennsylvania
6b	-5 to 0 F	-17.8 to -20.5 C	McMinnville, Tennessee; Branson, Missouri
7a	0 to 5 F	-15.0 to -17.7 C	Oklahoma City, Oklahoma; South Boston, Virginia
7b	5 to 10 F	-12.3 to -14.9 C	Little Rock, Arkansas; Griffin, Georgia
8a	10 to 15 F	-9.5 to -12.2 C	Tifton, Georgia; Dallas, Texas
8b	15 to 20 F	-6.7 to -9.4 C	Austin, Texas; Gainesville, Florida
9a	20 to 25 F	-3.9 to -6.6 C	Houston, Texas; St. Augustine, Florida
9b	25 to 30 F	-1.2 to -3.8 C	Brownsville, Texas; Fort Pierce, Florida
10a	30 to 35 F	1.6 to -1.1 C	Naples, Florida; Victorville, California
10b	35 to 40 F	4.4 to 1.7 C	Miami, Florida; Coral Gables, Florida
11	above 40 F	above 4.5 C	Honolulu, Hawaii; Mazatlan, Mexico

PLATE 31. USDA weather maps are readily available on websites and in gardening books.

The Roosevelt Island Rose Garden

MARJORIE MARCALLINO

The Roosevelt Island Rose Garden is perhaps New York City's only totally organic or natural rose garden. It is part of a larger residential garden consisting of individual plots on Roosevelt Island in the East River between Manhattan and Brooklyn. Weather is generally a couple of degrees milder than either Manhattan or Brooklyn. The rose garden, which was established in 1992 but not planted with roses until 1993, currently consists of some 75–80 varieties.

The garden is never sprayed. Normally, the garden is treated with Espoma Rose-Tone—and manure and alfalfa meal are added when available. Blackspot is the main problem. I pretty much ignore insects, and they don't seem to do much harm.

Some of the varieties that do well here on Roosevelt Island with no-fuss treatment are 'Darlow's Enigma', (SEE PLATE 20) 'Martine Guillot', 'Elina', 'Sweet Juliette', 'Mme. Alfred Carrière', 'Astrid Lindgren', 'The Generous Gardener', 'Eloise', 'Redouté', 'Bishop's Castle', 'Golden Wings', 'Baby Blanket', and 'Phyllis Bide'. 'Bella Roma' and 'Floral Fairy Tale' can be victims of blackspot very early in the season, but usually recover by fall.

David Austin English Roses, top to bottom: 'Heritage', 'Cressida', and 'Graham Thomas'. The "Austin Revolution," beginning about 1980 (and continuing to the present), can be seen as a response to nostalgia for "old rose" form — but represented by new varieties having repeat bloom and the more brilliant modern color range.

Health in David Austin's English Roses

MICHAEL MARRIOTT

Most gardeners around the world are now demanding that any roses they plant in their garden be as healthy as possible. They don't want to spray them, at least not with chemicals that can potentially harm both themselves and the environment. Growing them as well as possible and mixing them up with other garden plants will certainly help a great deal in achieving this goal, but the most important starting point is choosing a variety that has a naturally high degree of disease resistance. There is such a huge choice on the market it is always worth doing some research before making a final choice, trying to identify the healthiest varieties for your area.

Many years ago David Austin recognised that gardeners didn't want to spray their roses and so started to place maximum health as one of the top priorities in his breeding programme. Importantly though, he tried to do this without compromising the characteristics that are so important in the English Roses and, ideally, in all roses — beautiful blooms, wonderful fragrance, and attractive growth.

To achieve healthier roses you can simply decide during the selection process to choose only varieties that achieve a certain level of health. However, to achieve really significant improvements on all counts you have to start with the parents, which means finding or developing parents that will produce healthy seedlings. As it takes 8 or 9 years from crossing to introduction, this can potentially take a very long time.

Most roses cross very readily, and this is one of the reasons why there are so many varieties available. But different parents can produce a very different number and quality of seedlings. Some parents may readily cross, and the seeds germinate well, but the seedlings are all of little interest. Other parents may be the reverse; they cross with difficulty and germinate poorly, but a high proportion of the seedlings are of interest. The challenge is to discover or develop parents that readily produce many seedlings of high value either for introducing directly or for incorporating into the breeding programme. So, while the general level of health of the English Roses has increased greatly in

Mixing roses up with other plants like perennials, biennials or annuals will hinder the spread of pests and diseases and help to attract beneficial insects.

the last few years, David Austin promises great improvements in the next few years with both improved parents and seedlings that are still going through the trialing and bulking up process.

The seedlings in the trials at our nursery in the United Kingdom have a very hard time. Of the 150,000–250,000 seedlings that are produced each year, only around 10,000 survive the first screening while still in the greenhouse, which is based purely on aesthetic characteristics. The selected few are then budded onto rootstocks out in the field, and this is where their relative health as well as their ability to cope with the English weather can be assessed. As they are not sprayed at all and are grown very closely together, many varieties quickly succumb to disease and are removed. Those remaining can go on to the next level, and the numbers of each seedling can be bulked up. This process is repeated a few times with no spraying until we are down to a selected very few and the numbers having been bulked up to a few thousand of each. It is then that the final decision can be made as to which are to be introduced. As I said it is a hard time being a rose seedling; out of the original 150,000–250,000 seedlings only 3 to 6 are introduced each year!

All this trialling is relevant to the climate in the United Kingdom, but the question then is, How well does it apply to the very varied climates around the world and especially to that of the States? The answer is sometimes it does and sometimes it doesn't, which is not very satisfactory! So, now we have to set up nine trials around the States to get an idea as to which ones to recommend in various key regions. Like the trials in the United Kingdom the roses are not being sprayed at all or at least only if absolutely necessary in a particularly tough area. This is already yielding very interesting results, which of course we are passing on to gardeners.

Having chosen a healthy rose for your climate, the other way to encourage maximum health is to choose a favourable position and then prepare the soil and look after it as well as possible.

Whatever your soil type, you should always add plenty of humus to it before planting. Always make sure whatever you add is well rotted. If possible, incorporate to a depth of 18". It is always worth putting plenty of effort into this stage—remember you will be hopefully keeping your rose for at least 15 years. Each spring mulch with the same to keep humus levels up.

It is a hard time being a rose seedling; out of the original 150,000–250,000 seedlings only 3 to 6 are introduced each year!

A garden or bed purely of roses can look superb, but it is a monoculture, which benefits the spread of pests and diseases. Mixing roses up with other plants like perennials, biennials or annuals will hinder the spread of pests and diseases and help to attract beneficial insects.

To look after your roses as well as possible you have to feed and water them well. But look after your soil too—it really is absolutely crucial to the success of roses and indeed just about every plant in your garden, so always try to use an organic or organically based fertiliser. A foliar feed, especially one containing seaweed, can also be extremely helpful. And roses love water, but do be sure to apply it at a time when the leaves will dry out quickly; otherwise it is the easiest way to encourage blackspot.

From years of reports from home gardeners and our recent trials, we recommend the following varieties in various key areas.

CALIFORNIA

Ambridge Rose	Benjamin Britten
Carding Mill	Charlotte
Darcey Bussell	Gentle Hermione
Golden Celebration clg	Grace
Graham Thomas	Huntington Rose
Jubilee Celebration	Jude the Obscure
Lady Emma Hamilton	Lady of Megginch
Molineux	Pat Austin
Scepter'd Isle	Snow Goose
Sophy's Rose	St Swithun
Tamora	Tess of the d'Urbervilles
The Alnwick Rose	The Dark Lady
Wildeve	William Shakespeare 2000

LOUISIANA

Abraham Darby	Benjamin Britten
Graham Thomas	Heritage
Huntington Rose	James Galway
Jude the Obscure	Molineux
Sophy's Rose	Tess of the d'Urbervilles

NEW YORK AND NEW JERSEY

Charlotte	Darcey Bussell
Grace	Lady Emma Hamilton
Lichfield Angel	Molineux
Mortimer Sackler	Queen of Sweden
Sophy's Rose	Teasing Georgia
Tess of the d'Urbervilles	The Generous Gardener
The Pilgrim	

OHIO

A Shropshire Lad	Abraham Darby
Benjamin Britten	Charlotte
Comte de Champagne	Corvedale
Crocus Rose	Crown Princess Margareta
Gertrude Jekyll	Hyde Hall
James Galway	LD Braithwaite
Mortimer Sackler	Scepter'd Isle
Tess of the d'Urbervilles	The Generous Gardener
The Mayflower	

OKLAHOMA

Abraham Darby	Ambridge Rose
Benjamin Britten	Carding Mill
Darcey Bussell	Falstaff
Gentle Hermione	Golden Celebration
Graham Thomas	Huntington Rose
Jude the Obscure	LD Braithwaite
Molineux	Pat Austin
Scepter'd Isle	Sophy's Rose
Teasing Georgia as climber	The Alnwick Rose
The Dark Lady	William Shakespeare 2000

OREGON

Benjamin Britten clg	Falstaff
Gentle Hermione	Graham Thomas clg
Jude the Obscure	Lady Emma Hamilton
Scepter'd Isle	Tamora
The Alnwick Rose	The Dark Lady
The Generous Gardener	The Mayflower
Wildeve	

The Great Rosarians of the World™ Lectureship Program was created by Huntington Botanical Garden's Curator of Roses Clair Martin to recognize and showcase the contributions of outstanding rosarians internationally. The distinguished honorees have been:

2001 . . . . Peter Beales . . . . United Kingdom

2002 . . . . Ralph Moore . . . . United States

2003 . . . . Miriam Wilkins . . . . United States

2004 . . . . Roger Phillips & Martyn Rix . . . . United Kingdom

2005 . . . . Peter Harkness . . . . United Kingdom

2006 . . . . Girija & Viru Viraraghavan . . . . India

2007 . . . . Wilhelm Kordes III . . . . .Germany

2008 . . . . William Radler . . . . United States

2009 . . . . Stephen Scanniello . . . . United States

Marilyn Wellan . . . . United States

2010 . . . . David Austin . . . . United Kingdom

In 2007, for the first time, the event became "bicoastal," being held first on the West Coast at the Huntington Botanical Garden and later in the year on the East Coast under the sponsorship of the Manhattan Rose Society. The events were called GROW™–West and GROW™–East, respectively.

In 2009, the GROW™ Chairman and Executive Committee decided to similarly honor outstanding rose gardens with the International Hall of Fame Rose Garden Award. The honorees have been:

2009 . . . . The San Jose Heritage Rose Garden . . . . United States

The Sacramento Historic Rose Garden . . . . United States

2010 . . . . Mottisfont Abbey . . . . United Kingdom

The Peggy Rockefeller Rose Garden . . . . United States

David Austin Rose Garden (private) . . . . United Kingdom

Peter Beales Rose Garden (private) . . . . United Kingdom

In 2010, an additional award recognizing outstanding service by Americans to the GROW™ program and to promotion of U.S.–International rose culture was given. The first recipients were William A. "Bill" Grant and Ambassador Faith Whittlesey.

Mankind's Second-Oldest Occupation (Cont'd.)

CLAIR G. MARTIN III

*"It is no use asking me or anyone else how to dig
… Better to go and watch a man digging,
and then take a spade and try to do it."*

GERTRUDE JEKYLL

Evolution is not about life forms evolving from the primitive to more complexity. It's just that all living things change and adapt to current conditions over time, or die out. Gardeners are no different. We have to change our ways of doing things to keep up with the changes in weather and the environment.

Fads come and go, but gardeners are usually in it for the long haul. The problem for many of us is that there are so many different ideas and ways of gardening being promoted that we are surrounded

Observation, and taking note of what works and what does not, is what sustainable gardening is all about.

with a cacophony of conflicting ideas. Making a choice between going totally organic or resorting to chemical interventions can be difficult and confusing.

Today, most urbanites sense a disconnect from Mother Nature. We worship the cult of the natural, buy organic produce and milk, make a commitment to be as green as possible, recycle, reuse, and yet still we realize we are not as connected to the land as we would like. Somewhere along the way we have lost our direction and are having trouble regaining our hold on the land and our connection to it.

I remember giving a pruning demonstration at the garden center where I trained, and while addressing questions on pruning fruit trees I happened to mention that cherry trees didn't produce well here in mild-wintered southern California. Of course, an elderly gentleman at the back of the audience had to interject that he had "had a cherry tree in my yard for 30 years and I get bushels of cherries every year!" The only answer to something like that is, "I don't argue with success, but for the rest of us planting a cherry tree where it will not receive enough chill to set fruit isn't a viable strategy."

Gardeners—and by that I mean everyone who grows a few plants in containers on a balcony or patio to someone who plants a few roses along the driveway, or someone who plows up their front and back lawns and replaces that with vegetables and fruit trees—are looking for ways to reconnect with the land and yet simplify their efforts. Gardening is a get-down-and-dirty occupation. If you don't plan to get your hands in the muck, then you cannot call yourself a gardener.

As fads come and go, the best advice I can give a novice gardener is to focus on the tried and true ways. I remember a time when we were told to plant by the cycles of the moon, plant low, and then plant tall. The one thing every gardener has to learn is to observe what is going on in his garden. Take note of how the plants are responding to what you do, or don't do. How do they respond to pruning, fertilizing, watering? We may not be as connected to the land as our ancestors, but we can take notice of what is going on around us in our own gardens and make adaptations and change accordingly.

Observation, and taking note of what works and what does not, is what sustainable gardening is all about. Sustainability in our rose gardens is only attainable if we take note of our environs, soil, water, and so on — and then make informed plant selections.

By taking note of our environs, I mean observing local conditions, like the exposure to sun and heat and cold. Is there good air movement through the plants to help minimize disease and insect infestations? We can take advantage of microclimates that will maximize our efforts. For me in the mild and dry Southwest, we have trouble getting some Gallica roses to bloom because we cannot provide them with enough winter chilling, but by planting them in a place where the cold air is trapped we can get them to bloom. Planting our roses in rows that take advantage of the prevailing winds will also help keep disease down.

Today, most urbanites sense a disconnect from Mother Nature. ... Somewhere along the way we have lost our direction and are having trouble regaining our hold on the land and our connection to it.

Our dry hot summers prevent blackspot from becoming a major problem, but many roses do not take well to our intense sun and heat. Planting selected roses where they receive some relief from these conditions may help promote better and more abundant bloom; it can be as simple as that.

Sustainable gardening also requires we develop a healthy respect for the soil as a living organism. We tend to think of soil as not organic but rather an inorganic composition of weathered rock. A good soil is alive with micro- and macro-organisms working at devouring each other!

Soil is the base we depend on to build our gardens. It is the place we must start before we can begin to grow crops or our gardens. The realization that soils are alive is the key to understanding the interconnectedness of life in our gardens.

The 20th century was a time of great advances in the science of agriculture, but we sometimes forget that science, while wonderful, is not always right. What we failed to realize was that there is a connection between all living things, and sometimes we let science with its miraculous new chemical interventions get between us and the life around us. To get better and larger crops we resorted to chemicals that almost guaranteed us bountiful production of foods and flowers, but that initiated a slow decline in the life of our soils and nature itself.

For most of us, once we have planted a rose it will remain in that spot for years; so, it is incumbent on us to improve the soil so that our rose can continue to grow and thrive.

Here with our coastal semi-desert soils it is necessary to add large amounts of organic material to match the needs of our roses and gardens. This organic component can come in the form of animal manures, store-bought soil amendments, or our own homemade compost. Composting our green waste is a great way to cut down on our personal contribution to landfills and is a productive way to recycle garden waste back into the garden.

Of all the components for developing a sustainable rose garden, selection takes the most thought and dedication to succeed. We need to focus on discovering the best roses for our environs, roses that will thrive in our unique conditions.

Composting need be no more complicated than piling up lawn clippings and leaves into a bin or container and keeping the contents moist while turning the pile from time to time to keep oxygen mixed in to allow the natural bacteria and fungi to break down the green matter into organic compost. I have even added my kitchen waste, including coffee grounds and the filter paper, banana peels, egg shells, and just about everything excepting bones and meat leftovers, and have produced a great compost in 4–6 weeks. I have even recycled the waste from bird cages in this way.

Adding your own compost while planting and using it as a top dressing to work into the garden is so satisfying. You receive a double feeling of doing something good for your garden and the environment!

Here in our dry summers we need to irrigate our gardens on a regular schedule to get our plants through our dry periods. Gardens here can do well on less water, but they still need supplemental irrigation to survive.

Drip irrigation, which provides water to just the plants you intend to get the water, can substantially cut back your water usage and help limit the growth of weeds.

But maintaining sustainability in our gardens has yet one more component: selection. We are easily seduced by the latest beauty growing in a container in our local garden center or printed on the pages of all the winter catalogs we receive almost daily. The problem with this seduction is that we ignore the fact we are developing a long-term relationship with our lovely beauties!

Of all the components for developing a sustainable rose garden, selection takes the most thought and dedication to succeed. We need to focus on discovering the best roses for our environs, roses that will thrive in our unique conditions. So, how do we go about identifying these unique roses? Do research, talk to your fellow gardeners, explore local public gardens to see which roses there would meet your needs and desires—these are some ways you can find the right roses. Join a local rose or horticultural society and network with fellow members, who are willing to share their successes and failures. And don't be afraid of failures, for we often learn more from these than we think.

With the advent of the digital camera and the cell phone camera, it is possible to take photos of roses we like just about anywhere and build up a library of possible selections for our own garden. And if the rose is labeled, then take a picture of the label to document the name. Or you can do it the old-fashioned way and keep a small notepad with you and jot down the names of the roses you like for further research.

The United States is just so big and accommodates so many diverse climatic zones that it is next to impossible for one rose to do well in all regions, but with research and observation it is possible to make informed selections for our gardens.

The other side of selection is being realistic and knowing when a selection is not doing well and removing it. Pruning with the shovel is the gardener's answer to varieties that are not performing to expectations. Great gardeners have to harden their hearts and remove plants that are not performing for whatever reason.

We will also have to challenge our expectations and live with some problems. Gardening isn't a pristine art; we are working with nature, after all. I can live with some powdery mildew or aphids. It is a matter of reality and developing a sense of how much of a problem you can tolerate—and gardening within those boundaries.

Sustainable gardening is not a fad. Gardeners need to recognize that we have to be conscious of the life of our soils as well as the garden they support. We gardeners cannot simply resort to using harsh and poisonous chemicals without thinking about what our actions are doing to the life around us. We are not independent but connected to everything in strange and wonderful ways. Horticulturists have not always been aware of these connections, but it is our responsibility to make sure we give back to the land as much as we take.

The Birth of a Rose Garden

KARL MCKOY

My rose gardening takes place on wet soil, not by choice but because I was given the heritage of a thousand mostly unlabeled Hybrid Tea roses, many donated by Jackson & Perkins. Our relationship to this formerly family nursery dated back to shortly after the 1939 World's Fair when the exhibit "Parade of Modern Roses" and other prized trees and shrubs from the World's Fair were relocated to the place we now call Queens Botanical Garden.

I inherited this rich rose gardening legacy without any of the original plants, of course!

But I did get the wet, overly silty soil … a reminder of the tidal wetlands that predominated throughout this area. I also acquired a mature woodland forest which 30 years ago would have been a well-proportioned boundary planting, but now the trees have become overarching monsters, shading out half the garden in the afternoon. However, the best gift of all was the mandate I was given to care for the roses without the use of fungicides, pesticides or synthetic fertilizers of any kind. Now that got my interest!

With the promise of funding from the Stanley Smith Horticultural Trust and the support of our Director to relocate the original rose garden, I set about creating new garden layouts. Many plans were discarded due to potential high construction costs or the difficulty of maintenance. The

WHAT EXACTLY ARE "VINYL COPOLYMER EMULSIONS"? SOILTAC IS ONE OF THEM. HERE IS A —MAYBE EXPLANATORY—LINK: www.nicnas.gov.au/publications/car/new/na/nafullr/na0300fr/na394fr.pdf. BELOW ARE TWO INDUSTRY LINKS THAT MIGHT ALSO HELP. (GOOGLE SOILTAC MANUFACTURE) www.soiltac.com/material-safety-data-sheet.aspx, www.powderedsoiltac.com/docs/powdered-soiltac-complete-information-packet.pdf   —EDITORS

scheme we settled upon was a simple series of raised circular beds radiating around a central island, almost resembling that classic wave pattern seen when a pebble falls into a still pool of water.

Our intention was to showcase the exciting work of rose breeders such as William Radler, the Kordes firm, and Ping Lim who, in their quest to change the perception about roses as being inevitably difficult plants requiring chemicals to keep them healthy, were creating hardy, disease-resistant shrubs that bloom all season long.

So the plan was to raise these shrubs high above the problem soil, up to 24" in places, but all within a narrow footprint of pathways. This led to steep-sided mounds, which began to erode rapidly during rainfall or as a result of our conscientious watering of the young roses. The jute covering and carpet planting of sedum intended to hold everything together was not up to the task. In actuality, the sedum was being washed off the side of the mounds before it could grow roots to secure itself.

What pulled our well-intentioned project back from the slippery slope was a product we discovered called Soiltac, created to stabilize mineral soils by forming a polymer matrix around the individual soil particles. Soiltac, too, was regarded as being environmentally friendly in terms of its low impact on plant and animal ecosystems. It seemed a dream come true when we received the 5 gallon tanks of liquid. We mixed it with mineral soil to form a thick paste which was applied to the mounds and allowed to bake in the hot sun. It cracked and fissured, which was perfect for our requirements. This allowed both air and water exchange to take place while still providing a stabilizing layer that looked like a semi-permeable mulch covering.

The scope and ambition of our future plans at Queens Botanical Garden far exceed our current resources, but we are optimists, so, as I eagerly await the arrival of the new roses for trial—30 climbers including

(R. 'Amadeus' and R. 'Moonlight'), the healthiest varieties of the Austin English rose collection, and a special selection of 40 Tea roses featured in the best-selling book, *Tea Roses: Old Roses for Warm Gardens,* which will be tested for hardiness in New York — all that comes to mind is, where will we put them all?

(See page 222 for the Queens Tea Rose Test Garden project.)

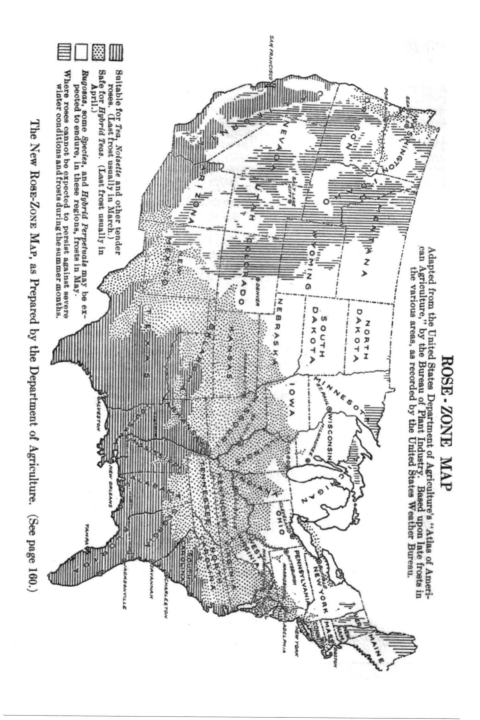

ROSE · ZONE MAP

Adapted from the United States Department of Agriculture's "Atlas of American Agriculture," by the Bureau of Plant Industry. Based upon late frosts in the various areas, as recorded by the United States Weather Bureau.

Suitable for *Tea, Noisette* and other tender roses. (Last frost usually in March.)

Safe for *Hybrid Teas.* (Last frost usually in April.)

Bugosas, some *Species,* and *Hybrid Perpetuals* may be expected to endure, in these regions, frosts in May.

Where roses cannot be expected to persist against severe winter conditions and frosts during the summer months.

The New Rose-Zone Map, as Prepared by the Department of Agriculture. (See page 160.)

The Rose Zone Map was a precursor to many other maps drawn over the following decades to assist rosarians in selecting roses suitable to their climates. "Hardiness" was the guiding consideration. From the American Rose Annual, 1920.

Soil and Water and Roses

DAN MILLS

One thing that all rose lovers can agree on is that we want our roses to bloom and rebloom as much as possible throughout the growing season. Most of our modern roses and many of our OGRs are quite capable of repeat-blooming with consistency as long as their basic needs are met. These needs include adequate sunlight, air, water, and mineral nutrients. It is our job as growers to first provide a planting site with full sun and good air circulation, and then make up for inadequacies in water and nutrients as the growing season progresses.

As pointed out in the ARS *Consulting Rosarian Manual*, nearly all water and nutrients taken up by roses come from the soil. Therefore, it makes sense for us to try to understand the nature of our *native soil* and then try to manage it to provide our roses with the needed water and nutrients as efficiently as possible.

This is an especially challenging task for most of us living in the Central and North Florida area because our native soil is so sandy. Soil scientists have determined that the *ideal soil texture* for growing roses is 60% sand, 20% silt, and 20% clay. Most of our soils in Central and North Florida are 80–90% sand. This means that water and dissolved nutrients drain out of the root zone too fast.

One consequence of this excessive drainage is that we have to water and fertilize more frequently than if we had a more ideal texture. Another

JUST ABOUT EVERY STATE MAINTAINS SOIL TESTING LABORATORIES AND OFFERS SOIL TESTING SERVICES AT NO CHARGE AS PART OF THEIR AGRICULTURAL EXTENSION PROGRAM. FOR INSTANCE, THE UNIVERSITY OF FLORIDA EXTENSION SOIL TESTING LABORATORY WILL TEST YOUR SOIL AND TELL YOU YOUR SOIL'S PH, THE FERTILITY LEVEL OF PRINCIPAL NUTRIENTS, THE LIME LEVEL OF YOUR SOIL AND WHAT NUTRIENTS YOU NEED TO ADD TO YOUR SOIL. CHECK WITH YOUR EXTENSION SERVICE TO FIND HOW TO PREPARE SAMPLES AND GET AN ANALYSIS. THERE ARE ALSO NUMEROUS PRIVATE PROFESSIONAL SOIL TESTING COMPANIES.   —EDITORS

consequence is the added pressure put on local water supplies and the quality of ground and surface waters.

So the obvious question is, What can we do to improve our native soil's water and nutrient retention capacity? Before an answer to that question is offered, let's first take a brief look at the make up of a good garden soil and get an idea of how its various components interact to help provide the needs of plants.

COMPOSITION OF A GOOD GARDEN SOIL

A good garden soil for growing roses consists of approximately 25% water, 25% air, 45% inorganic material (often called mineral material), and 5% organic matter. In view of our tendency to think of soil basically as a solid, it seems rather remarkable that the top several inches of good garden soils are actually about half water and air by volume. This fact alone makes it clear that water and air are very important in proper soil function.

Water is essential to all living organisms within the soil and to all plants rooted in it. Water keeps plants turgid and is a vital component of photosynthesis. This is the process whereby plants make their own food by utilizing the energy of sunlight to convert CO_2 and water into carbohydrates. Water also transports in solution from the soil virtually all of the mineral nutrients that are utilized by plants as they grow and maintain themselves.

Air is required for respiration by all living organisms in the soil, including roots, earthworms, and microorganisms. Therefore, air along with water should be fairly evenly distributed throughout all portions of the soil that are biologically active.

The relative proportions of air and water in the soil can fluctuate significantly between successive rainfalls and between wet spells and dry spells. We typically compensate by having some kind of irrigation system to maintain a continuously moist soil. The amount and frequency with which we have to irrigate between rainfall events depends mostly upon how well the soil retains water. In this respect, both inorganic and organic materials play very important roles.

Inorganic material is made up mostly of tiny rock particles called sand, silt, and clay. Sand particles are the largest and are visible to the naked eye. Silt and clay particles are microscopic, clay being the smaller of the two. As pointed out earlier, the ideal combination of soil texture for growing roses is 60% sand, 20% silt, and 20% clay.

The 60% sand is ideal for adequate drainage of water, even during periods of excessive rainfall. Otherwise, roots could suffer or die from lack of oxygen as water pushes out air and fills up pore spaces (producing the "wet feet" syndrome).

The 20% silt is ideal for retaining sufficient *available* water and freely giving it up to plant roots as needed. In fact, soil science has determined that much of the water taken up by plant roots comes directly from silt-size particles.

The 20 % clay is ideal for holding water and mineral nutrients *in reserve*. Collectively, as individual particles and lattice-like groups, these microscopic particles constitute a huge surface area on which a relatively large volume of water can accumulate and be held very tightly. They also carry a negative electrical charge, which accounts for their tendency to attract and hold mineral nutrients that are positively charged ions.

Thus we see that the 60–20–20 combination of inorganic particles is the near perfect balance to help provide optimum water and mineral nutrient needs of roses.

Although the proportion of organic matter in a good garden soil is much smaller than the proportion of inorganic material, 5% vs. 45%, it nevertheless plays vital roles in nutrient cycling and in building and maintaining good soil structure. At this point it is worth mentioning that our native sandy soils (here in North and Central Florida) typically contain only about 1% organic matter compared to the 5% ideal.

The living portion of soil organic matter (mainly the microorganisms and earthworms) is constantly at work breaking down the dead portion (organic waste) into (1) carbon dioxide and water (a process that is just the opposite of photosynthesis), (2) mineral nutrients, (3) a wide variety of organic compounds, and (4) relatively stable end products called humic substances, or humus.

One way of looking at what we are trying to accomplish ... is to view it as a sort of restoration of the natural cycle of growth, leaf fall, decomposition, and recycling of nutrients that is found in forests and grasslands. Nature is the model ...

During the decay process, some of the released mineral nutrients eventually may be taken up by roots and utilized by plants. Some may be reabsorbed by microorganisms and cycled again through the process. Others may be held in storage by clay particles, or by humic substances, or by the combined action of the two. And still others may leach out of the root zone, along with excess soil water.

The humic substances tend to persist in the soil and provide a variety of very important benefits, including the coating of inorganic particles (sand, silt, and clay), which promotes the grouping together of individual particles into aggregates.

Aggregation leads to good soil structure, which in practical terms means greater pore space and better water, nutrient, and air retention. To convey this important concept in layman terms, soil scientists sometimes make the analogy between well-aggregated soil and a sponge.

Technically, humus is the very end, stable remains after virtually all degradable material has been removed. Because it resists further decay, humus tends to slowly accumulate in the soil as long as conditions under which it formed remain the same.

In our warm climate, exposure of soil to excessive heat from direct sunlight by frequent or permanent removal of vegetative cover can lead to a rapid decline in humus content. Thus, humus tends to survive or accumulate best under the canopy of a forest or a thick blanket of mulch in the garden.

Humus particles are dark brown to black and very similar to clay particles in terms of their size and in terms of their tendency to attract and hold water and mineral nutrients in reserve. According to some sources, soil organic matter can hold up to 20 times its weight in water.

IMPROVING THE WATER AND NUTRIENT RETENTION CAPACITY OF OUR SOIL

From the discussion above, there appear to be two obvious possibilities for improving the water and nutrient retention capacity of our native sandy soil. We can either increase the amount of clay in the soil or we can increase the amount of organic matter. Both options are achievable, depending on how much time, expense, and effort we are willing to give.

Since the right kind of clay is often difficult to locate and transport, heavy to work with, and hard to incorporate into the soil, nearly all gardeners opt for using organic materials. In addition to improving the water and nutrient retention capacity

The slow, continuous decay of mulch will contribute to the build up and maintenance of the organic level of the soil. The accumulation of humus is essential to achieving our goal of improving the soil's water retention capacity.

of soil, regular additions of organic matter will also provide a steady supply of plant nutrients, better aeration and more even temperatures, and support a larger population of soil life.

In an ideal situation, organic materials probably should be incorporated into our native sandy soil and allowed to age for at least a few months *before* any roses are planted. In theory, this would get benefits from extra organic matter started in the root zone before planting. However, as a practical matter many rose growers likely do not become aware of the potential benefits of organic material until *after* they have planted roses.

For either situation, there are ways to apply organic materials effectively. Some suggestions on kinds of organic materials to use and ways to apply them are presented below.

ORGANIC MATERIALS TO USE

Most organic materials are useful for improving water and nutrient retention capacity of sandy soil. As a rule, the greater the variety of material used, the greater the variety of potential nutrient release for future plant use. Some commonly available organic amendments in our area include (1) "nitrogen-rich" materials like food wastes, homemade compost, straw and manure, shavings and manure, mushroom compost, worm castings, various processed meals (blood, cottonseed, fish, and alfalfa), seaweed, packaged manures and compost, and (2) "carbon-rich" materials like peanut hulls, fallen leaves, wood chips, sawdust, shredded newspaper and cardboard.

The nitrogen-rich materials contain sufficient nitrogen to support the microbial activity necessary to break them down in the soil. However, the carbon-rich materials are nitrogen-deficient and, if used alone, require 1–1.5 pounds of nitrogen per 100 pounds of material, to be mixed in at the time they are incorporated into the soil or applied on top of it. Otherwise, the decay organisms may actually rob the soil of needed nitrogen, causing a nitrogen deficiency in plants growing in the soil. This sometimes happens when fresh wood chips are used alone as mulch.

In addition to improving the water and nutrient retention capacity of soil, regular additions of organic matter will also provide a steady supply of plant nutrients, better aeration and more even temperatures, and support a larger population of soil life.

Ideally, a mixture of nitrogen-rich and carbon-rich amendments should be used together in such a proportion that a slight excess of nitrogen is released into the soil as decomposition progresses. A similar concern for the carbon to nitrogen balance must be taken into account when attempting to make compost.

WAYS TO APPLY MATERIALS

For new rose beds many different approaches are possible — depending in part on how much time and effort one is willing to exert. One possibility involves first killing all grass and weeds so thoroughly as to eliminate future sprouting of root remnants of aggressive grasses such as Bahia and Bermuda.

After the dead grass and weeds are removed or tilled in, the desired organic amendments should be spread evenly in thin layers over the entire bed, alternating nitrogen-rich and carbon-rich materials, to a maximum depth of 6–8 inches. Each layer should be moistened as it is applied. The whole mass of amendments should then be spaded in or tilled in with a rotary tiller to a depth of several inches. This method amounts to composting in the ground instead of in a pile. If the soil pH at the time of treatment is under 6.0, sufficient lime should be added and tilled in with the amendments.

After several months of resting, the bed should be ready for planting. Just before planting, the pH should be checked again and adjusted if necessary. Sometimes a large treatment with organic material will acidify soil significantly because of the organic acids generated by the decay process. This tends not to be a serious problem in Central and North Florida because most of our soils are underlain by limestone rock, which naturally tends to counteract acidity. If weeds start to grow in the bed before roses are planted, they can be mowed and the residue left in place. The whole bed should be mulched thickly after the roses are planted.

A simpler version of the method described above is to skip "tilling-in" the layered amendments. The materials would decay "in place" on top of the soil, if kept moist. This method of composting is called *sheet composting*, and there is substantial evidence attesting to its effectiveness.

Some who use sheet composting also control or eliminate weed growth by covering the top layer of amendments with overlapping sheets of newspaper or cardboard and keeping the mass constantly moist until it "mats" in place. A better technique might be to crisscross the paper or cardboard with baling twine anchored down by ground-cover u-nails. After several months have elapsed, holes can be dug right through the composting material and roses planted.

Soil scientists have determined that the ideal soil texture for growing roses is 60% sand, 20% silt, and 20% clay. Most of our soils in Central and North Florida are 80–90% sand.

When bushes are planted, the planting holes may be amended in the usual way (by adding extra compost or aged manures, slow-release fertilizer, rock phosphate or superphosphate in the bottom of the hole, etc.). This is common practice to help new bushes get off to a good start. The real benefits from having treated the *whole* bed with organic materials prior to planting will show up in future years as the bushes outgrow their original planting holes.

Immediately after bushes are planted, the entire bed should be mulched to a depth of 3–4 inches with coarse organic material such as pine bark or pine straw. This thickness of mulch should be maintained continuously by periodic replenishment as needed. The slow, continuous decay of mulch will contribute to the build up and maintenance of the organic level of the soil. The accumulation of humus is essential to achieving our goal of improving the soil's water retention capacity.

For rose beds that have *already* been planted, organic amendments may be applied evenly on the soil surface around each bush after the mulch has been raked back to the drip line or a little beyond. After the amendments have been applied, they should be covered with new mulch. It is *not* recommended that amendments be scratched in or dug in, because damage to rose roots could occur.

There is evidence that surface applications of organic amendments have similar effects to "incorporation." It just takes longer. The old mulch that was raked back to make way for the amendments can be spread evenly over the space between bushes to help maintain an even thickness over the entire bed.

Perhaps the best time to do this "organic treatment" each year is immediately after late winter or early spring pruning is completed. This provides a month or two for the microbes to begin work on the new amendments before spring growth begins on the roses. Some rose growers do a second annual organic treatment in August immediately after the light pruning for the fall flush. These annual organic treatments should prove beneficial to all rose beds established in our native sandy soil.

BE PATIENT! IT MAY TAKE A WHILE*

One way of looking at what we are trying to accomplish here by building up the organic component of our soil is to view it as a sort of restoration of the natural cycle of growth, leaf fall, decomposition, and recycling of nutrients that is found in forests and grasslands. Nature is the model and we are trying to simulate it in our garden by artificially replenishing a major missing component, organic matter, and supplementing the process with sufficient water (when necessary) to make it work. It takes nature perhaps hundreds of years to evolve an effective forest or grassland in a suitable climatic zone. So let's be patient and give our efforts a little time (several months or a few years) to start yielding nature's benefits. They *will* begin to accrue, and our rose bushes will appreciate it!

Ideally, a mixture of nitrogen-rich and carbon-rich amendments should be used together in such a proportion that a slight excess of nitrogen is released into the soil as decomposition progresses.

---

* Assessments of the time factor for achieving results are provided by:
(1) Toor and Shober, University of Florida, IFAS Ext. Service, SL273, p. 3. "Building soil organic matter is a slow and gradual process …It may take a decade or more for organic matter levels to significantly increase. Fortunately, the beneficial effects of the changes in organic matter can be seen after few additions of organic residues/compost."

(2) Pleast and Morton, The Complete Compost Gardening Guide, *2008, p. 20. "In most soil, attaining an ideal level of 6 to 8 percent of stable and active organic matter usually takes three years if you mix in a 3" (7.6 cm) thick blanket of compost annually and use biodegradable mulches."*

(3) Our experience at The Weed Patch, near Fairfield, Florida. Prior to 1998 the native soil had been used for the production of watermelons, various vegetables, and Bahia grass for 65 years or so. The organic matter content of the soil was about 1.0%. By 2009, following annual organic treatments and the maintenance of a continuous mulch cover, the organic matter content of rose bed soil averaged 3.7%.

Notes from the Sacramento Historic Rose Garden

BARBARA OLIVA

In the Sacramento Historic Rose Garden, we never use complex synthetic chemicals. We use only some horse manure and alfalfa pellets.

I'm pretty sure that the roses that are most trouble free in the Historic Rose Garden are the ones well-suited to our climate—the Chinas, Teas, Noisettes and Tea-Noisettes. Prime examples include 'Lady Hillingdon', 'Mons. Tillier', 'Duchesse de Brabant', "White Pearl in Red Dragon's Mouth", 'Louis Philippe', 'Cramoisie Superior', and many others.

 THE SACRAMENTO HISTORIC ROSE GARDEN WAS NAMED TO THE ROSE GARDEN HALL OF FAME IN 2009 FOR ITS ACHIEVEMENT IN GATHERING TOGETHER THE ROSES OF HISTORIC CALIFORNIA AND GROWING THEM TO THEIR NATURAL PROPORTIONS IN THE OLD CEMETERY. HAPPY ROSES!   —EDITORS

The rose pathogen of most concern to us is crown gall, because the crew members will use weed eaters and hoes against the center of the bush. Others, like mildew, spider mite and blackspot, aren't a major problem, although we see some now and then. Otherwise of little concern to us, we do see some rust on Hybrid Perpetuals and senescent leaves at the end of the season. One point here—a plant, "Petite Pink", that has spider mites now and then in the cemetery when it is dry and dusty, doesn't ever get them in my garden. I water with sprinklers—the cemetery is bubblers.

Blush Noisette is an especially beautiful and popular representative of the free-flowering Noisettes, a rose class that originated in South Carolina in the first part of the 19th Century when the 'Old Musk Rose' *(Rosa moschata)* was crossed with 'Old Blush', a Chinese import.

A Life Filled with Roses

WILLIAM M. PATTERSON

Thinking back over the 44 years that I have enjoyed roses in South Carolina since my childhood, I recall the best of my gardening experiences, starting with the first rose I grew and called for years, "Aunt Belle's Tea", in honor of my great aunt who helped dig the old own-root rose from her mother's garden and pass it on to me. Oh, what joy there is in sharing plants and gardening tips! In later years, I was able to identify that rose as the old China, 'Jean Bach Sisley'. That very plant is still growing and blooming here after some 100 years in the family garden. For me, "Aunt Belle's Tea" reflects the enduring essence of a sustainable rose.

Experience has taught me over the years that I need to ask the following questions before selecting roses for the garden.

What am I looking for in a rose?
What color and style of bloom would I like?
Do I prefer color in the garden, or roses to cut and share?
Is fragrance important to me?
What am I trying to accomplish with my landscape?
What location will be best for my roses?
What size bushes will fit my landscape?
How much winter protection will my plants need?
How much time and physical energy am I willing to spend
in the garden?

The time and physical energy one expects to expend have a great influence on the varieties to be selected. If one has little time for gardening activities, one should steer more toward the easy-care varieties that offer greater than average disease resistance. Throughout the years, experience has taught me that very few roses are disease free; however, many can be sustained with minimal effort. Each class holds many members that are well worth growing. Some varieties offer only one cycle of bloom, whereas others knock themselves out with continuous bloom. Let me share my list of outstanding varieties, those which grow and perform well for me with little to no disease problems.

'Applejack'	1973 Griffith Buck Shrub rose of medium pink, intense fragrance, but only a spring bloomer in my Southern garden
'Awakening'	1935 light pink sport of New Dawn, the best modern day climber, continuous bloom, slight. occasional but manageable blackspot
'Chestnut Rose'	1814 Species with medium pink blooms packed with petals, a nice repeat, unusual sepals, and outstanding exfoliating bark
'Darlow's Enigma'	introduced 1995 Hybrid Musk with intense fragrance from pure white flowers with golden stamens
'Jean Bach Sisley' & 'Le Vesuve'	1898, 1825, respectively, pink blends from the China class; what few leaves get blackspot fall right off as the plants continue to thrive and bloom all season
'Mme. Antoine Mari'	1901 Tea with lilac pink blooms, slight mildew problem under certain weather conditions, outstanding Earth-Kind™ rose
'Mrs. B.R. Cant'	1901 Tea with medium pink flowers, grown for years as "Senn's Pink", a mystery rose found

	growing in an old cow pasture with no care for over 50 years
'Pink Pet'	1928 lavender pink China with clusters of small blooms
'Sander's White'	1912 rambler with glossy green foliage, spring bloomer that reminds me of a Christmas tree decorated with 10,000 white lights
'The Gift'	1981 Polyantha with single white blooms that produce lovely orange hips but continuous bloom if deadheaded regularly

Other outstanding varieties on my short list of those worth growing include 'Alberic Barbier', 'Alister Stella Gray', 'Archduke Charles', 'Carefree Beauty', 'Cramoisi Superieur', 'Dr. Grill', 'Duchesse de Brabant', 'Green Rose', 'Mlle. Franziska Kruger', 'Mme. Joseph Schwartz', 'Mozart', 'Mutabilis', 'Penelope', 'Sea Foam'.

For those who must have the modern Hybrid Tea look, I would suggest:

'Belinda's Dream'	1992 Shrub with medium pink, 4-inch flowers with a raspberry fragrance, a well deserved Earth-Kind™ designated rose
'Elina'	1984 light yellow Hybrid Tea that received the coveted 1987 ADR award

Remember that, as with all things, the more tender loving care you give, the greater the reward in rose growing. Modern rose classes tend to require more spraying and grooming than the Old Garden varieties. Typically (but not invariably), the glossier the foliage, the more disease resistant the variety will be.

Choose your varieties according to your time schedule and enjoy what nature has to offer.

This print (reproduced above in black and white) of *R. centifolia* 'Cristata' from the first edition of *The Rose Garden* by William Paul, like other of the book's prints, was painstakingly hand-colored for each book by artisans who consulted the original watercolor drawing. One person would lay in the greens; another person the pinks, and so on. The artist who created the original watercolor, James Andrews, was responsible for a number of gracefully drawn images in *The Rose Garden*'s first edition.

The Pillar Rose

WILLIAM PAUL (1822–1905)

Perhaps there is no form of the Rose more effective than the Pillar Rose, and if this method of fashioning the Queen of Flowers was more thoroughly understood, Pillar Roses would probably be more plentiful in our gardens.

A Pillar Rose when fully grown should be 8 ft. high, broader at the base than at the summit, and in the blooming season it should be clothed with flowers over its entire height. The Hybrid Chinese and Hybrid Bourbon are the best kinds for the purpose, on account of the masses of large brilliant flowers which they produce. The Ayrshires, Sempervirens and Boursaults stand next in order of merit, and these will attain the height of 10 ft. or 12 ft. if required; while the strong-growing Hybrid Perpetuals, Noisettes, and Bourbons, are

PAUL'S LANDMARK BOOK, *THE ROSE GARDEN*, RAN THROUGH 10 EDITIONS, THE FIRST IN 1848, THE LAST IN 1903. IN *ROSES* (1978), JACK HARKNESS WROTE, "THE OUTSTANDING FEATURE OF PAUL'S BOOK IS THOROUGHNESS. HE SWEEPS UP EVERY CRUMB OF FACT ... IT IS THE VERY TOUCHSTONE OF AUTHORITY." "THE PILLAR ROSE" IS REPRINTED FROM *THE FLORIST AND POMOLOGIST* (OCT., 1870, PP. 241–43), ONE OF THE MANY LIVELY HORTICULTURAL JOURNALS OF THE TIME.

—EDITORS

available in positions where a maximum height of 6 ft. suffices. The three latter groups, however, offer fine varieties that will form well-furnished pillars more than 6 ft. high, and they bloom only by driblets after the first flowering; still, where it is desired to have flowers in the autumn, rather than in the summer, they may be preferable, and they form by no means inelegant objects.

Pillar Roses may be placed singly on lawns, in groups, or in avenues, and in the latter case, if the walk is of grass the effect is materially heightened.

It is by no means difficult to form a Pillar Rose; time and patience are the chief requisites. Choose from the nurseries the tallest and strongest plants, whether on their own roots or otherwise, and here, as elsewhere, be sure to obtain suitable sorts. This is a point of primary importance, and no amount of skill and patience will avail if it be neglected.

Pruning and training are the principal means by which we expect to carry forward our operations with success; but manuring must not be neglected.

After the plants are fairly set in the ground, some recommend cutting back the shoots to one or two eyes, to induce the formation of a few strong shoots the first year. I have no grave objections to urge against this practice; and if the roots have been injured or curtailed in removal I recommend it; but under other circumstances my experience is in favour of leaving the plant unpruned the first year, or at the most restricting the operation of pruning to the removal of the weak, misplaced, and ill-ripened wood. Tie up the shoots to a neat stake immediately after transplanting, and the first growth springing from the top will further extend the height of the plant. This completed, the second or summer growth will probably arise from eyes nearer the base hitherto dormant, and while the former were weak and short, terminated with flowers, the latter will be vigorous wood-shoots available for forming the plant, and giving flowers the next year. Pruning and training are the principal means by which we expect to carry forward our operations with success; but manuring must not be neglected. Be it remembered that a Pilllar Rose has more to support and develop than a dwarf or standard, and a liberal diet should be accorded to it. Manure twice annually, in February and in July; and if convenient, water frequently with weak liquid manure in the growing season, especially in dry weather.

But we have something to say on pruning and training. When the plant has been a year or more in the ground (in the spring of the second year) pruning is absolutely necessary. Cut all weak, ill-placed and crowded shoots, and shorten back such as are indifferently ripened to the first solid eye, taking care not to lower the height of the plant more than is necessary in carrying out these principles. The well-placed and well-ripened shoots should be pruned sparingly or moderately, in no case severely. After pruning, tie the branches round the stake with willow-twigs or tar-twine.

The operations of manuring, pruning, and tying, are to be repeated from year to year. About the third year the stake may be replaced by a small birch pole, with the snags left protruding some six inches from the sides, which have a pretty rustic appearance, and serve to protect the branches from the action of the wind. Thus is the Pillar Rose formed, and few objects in the garden present a more gorgeous appearance.

… to form a Pillar Rose … be sure to obtain suitable sorts. This is a point of primary importance, and no amount of skill and patience will avail if it be neglected.

When the pillar is five or six years old, now and then an original and main stem will show signs of debility. Such should be cut away close to the ground, and replaced by the young shoots which occasionally spring up at or near to the ground-line. By this practice the plant is rejuvenized and retained in perfect keeping over an indefinite period.

Wilhelm Kordes IIII and the Kordes firm manager Thomas Proll in a field with tens of thousands of Kordes seedlings. A select few of these seedlings will be entered in the rigorous ADR (All German Rose) Trials, where they will be tested for 3 years in 11 test gardens all over Germany without any spray program for qualities such as beauty, presentation, flowering, growth and—foremost—disease resistance. No synthetic pesticides or fungicides will be applied. For more about the ADR trials, see www.newflora.net.

Report on Kordes® ADR Roses in the United States, 2010

GARY PELLETT

The ADR rose evaluations are conducted by the German Nursery Growers Association at eleven trial stations throughout Germany. Judging occurs over three growing seasons for all rose varieties that are entered. Many consider these evaluations the most challenging in the world, in that fungicides have not been used since the 1997 season. We continue to have interest in the parallels between performance in Germany and the performance in the eastern U.S. locations, knowing that there are different races of blackspot and mildew around the world. Kordes varieties did well in the ADR judging of 2009 with 7 varieties gaining ADR certificates.

We have submitted a number of the ADR varieties into both the Minnesota and the Texas trials. David Zlesak has assisted us greatly in this. Varieties were first received into the Minnesota program in spring, 2008. Apparently, they performed quite well, but David would be the one with more details. We have submitted varieties to the Texas trials just this winter.

The Kordes® varieties also have performed quite well at the NYBG gardens with Peter Kukielski, with 16 of the 'Top 30—Superior Roses' having come from Kordes® Also, evaluation of Kordes® varieties is ongoing in a number of important trial gardens in the U.S. and Canada, including the Missouri Botanical Gardens, Montreal Botanical Gardens, Boerner Botanical Gardens, to name a few.

ROSES OF THE SAN JOSÉ HERITAGE ROSE GARDEN

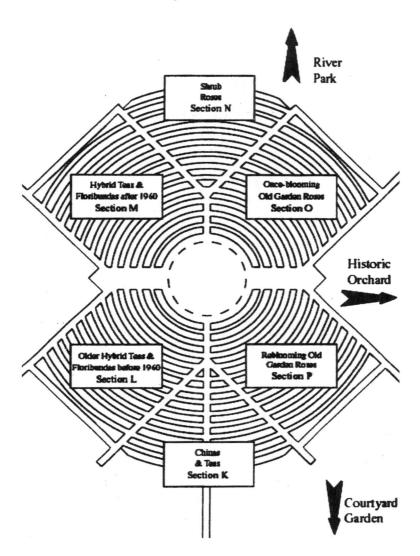

A schematic showing the lay-out, largely along historical lines, of the San José Heritage Rose Garden's rose beds. "The Heritage" as it is often called is—in terms of number of varieties grown (more than 3,000), not number of plants—the largest rose garden in the U.S. It is as close as we come on this side of the Atlantic to a true rosarium such as, for instance, Germany's Sangerhausen. The Heritage is a creation of inspired amateur rosarians working together with the City of San José.

Sustainable Gardening Practices at the San Jose Heritage Rose Garden

JILL PERRY AND BRIAN DEBASITIS

Part 1: Background

JILL PERRY, CURATOR

When the City of San Jose was planning the Guadalupe River Parks and Gardens (GRP&G), a group of Heritage rose lovers in the South Bay Heritage Rose Group planned the Heritage Rose Garden as a part of it. The plan was to show and preserve roses of all periods in rose history. Budwood was imported from many gardens in the United States and Europe. Cemeteries around California were also searched for old roses, and found roses make up about 15% of our varieties.

You cannot spend very long in the garden without having planes flying over just before landing. The location of GRP&G is just south of the runway for San Jose's Mineta International Airport. There used to be a housing development here, but when the airport expanded, the houses were torn down. In digging to plant roses, we often come across remnants of the housing tract—bits of pavement or concrete, pieces of brick or metal. The soil is heavy clay.

THE SCIENTIFIC EVIDENCE IS INCONCLUSIVE ON WHETHER MYCORRHIZAL COLONIZATION CAN BE SUSTAINED FOLLOWING INOCULATION. SEE, FOR INSTANCE, "MYCORRHIZAL FUNGAL INOCULANTS TO SOIL—NO ANSWERS YET" (www.ipm.iastate. edu/ipm/hortnews/2004/4–23–2004/ spores.html) FOR AN ASSESSMENT THAT MIGHT BE OF INTEREST TO GARDENERS. IF THERE IS NO RELIABLE "QUICK FIX," THEN CREATING A BETTER SOIL THROUGH REGULAR COMPOSTING, AND SOIL TESTING FOR THE PRESENCE OF MYCORRHIZAE, MAY BE THE ROAD SUSTAINABLE GARDENERS MIGHT BE ADVISED TO TAKE.   —EDITORS

The garden comprises six sections laid out in a circle. The first rings by the center of the circle contain our Minis and Polyanthas. Behind these two rows, the six sections each contain different types of roses. The first section (O) has Species roses, Hybrid Species such as Eglantines and Spinosissimas, and OGRs—Albas, Gallicas, Centifolias, Damasks and Mosses. The next section (P) contains classes influenced by the Chinese imports—Bourbons, Portlands, Hybrid Perpetuals and Hybrid Rugosas. Next come the Tea and China roses in Section K. I would like to collect every Tea rose in existence. Section L contains Hybrid Polyanthas and older Floribundas in the front part, and older Hybrid Teas and Pernetianas in the back part. More recent Floribundas and modern Hybrid Teas are in Section M. Shrub roses are in Section N—Lambertianas, Hybrid Musks and Austins, among others. Adjacent to the pathways in the garden the end rose in each row is a climber, and most of our Noisettes are found along these row ends. Some of the bush Noisettes are at the back of Section K. A few Hybrid Giganteas are there as well. There are not enough locations for all the great ramblers and large climbers, and the airport will not allow us to build large structures for them, so an arrangement was made with Santa Clara University for us to cover a half mile of fence there with climbing and rambling roses—about 250 varieties of them.

The garden was planted in January 1995. In the years since, we have learned much about growing these roses. First, we have come to realize that the initial spacing was often too close. Many roses were much more vigorous than expected, and crowded out the adjacent plants. We have had to designate a large number of locations as "not available." Another realization is that planting a young rose out among the mature plants led to high losses of new plants. A nursery was added to grow out young plants until they are big enough to survive in the garden.

The most serious problem we've had took a long time to figure out, and was happening at the time I took over as Curator in January 2005. Roses started dying at a high rate—several hundred that year. We had no idea if the symptoms we were seeing were caused by a disease, contaminated pruners spreading disease, bad or poor soil, fungi, wrong fertilizers, aging plants or the use of reclaimed water. This led to a lot of discussion, thoughts of experimenting in different parts of the garden with fungicide, more fertilizer, and so forth, but it was finally decided to get some good soil testing done before doing anything else. Brian Debasitis stepped in as a volunteer at this point.

Part 2: Soil Improvement Program
BRIAN DEBASITIS, SOIL ECOSYSTEM CONSULTANT

There had never been a comprehensive assessment done on the soil at the San Jose Heritage Rose Garden (HRG). The project started with a complete soil analysis, including testing soil chemistry, soil physical properties, soil microbiology and water chemistry since the garden is irrigated with recycled water. HRG volunteer supervisors were interviewed to get as much history as possible. The approach was to determine how all factors might be affecting the roses and causing the problems contributing to poor plant health.

INITIAL FINDINGS

Overfertilization. This was caused by applying the slow-release fertilizer more often than specified in the instructions, in combination with the extra fertilization being provided by the recycled water. Our recycled water provides significant amounts of N, P, K as well as calcium, sodium, sulfur, zinc silicon, manganese, magnesium and boron. Some of these nutrients are provided in quantities higher than required and need to be watched and managed to prevent build up in the soil.

Severe soil compaction in parts of the garden. Compaction prevents good root growth and causes water to pond on surfaces. Compacted soil *can become* anaerobic and anaerobic conditions provide a breeding ground for plant pathogenic organisms.

Poor soil microbiology makeup. The microbiological ecosystem was incorrect for roses. The soil had excessive levels of bacteria and few beneficial fungi. Roses grow better in a soil that is dominated by fungi, including mycorrhizae, which help roots absorb nutrients from the soil. There were also few protozoa and they are key to cycling nutrients from the soil to the plants.

STEPS TAKEN

The first step was to apply a thin top dressing of compost. The compost used was amended to increase the fungal biomass before application. The amendments used were humic acid, chitin, pulverized oyster shell, and some organic oats. The compost provided an inoculum of organisms as well as foods and habitat for the additional organisms being encouraged to grow in the soil.

The beds were mulched with wood chips to increase the organic matter in the soil. Wood chips, being a high carbon material, are also a good food for soil fungi.

Aerated compost teas were, and continue to be, applied as foliar sprays, soil drenches and as a root injection with mycorrhizae. The compost teas were produced with fungal dominant compost to deliver as many fungi to the soil as possible. A protozoa inoculum was added to the compost teas to increase the number of protozoa in the soil.

Sunflowers were planted in some beds to help break up the compacted soil. Sunflowers were chosen because they have a deep taproot, have no known antagonisms to roses and form mycorrhizal relationships so they wouldn't set back mycorrhizal colonization on the rose roots.

RESULTS TO DATE

The first measurable improvement was the return of protozoa to the soil. With sufficient protozoa returned to the soil, the roses were getting all the nutrition they require without any additional fertilizers. What is being provided by the recycled water and the soil microbiology is sufficient. Fertilizer is no longer required in the garden.

Soil compaction is less severe. The reduction of soil compaction will continue as long as the soil maintenance practices now in place continue. There have been no ponding incidents over the last two winters. Even though the winters were relatively dry, there have been single storms with significant rainfall with no surface water build up.

The soil had excessive levels of bacteria and few beneficial fungi. Roses grow better in a soil that is dominated by fungi, including mycorrhizae, which help roots absorb nutrients from the soil.

The bacterial levels in the soil have dropped. This helps put the fungi to bacteria ratio into better balance. Worms have returned to the garden. Early on, it was reported, worms were not found in holes dug for new plants. Now worms are found regularly when planting holes are dug. Fungal biomass has increased in the soil. Increased fungal biomass will help with disease resistance. Beneficial soil fungi help increase disease resistance in two ways. First, the beneficial fungi out-compete pathogenic fungi, reducing the possibility of infection. Second, since roses prefer a soil dominated by fungi, the increased fungal biomass improves the overall health of the roses, allowing the plants to better withstand any minor infections.

To date, mycorrhizal colonization has not improved to adequate levels. The level changed from 4% colonization to 8% colonization. The goal is a minimum of 40%. Considering overall soil conditions are more conducive to fungal growth, the recycled water is being looked at as a *possible* inhibiting factor. Recycled water provides soluble nitrates and sulfates in fairly high quantities. Sulfur is a fungicide and may be inhibiting mycorrhizae. Reports also have shown mycorrhizae may disassociate when there is an excess of nitrate available. These issues are still being evaluated in the garden. The goal of adequate mycorrhizal colonization has not been abandoned and recycled water is here to stay. A different approach is being planned for getting mycorrhizae to the roses.

Overall, plant health appears good. There are still a few areas where powdery mildew occurs regularly, and that is being worked on. Aphids come to the garden, but not to a point where plants are being damaged, and the predators are abundant and keep them in check.

Memoirs of a Condo Rose Grower and Composter: Containers for Roses

Revised and Enlarged

ELLEN SPECTOR PLATT

COUNTRY MOUSE

For 14 years I grew and cut flowers for resale on 5½ acres in Orwigsburg, Pennsylvania, at Meadow Lark Flower & Herb Farm. Most of the over 500 varieties were for drying, and I farmed without herbicides or pesticides. Compost was the principle ingredient for enriching our rocky soil. My own compost production consisted of an "official" wire bin for kitchen scraps, weeds and clippings, and lots of piles in the tree-line where hand-pulled weeds from the raised flower beds met their timely disintegration. My thoughtful son Mike presented me with sacks of composted horse manure as a holiday gift, and I bought additional brown-gold from a local farm by the dump-truck load as needed.

CITY MOUSE

When I moved to Manhattan in 2002 and took over gardening chores for my condo building of 100 units, I designed a rooftop garden with trees, shrubs, perennials, bulbs, and annuals, all living in some 80 containers. Plenty of roses were in the mix. No longer having to worry about deer, groundhogs, rabbits, moles, voles, or even Japanese beetles 18 floors above Third Avenue, at first it seemed easy to garden organically. The building paid to install automatic drip irrigation, a must in such hot and drying conditions. The heavy winds provide excellent air circulation for roses and lavender, and the full sun permits a wide selection of plants. I can grow enough culinary herbs to supply anyone in the building who wants them for cooking. It's a lovely place to relax away from the noise and confusion of the street. Young children have a large safe play area after they learn not to grab at the roses with prickles. Their elders host dinner parties and brunches in the small garden rooms separated from one another by hydrangeas and buddleia. In-betweeners sun themselves and hold evening parties away from parental eyes.

But rooftop gardening has its own concerns. By trial and error I learned:

(1) Measure the elevator before selecting a perfect tree for a rooftop garden.

(2) When purchasing prebagged potting soil and compost, it takes many, many, *many* bags to fill and feed 80 containers.

CITYSCAPE: CONTAINER ROSE GARDENING

In the downtown of a large city, tall buildings cast deep shadows on those lucky enough to have a backyard. Natural soil is often highly compacted from years of hard use. Balconies, also for the few, can be small. Gardeners who snag a space in a nearby community garden consider themselves fortunate, then try to cram in as much as possible: a few tomato plants, some vegetables and herbs similar to those grown in childhood, often in far-off countries. They covet spring and summer flowers, perhaps a rose or two. Looking up from street level, passersby notice highly illegal containers on fire escapes, sometimes the only area available for desperate gardeners.

Large pots help city dwellers with minute space allotments to select their own soil, layer the plants to cram more in, and allow them to place roses in the sunniest spots available even if there's no natural soil there. In my present life, I've had to adapt to grow everything in containers and to discover the virtues of an all-containerized garden. Suburban gardeners will find that a couple of large pots on a terrace or deck will be equally enthralling. The aroma of roses will be nearby as you relax, read, or enjoy your company. And in a pot you can control the soil and use a mix that drains well instead of your natural red clay or shale.

Since weight of filled containers is often an issue on rooftops, a soilless mix is preferable. I use a light bagged potting soil without added fertilizer, since I want to feed with only organic stuff.

MANAGE YOUR EXPECTATIONS

Experts reckon that trees and shrubs grown in containers will be ⅓ to ½ of their natural in-ground size. Bear this in mind so you won't be disappointed when the 15-foot climber promised by the grower reaches but 9 feet on your terrace. When the rose expert from Pasadena showed slides of his 15-foot 'Graham Thomas', I could be well satisfied, not disappointed, that mine was at least 8 feet tall.

THE RIGHT POT

The container should be able to stand up to your coldest winter temperatures. There usually is no room in a city apartment to wheel sensitive plants or pots indoors to winter over in a more compatible environment. Look for high-fired clay, fiberglass, or one of the excellent terracotta reproductions. The size should be no less than 20 inches in diameter, 24–30 inches for the biggest plants. If you've had trouble with winter-kill before, line rectangular or square pots with sheets of Styrofoam and round pots with pieces of bubble wrap before adding soil. The extra insulation will help prevent the roots from freezing. But be sure you have a big enough pot to start with as insulation takes up extra room from the roots.

THE RIGHT WATER

I think that water is more important than food for plants, and roses are no exception. You MUST install drip irrigation on a timer for city container gardens. The atmosphere can be very windy and drying especially on those upper balconies and terraces. You may promise yourself, your spouse or your friends that you'll water faithfully twice a day when necessary, but don't lie to your roses. They won't tolerate being dried out.

Large pots help city dwellers with minute space allotments to select their own soil, layer the plants to cram more in, and allow them to place roses in the sunniest spots available even if there's no natural soil there.

THE RIGHT PLANT

It's a no-brainer to think that Miniature roses are perfect for containers, and so they are. But since I've never been a big fan of Minis, I look for my favorites and go on from there. It's my theory that ANY rose will grow in a nice big container with proper water and plant food. If a rose or any other plant doesn't appreciate my conditions, I'm hard-hearted and yank it out to try something that will value my 18th-floor garden with a view of the Empire State Building and other less fabulous rooftops. Currently I have my favorite 'Graham Thomas', another David Austen rose 'Crown Princess Margareta', two 'Knock Out'®, a large 'New Dawn' climber, 'America', OSO Easy™ groundcover roses 'Paprika' and 'Pearly Cream', 'All the Rage', and a sentimental favorite, 'Harison's Yellow'. Some of these, like 'New Dawn' and 'Harison's Yellow', bloom but once—in spring—but so does my wisteria, the iris, and peonies. I cannot fault the roses any more than I can these other cherished plants. Being realistic in your expectations will make you well satisfied.

'All the Rage' (center) in a container on my Manhattan rooftop garden.

Peter Kukielski, Curator of the Peggy Rockefeller Rose Garden and Rose Collections here at the New York Botanical Garden, recommends Drift roses for containers and large hanging baskets. He's super-thrilled with all of the Kordes roses, 'Mystic Beauty' from Pat Henry, and many of the David Austen's as well. Their catalog lists 11 shorter roses as excellent in pots, but ever the contrarian, I'm growing two of their climbers instead with great success.

PESTICIDES

NONE. I do no spraying whatsoever. These are roses that work well in our climate and need nothing, or I wouldn't allot them any of my precious space. Selecting roses that have high disease resistance is paramount from the start. The 'America' occasionally gets a few leaves with blackspot that I remove and discard immediately. The constant wind, even in summer heat, is an advantage, keeping leaves dry in our humid Julys and Augusts.

THE RIGHT SOIL

Since weight of filled containers is often an issue on rooftops, a soil-less mix is preferable. I use a light bagged potting soil without added fertilizer, since I want to feed with only organic stuff. Generally it's any brand I can get my hands on, since I'm without a car in the big bad city and must rely on delivery from one of several sources in distant neighborhoods. I'd rather not cart home on the bus with a bag on each shoulder. I also add compost that I'm now producing in-house (see below).

If you've had trouble with winter-kill before, line rectangular or square pots with sheets of Styrofoam and round pots with pieces of bubble wrap before adding soil. The extra insulation will help prevent the roots from freezing.

THE RIGHT FOOD

I use any organic plant food I get my hands on according to package directions and try to be regular with the feeding through late August. I stop feeding then to discourage new growth that might be killed at the first heavy frost.

CONFLICT

I designed, planted, pruned, and groomed and had a pretty respectable collection of plants, but my stomach churned every time I packed up a big plastic bag of green garden waste to haul down to the basement, where the building janitor threw it in with the other "garbage." The building then paid the garbage company to haul it away. You can see this makes no sense: I was buying bagged compost, then bagging garden waste and paying to haul away materials that could produce compost. I was also dumping down the garbage chute kitchen scraps that I had formerly composted.

EPIPHANY

In the summer of '07 this clash produced a rebellion within my soul. Pulling out yellowing pansy plants in early July heat, I cast around for a receptacle, and I found two. The EarthBox Company had sent me two large self-watering containers to trial. They were still empty. An EarthBox is a heavy plastic rectangular self-watering container, 28" long x 10½" high with a perforated shelf 4" above the floor and a black plastic cover like a shower cap that can enclose the entire top. The cover helps warm the soil for tomatoes, eggplant and other heat-loving plants. The boxes seemed

The EarthBox containers proved useful in reducing the time it took to create a rich compost to about 6 weeks, though the amount it produced at one time was limited. I've since purchased an "official" rotating composter.

heaven-sent. I loaded one with the half-dead pansies, weeds, shriveled tulip leaves, and lettuce that had bolted, sprinkled them with water, and covered with the plastic cap. For about 3 weeks I added materials as they were ready for discarding, reaching in to stir the pile by hand to aerate. In about 6 weeks with great pride I strewed my rich and nutritious Upper East Side Compost on my favorite children: Rosa 'Harison's Yellow' 'New Dawn', two Knock Out®s, the David Austin rose 'Graham Thomas', the climber 'America', and a gorgeous new rose from Bailey's, 'All the Rage' (Easy Elegance™).

Emboldened by my success with the first bin, I started another pile in the second EarthBox, this time adding beautiful kitchen waste, burying it near the bottom so that no onlooker would get upset by "garbage" on the roof. Granted, the rest of the summer produced just three buckets full, but I felt vindicated. I could expand my horizons and add this free compost to the iris, the clematis and the butterfly bushes.

WIGGLERS

With winter coming on, flyers from the Manhattan Compost Project and the Bronx Compost Project heralded courses in indoor worm composting, a natural for an Upper Eastside Condo. For a mere $10, subsidized by the city Dept. of Sanitation, class members received a pound of red wiggler worms *(Eisenia foetida),* and a ready-made plastic worm condo complete with ventilation, an irresistible deal! Thus started my adventure to transform garbage into worm castings that would be my new winter-produced organic compost. These worms are not earthworms but live normally in the decaying leaves under trees and shrubs. They cannot take freezing cold or hot sun and burrow to the bottom of the worm condo, needing air, food, moisture, and bedding to survive.

THE PAPER OF RECORD

Shredded, moistened *New York Times,* black and white pages only, with their soy-based ink, made the perfect bedding. My granddaughters, ages 5 and 7, giggled as they helped tear the strips of paper. We soaked them in a basin of water, wrung them out thoroughly and distributed them loosely in the condo, then dumped in the wiggling worms, which quickly burrow to the bottom. One pound of worms eat about three pounds of kitchen scraps a week, vegetable matter only, no meat, fats, or dairy; these guys are totally vegan. I collect my scraps in a mixing bowl set on the kitchen counter, with a plate for a lid. No need to buy anything fancy. My husband cooperates by adding all of his coffee grounds, but between his

Annabelle and Lucy preparing bedding for worm composting condo.

coffee and my five teabags daily, we wondered if they were getting over-caffeinated. The worms had a wonderful celebration at Hanukkah when they partook of the traditional latkes in the form of raw potato and onion peelings, and they loved it when 10-year-old Max visited and cut up watermelon rind. I know that because they gobbled it up within a week.

The worm condo itself stays on the floor of a powder room, transformed from its intended use, and now entirely devoted to gardening tools, vases, dried flowers, and the other necessities of this New York City gardener's existence.

PETS

Standing in the produce-aisle of my local Food Emporium, I considered whether the red wigglers would prefer browned leaves of iceberg or romaine, the rinds of lemon versus lime. I cooked up a huge pot of vegetable soup so they could sample carrot and parsnip peelings. Each time I feed them a new fruit or vegetable, I imagine their pleasure as they test an unfamiliar food. So, what's the harm in a little anthropomorphic reasoning? Dog and cat owners do it all the time.

When we went on vacation for 9 days, my compost teacher said the worms would be perfectly fine, provided I left them a few scattered piles of food at the bottom of the container. It's harder to find a worm sitter than a baby or cat sitter but I did have a couple of offers if need be. Teacher was right. The worms continued to do their thing without any intervention while we were adventuring in the rain forest. But the red wigglers were eager to gobble up the next batch of scraps on offer.

TIPS ON WORM COMPOSTING

What smell? The compost won't have an unpleasant odor if you add only fruit and vegetables, with no meat or fat to go rancid, no cheese to turn sour, and no moldy scraps at all. Think of the oxymoron, GOOD GARBAGE.

Rain, rain, go away. The worms get needed moisture from the food and damp newspaper strips, but it shouldn't rain in their condo. If there's too much moisture, water drops will condense inside the lid and fall again in the box. When I saw that happening, I wiped the excess moisture with a paper towel and added a few handfuls of dry newspaper strips mixed in to help balance the moisture. Depending on how wet the food scraps were, I found myself doing this every 2–3 weeks. For a short-term measure, I left the lid off for several hours at a time to reduce overall moisture. In a plastic box the worms don't seem able to climb out. In a wood box, maybe they could.

One pound of worms eat about three pounds of kitchen scraps a week, vegetable matter only, no meat, fats, or dairy; these guys are totally vegan.

Ain't no flies on us. Fruit flies sometimes lay eggs on the rinds of tropical fruits and may hatch in your condo. At the first sign of trouble, fill a jar half-way with beer. Cut a 10-inch circle of wax paper or parchment, fold in half, then in quarters. Cut off an inch of the bottom point and open to form a funnel. Insert the funnel in the jar and fold ½ inch over the rim. Hold in place by slipping on a rubber band. Place the jar on the bottom of the condo, in the center. Any flies will investigate the beer and be trapped.

My worms ate my tax return. Worried about identity theft when discarding old tax returns with their revealing names and numbers, I pondered buying or renting a paper shredder. Lots of drawbacks here of cost and space, for the small quantity I needed to get rid of. I threw caution to the wind, I ripped off our names and Social Security numbers from 5 years of returns and added the papers to the worms bedding. All gone in no time! My apologies if the ink wasn't the preferred kind, but it was only a little tiny bit.

SPRING FEEDING

Four months from their December arrival, in the beginning of spring, I had a lovely bucket of worm castings to add to my rose containers. As my shrubs broke dormancy I dug a trowel full into the soil around each rose and other favorite perennials and imagined the pleasure of the roses as they fed on the gift from my worms.

For "Chocolate and Roses," also by Ellen Spector Platt. (SEE PLATE 21)

For more specific instructions on building and maintaining a worm box see: Worms Eat My Garbage *by Mary Appelhof (ISBN 0–942256–03–4)*

Ellen Spector Platt is the author of nine books on flower and garden topics including Easy & Elegant Rose Design: Beyond the Garden, *Fulcrum Publishing, 2004. She is also the co-publisher of the garden blog* www.gardenbytes.com.

Knock Out®, for many, started the "Sustainable Revolution" in roses about 2000, when it was introduced. It is tough, vigorous, free-flowering, and, especially, highly resistant to blackspot. Today, because of the success of Knock Out® with the public and landscapers, hybridizers have had to reorder their priorities, placing disease-resistant foliage at the top.

Talking about My Work with Roses

Revised and Updated

WILLIAM J. RADLER

When and how I became interested in gardening

It seemed to just happen. My Mom and Dad both gardened a little, as did Grandma Sternhagen. Grandpa Radler had a hillside garden which was rather "wild"—his thing didn't appeal to me as a garden. Mom credits herself as an influence for my gardening because she said that she did extensive gardening when she was carrying me ("with child"—Victory Gardens were in at that time). I was born on February 13, 1943.

I remember my first experience with seed. My brother, 1½ years older, and I (probably age 8) decided that we wanted to have a garden, and Dad gave us some leftover seed from when he and Mom had their Victory Garden.

Most of the seed was too old and didn't germinate well, but I remember how the experience caused me to begin my inquisitiveness on why some plants failed while others thrived, and how some things like lettuce went to seed before the growing season was finished. There seemed to be so much to explore.

Even though roses are my specialty, I love all plants. I do a little experimenting on new varieties of all types. In the future I hope to introduce a lily, a crabapple, and maybe a zone 5 hardy glad.

What attracted me to roses

At a time when children were seen and not heard, I fought boredom at my grandparents' home by looking through rose catalogs. Page after page, I was captivated by the various shapes, sizes, and colors of the roses.

My fascination continued. At age 9, I took my allowance money and went to the local A&P to purchase my first rose, for 49 cents. My parents warned me that the plant would die over the winter. I expected the rose to survive and flourish in my backyard—and I was right! Not only did it survive, it did even better the second year.

I remember the bloom of this first rose. The bud exploded into the most gorgeous thing that I had ever seen. And it was fragrant! Before long, I had to have more plants to experience the multitude of colors, sizes, and forms and the wealth of perfumed fragrances that my grandparents' catalogs had promised.

My garden, its climate and dimensions, and how it evolved

I acquired my present garden/yard in April of 1992. On the day of closing on the property I took to my new home a garden hose and a spray tank of diluted Roundup® to kill the grass for what were to be the first beds of the "Rosarium."

Seedling 89–20.1 (later to be named Knock Out®) was already 3 years old. I moved this rose along with 600 others to my new home. I also moved hoards of trees, shrubs, perennials, and houseplants as well as about 120 varieties of hostas.

The Rosarium is an acre and a half, but a lot of that acreage is too wet to be gardened with roses and other highland plants. As a result I garden intensively about 1/2 to 3/4 of an acre. The Rosarium consists of 14 beds of mixed plantings and 28 rows of roses. I keep a running number of 1,400 roses in inventory, discarding those that don't make the cut. The lowland setting causes the air to be moist throughout the growing season. Diseases of roses thrive in such a setting, a climate perfect for screening for disease resistance.

In the fall of 1993 an overhead photo was taken of my home and garden (the Rosarium). The garden layout has remained much the same. Only the permanent plants have grown much larger and some of the beds have expanded, but the rows where the rose testing occurs have remained much the same. For me a garden is never a static thing.

As I acquire more plants to satisfy my need to grow, the Rosarium changes. In 2009, groundbreaking occurred for adding onto my home and to make major changes with hardscaping. The end product was additional indoor space for the rose business, a root cellar, a small greenhouse, a spacious gazebo, enlarged patio, and paved walks throughout. Adding water features, music, and night lighting has made my bit of paradise so much grander.

My "unorthodox" way of developing roses

To ensure the disease resistance of my roses I developed a rigorous evaluation. I create an environment that guarantees diseases have ideal conditions to survive and thrive.

I collect diseased leaves early in the season and dry them on sheets of newspaper. The dried leaves are put into a kitchen blender to create a powder. This powder is sprinkled over the entire rose garden while the rose leaves are wet. The overhead watering adds additional moisture and creates an ideal environment for infection.

Compact-growing, disease-resistant roses are a natural for shade as long as you can keep them adequately watered. Avoid planting roses in the root zone of overly aggressive trees like hackberry, beeches and maples unless the roses are in containers.

Diseases like blackspot usually show themselves within 2 weeks of this inoculation. In any case, before the current growing season ends, a high level of disease resistance is easy to spot among the devastation in my garden. A friend of mine has called this practice "benign neglect"!

To screen for hardiness, winter protection is not used. Roses that do not overwinter are part of "survival of the fittest"—after all, 500 roses need to be discarded annually to make way for that year's crop of new rose seedlings.

In winter, roses are grown from seed in my basement under ordinary fluorescent 40 watt shop lights. Gardening for me is a year 'round thing even though I am in zone 4/5.

The Knock Outs and my other rose introductions

In 2011, I will have 22 low-maintenance rose varieties on the market—all known by their trade names (code/cultivar names follow, plus year of introduction). All are self-cleaning—not needing spent bloom removal and/or shortening of stem to continue to bloom and produce an attractively shaped plant naturally.

Knock Out® ('Radrazz') 2000. A highly disease-resistant, quick-breaking, tightly compact, low-growing, and wide-spreading, mounded plant. The semi-double flowers are a bright cherry red that is most lovely at low light levels when the color absolutely glows. The flowers are produced in small clusters; they are long-lasting and self-clean, and have a lovely sweet fragrance which, while mild, does drift into the air. The leaflets are long, leathery, and dark green with a burgundy hue, and densely produced. Knock Out® further rewards viewers at the end of the season with a sensational plum-purple autumn leaf display. The plants are resistant to leafhopper and Japanese beetles as well as tolerant to rose midge. Plants are crown hardy to -20°F. without winter protection and are tolerant of late spring frosts.

I grow plants with the minimum amount of care possible. My maintenance practices are determined by the basic needs of the plants.

Carefree Sunshine™ ('Radsun') 2001. A highly blackspot-resistant, low-growing, wide-spreading, and symmetrical mounded plant. The nearly single-petaled flowers are a bright light yellow; they self-clean, are produced in small clusters, and exhibit a mild sweet fragrance. The leaves are light green and densely produced. The plants are tolerant of leafhopper and dependably crown hardy to -20°F. without winter protection.

Ramblin' Red™ ('Radramblin') 2002. The nicest formed bloom of any of the repeat-blooming winter-hardy climbing roses. Hardy through zone

4. Once established, this is a very aggressive grower thatcan easily fill a space 20 feet wide. It can be kept much smaller through selective pruning. The double-petaled crimson-red flowers have a nice sweet scent, and the foliage is tolerant of blackspot.

Blushing Knock Out® ('Radyod') 2003. A pale pink mutation of Knock Out®. Identical except for color.

Pink Knock Out® ('Radcon') 2003. A medium pink mutation of Knock Out®. The coloring undergoes pleasing subtle changes as the flower opens and ages. Except for color, it is nearly identical to Knock Out®.

Double Knock Out® ('Radtko') 2005. A sister seedling of Knock Out® with the same coloring, yet different in the flower shape and with an increased number of petals. As a cut flower the blooms can last for 10 days. The plant is similar to Knock Out® but with greater winter hardiness but, alas, less resistance to Japanese beetles. Crown hardy through zone 4.

Lemon Meringue™ ('Wekradler') 2005. A lemon-yellow mutation of the popular rose Autumn Sunset™. Blackspot tolerant and crown hardy through zone 5. A climber which is perhaps warm-wall hardy through zone 5.

Brite Eyes™ ('Radbrite') 2006. Pink blend blooms with a prominent yellow center. Can be used as a tall freestanding upright shrub or as a restrained climber suitable for the smaller garden. The lemony-rose scented blooms undergo color changes from bud through full open bloom. Unfortunately, in 2009 a new strain of blackspot disease has challenged this plant's resistance. Nevertheless, the plant is winter hardy through zone 5 and possibly more, as well as resistant to rose midge.

Climbing Carefree Sunshine™ ('Radsunsar') 2006. A mutation of 'Carefree Sunshine™. This is a vigorous, productive blackspot-resistant climbing rose. Perhaps warm-wall hardy through zone 5.

Rainbow Knock Out® ('Radcor') 2007. All-America Rose Selections winner. A slightly smaller plant and flower than Knock Out® but with even more bloom power. The 5-petaled flower is a yellow centered light pink which ages to white. Crown hardy through zone 4 and resistant to rose midge.

Pink Double Knock Out®. A medium pink mutation of Double Knock Out®.

Sunny Knock Out® ('Radsunny') 2008 . Yellow blooms quickly age to white and have a moderate spicy fragrance. The plants are slightly more upright than Knock Out®, crown hardy through zone 5, and resistant to rose midge.

Carefree Celebration™ ('Radral') 2008. Coral-orange ages to white. A little more open in habit than Knock Out® with handsome colorful foliage. The pest resistance that you expect from a Radler rose and midge resistance, too.

Midwest Living™ ('Radliv') 2008. Velvety dark red blooms are especially nice in the bud. More open in habit than Knock Out® and perhaps shorter. The pest resistance is good, and midge resistance is excellent, too.

Morning Magic™ ('Radmor') 2008. This pastel-colored climbing rose ages to white with glossy foliage enhances the fragrant bloom and a fragrance that drifts in the air. This delicate-looking beauty is anything but delicate. Winter hardy through zone 4.

Winner's Circle™ ('Radwin') 2008. A climbing red that is more refined in habit than Ramblin' Red™, with better repeat bloom. This is a better climber for smaller spaces. In autumn, expect to be overwhelmed by profuse orange hips backed up with plum-purple glossy foliage. Winter hardy through zone 4.

Stark® Pink Lady ('Radsweet', sold in Europe as Alaska™) 2008. A pale pink sister seedling to Rainbow Knock Out®. Excellent midge resistant. Deserves to be more widely grown. In humid weather, the growth gives off a light scent of baked apples into the air. Unfortunately, it is only available through Stark Bro's (www.starkbros.com) as very small own root cuttings.

Cancan™ (Radcancan') 2010. A new color in roses. The deep pink and white bicolor blooms age with purple edges. This hardy, upright restrained climber has small clusters of bloom and repeats well. The pest resistance is what you expect from a Radler rose and midge resistance, too.

Milwaukee's Calatrava™ ('Radfragwhite') 2011. Intoxicatingly fragrant, this full-petaled white rose blushes in cool weather and as the blooms age. The upright, disease-resistant plants will keep you in heaven all season.

Peppermint Pop™ ('Radcarn') 2011. The double blooms are white with a broad pink edge. The well-behaved mounding plants blend beautifully with Knock Out® roses and other ornamentals in the landscape.

Bubble Double™ ('Radnov') 2011. A double pale pink variation of the Double Knock Out®.

White Out™ ('Radwhite'). The cream-colored buds open to pure white single blooms. The plant is compact and mounding. The closest thing to a white Knock Out®. Very winter hardy and midge resistant.

What gives me the most pleasure in my garden

Through proper care, selection, and placement, creating a beautiful picture—a bit of paradise. Seeing plants thrive and excel. Finding new things about how plants change and evolve and creating magic through the use of plants. The first rose seedling of the year to bloom under lights in my basement. The first plant to emerge in spring. Giving up on a plant only to be proved, by the plant, that I was wrong. Hearing that another plant of mine will be marketed. Anticipation. Continually learning.

My favorite perennials to grow as companions to roses

I love to combine roses with plants that are completely different. And they can be different in form, color or texture, or even fragrance or season of bloom. For instance, lilies are different in texture and fragrance. They add a vertical element and the blooms, a coarse texture. Trumpet, Oriental and Orienpet lilies are especially fragrant.

Blue and purple plants add a color dimension lacking in roses. Some of my favorites are Delphiniums, *Perovskia atriplicifolia* (Russian Sage), *Centaurea* montana (Mountain Bluet), *Salvia* 'Blue Hills' , *Veronica spicata* 'Royal Candles', *Veronica* 'Sunny Border Blue', *Heuchera* 'Palace Purple', *Polemonium* sps., Purple Pasqueflower, *Platycodon* 'Sentimental', *Nepeta*

I'm constantly "bending the curve" by going against popular horticultural advice. Sometimes I luck out. Sometimes I don't. I am always trying to stretch the capability of plants.

'Blue Carpet', vining Clematis of all kinds, especially 'Betty Corning', as well as *Clematis integrifolia* (Bush Clematis). I'm constantly looking for more to include in this palette. Then there are the minor bulbs like *Scilla siberica* 'Spring Beauty' and *Chionodoxas* that color the garden with drifts of blue before other plants emerge.

Foliage colors like the grey of Artemisia also add a fine texture. The blue-green leaves and coarse texture of *Euphorbia myrsinites* (Myrtle Euphorbia) are nice as well.

Some roses can be grown in shade
Roses like a lot of light. They don't necessarily need full sun. Compact-growing, disease-resistant roses are a natural for shade as long as you can keep them adequately watered. Avoid planting roses in the root zone of overly aggressive trees like hackberry, beeches and maples unless the roses are in containers. Besides the Knock Out® series, roses like 'The Fairy' and the Flower Carpet™ series also make great choices for shady locations. Some of the Meidiland and Dr. Buck roses will work also.

How long it takes for a rose to go from my backyard to garden centers
The shortest time span for me has been 7 years. For Knock Out® it was 11 years. It begins with sending budwood to a commercial nursery to clone the plant and to test and evaluate it (a license agreement for testing purposes only is recommended). The test begins with 4 to 25 plants. If these plants pass the 2-year test, additional plants are propagated and evaluation continues for additional years. More than one testing location is often chosen, and outside evaluators are sometimes used. If at the end of the testing period the introducer feels that the rose fills a niche or replaces an inferior rose in their inventory, the company will patent and trademark the rose for introduction. (If

Be sure to know the ultimate size of your rose (height and width). Unlike many perennials, once the rose is planted, it will not require dividing. The location you choose will be its permanent location.

the company decides to enter the rose into All America Rose Selections testing, add on an additional 3 years.) Even with all the time and money invested, it is still a gamble that the rose will be a moneymaker for the company. It is hard for any one rose to perform well in all climatic situations. Popular taste plays an important part in "survival of the fittest" in the rose industry.

Some special tips for growing roses well

I grow plants with the minimum amount of care possible. My maintenance practices are determined by the basic needs of the plants. I have an automatic watering system since supplying supplemental water can be an arduous task, especially when the season is droughty. This is especially true for plants in containers. Battery-operated water timers were the first godsend for my container plants. Now the whole garden is automated.

Think of your garden as an outdoor room with a floor, walls and ceiling. Work with the space to create the feeling you want. Then fit in the plants to accommodate the design.

I generally don't use insecticides and, because of this practice, I don't have a problem with spider mites. If sawfly larva or caterpillars are noticed, I usually handpick. I also handpicked Japanese beetles in the past—I now am prioritizing breeding for resistance to the beetles. I may use horticultural oil or soap but mostly for indoor plants.

I use lawn fertilizer for everything outdoors; once a year. I believe in mulching. I find the black-colored wood mulch to be best for me. It holds its color and is long-lasting.

My professional background

I have a degree in Landscape Architecture from the University of Wisconsin. After graduation, I worked for the Milwaukee County Park System, becoming the director of the Boerner Botanical Gardens in 1980. I took early retirement in 1994. Six employees now help me with the rose research and development.

The biggest challenge in my garden

With any garden the biggest challenge is keeping ahead of the weeds. I'm not especially fond of dividing plants and prefer plants that tend to need dividing less. Creating the picture of my dreams is always a great challenge to a plant collector.

Horticultural mistakes that taught me a lesson

We all make mistakes. I've learned to accept that a mistake can be a good thing when it teaches us. If we didn't make mistakes, we wouldn't learn. Of course, it's better to learn by the mistakes of others, but on the other hand, there is something to be said for firsthand experience. I'm constantly "bending the curve" by going against popular horticultural advice. Sometimes I luck out. Sometimes I don't. I am always trying to stretch the capability of plants. For instance, I plant sun-loving plants in shade to see if they are tolerant. In certain microclimates, plants can succeed where normally they wouldn't. So I lose some plants. Nothing ventured; nothing gained. I enjoy the process of gardening. If I'm not happy with the "picture" I paint, there's always next year.

How I would describe my house

Contemporary English Tudor.

What I am currently working on

Rather than spending my time on showing other people's roses and growing them to perfection, I prefer to create a less demanding, more forgiving plant—constantly striving to develop the "perfect" rose. My current goal is producing absolute midge resistance in roses. The rose midge is a tiny native insect that causes ever-blooming roses to not bloom in the summer—the larva of this insect causes tip growth to abort.

Along with this goal I am working on fragrant roses. I am especially pleased with my 2011 introduction, Milwaukee's Calatrava™. In addition,

I am continuing to work on the colors yellow, orange and purple. Yellow is one of my favorite colors and is not well represented in low-maintenance roses. And, previously, I mentioned Japanese beetle resistance.

Where the name "Knock Out" came from

I believe Angela Treadwell came up with the name. Conard-Pyle (C-P) was trying to come up with a distinctive name for Rad89–20.1/C-P 4642/95R503. She was thinking of the name "Razzleberry," which was trademarked for some other plant by the Monrovia Nursery Company. Permission to use the trademark was not granted. Angela called me soon after this to see how I would like "Knock Out," which I totally loved. Unbeknownst to me C-P was thinking of the word "knockout" as in "she's a knockout," but they misspelled it as two words which means the prizefighting knock out. The misspelling became the permanent name since the registration process had already been completed. At the first trade show booth used to promote Knock Out®, C-P designed a prizefighting ring from horticultural materials (garden pots and stakes for instance) and the salespeople had "black eyes."

> *I love to combine roses with plants that are completely different. And they can be different in form, color or texture, or even fragrance or season of bloom.*

Some tips for designing with roses in the perennial garden

Be sure to know the ultimate size of your rose (height and width). Unlike many perennials, the rose, once planted, will not require dividing. The location you choose will be its permanent location. And like perennials, the rose performs better its second year. So do your homework, making sure that the right rose is chosen for the location.

Be sure to plant the rose deeply. Where the branches emanate should be about 1½ inches below ground. This will better guarantee winter survival of crown hardy rose varieties.

Rose varieties that continue to bloom even when spent bloom is not removed will require far less maintenance. Your garden will always look kempt if varieties are selected that drop their petals rather than holding on when they turn ugly.

The best garden advice anyone's ever given me
Think of your garden as an outdoor room with a floor, walls and ceiling. Work with the space to create the feeling you want. Then fit in the plants to accommodate the design.

Something more ...
For people who tell me they're afraid to grow roses, I tell them that they don't need to be afraid to grow Knock Out®. I developed this rose specifically for my retirement years so that I didn't have to give up my hobby because it required too much work. Once I realized that I was nearing my goal, I felt the need to share my results with others. Knock Out® was specifically developed to satisfy the need for a dependable flowering garden plant that didn't require a lot of maintenance. With Knock Out® many people have learned to forget what you heard about roses being difficult.

The Days of ... Chickens and Roses?

RON ROBERTSON

Roses seem to go with everything, don't they? Who hasn't heard of "Wine and Roses"? There's even a band by the name of "Guns 'n' Roses," so maybe it's not so far-fetched to talk about Chickens and Roses. I've been fortunate enough now twice in my life to have space for both roses and chickens.

THOSE WISHING TO EXPLORE THIS SUBJECT FURTHER COULD DO WORSE THAN TO CONSULT "HENDERSON'S HANDY-DANDY CHICKEN CHART" AT www.ithaca.edu/staff/jhenderson/chooks/chooks.html. —EDITORS

I know, there are two big negatives people have about chickens—one is their scratching, the other is the "noise" they make. The former I can understand. It actually is a problem, and when I'm planting I put things that are easily scratched up either away from where chickens typically roam or put wire on the ground around the plant. We have a bigger problem with gophers here, so anything that's in a gopher basket will not be bothered by chickens' scratching. The chickens happily pick at bugs or weeds next to the plant. The main noise problem comes from roosters. My partner is one of those who is bothered by crowing. I always point out that it's not louder than a dog barking or two cats fighting, and that, in a way, it's a sign of peacefulness. Roosters won't crow if they sense there's any danger near.

Negatives aside, what do chickens bring (at their request, I did not add "to the table" to that phrase)? They are formidable bug and pest eaters. Favorite delicacies include snails and slugs, and grasshoppers are a treat they'll run hundreds of feet to catch. They also eat a wide range of weeds, especially grasses. Chickens will not harm roses of any size, having no interest in their foliage or flowers, though I've seen them inspect the undersides of the leaves for aphids and other small bugs. I love watching them as they run from place to place in our garden, nearly always busy and enterprising in their search for tasty tidbits. Nothing is as charming as a hen with her brood of chicks making their way around the roses. Chickens, like other birds, seem to gravitate toward roses, sensing a measure of protection offered by the roses' prickles and camouflage offered by their foliage and stems. Plant a row of climbing roses and you'll have an automatic bird magnet.

The main caution about having chickens with your roses is that you'll want to carefully think about any chemicals you use. Even though our property has over 10,000 roses, we use no chemicals (we use a combination of compost and Actively Aerated Compost Tea that we brew on the property for our fertilizer and pest control), so the chickens, bees, and other wild and domestic life are in no danger; nor, I might add, are our visitors or ourselves.

We get far more eggs from our chickens than we could ever eat, so I end up giving or selling the excess. These genuinely free-range-produced eggs make mass-produced eggs seem a pale imitation by comparison in every way, from the color of the yolks to the taste in your mouth. So, if you have the space, and your neighbors don't mind, try out some chickens in your rose garden. They give much more than they take and add an element of liveliness that's hard to beat.

One last thing. Do chickens have a favorite rose? Well, the translation from their lips to my ears was a bit difficult, but it seems that the Polyantha 'Marie Pavie' is their favorite in our garden. They seem to like its full, dense growth from the ground to well above their heads, the fragrant flowers (they've seen me sniffing them from time to time), and last, but certainly not least, it's next to where I feed them. Judging by how well 'Marie Pavie' grows in that spot, the admiration is mutual.

Garden Valley Ranch
Compost Tea Program

RON ROBERTSON

We use a product called "Active Aerated Compost Tea" (AACT for short) as the only spray for our roses. This is produced by putting a complete compost (worm castings, humus from Alaska, and a special compost rich in microbes) in a bag that is immersed in water. The water is aerated with a large airstone continuously for 48 hours (most of the country can have it brewed in 24 hours, but due to our cools nights in Petaluma in northern California—typically around 45°F, even in summer—it takes us longer to get sufficient microbial growth.) This is mixed in our spray tanks with 5 parts water to 1 part tea, as well as fish emulsion with kelp to feed the microbes and the plants, and sprayed over the entire plant. That is how the AACT is made.

The science behind it is a little more elaborate, but basically what we're doing is introducing sufficient quantities of good fungus and bacteria that they out-compete the pest organisms that are always present. I tend to think of them as the "good organisms and bad organisms," and by introducing and keeping healthy a population of "good organisms," we are able to keep our roses growing very well and productive. All of these organisms compete for food, and when there are not enough of the good ones, the bad ones are able to spread and make plants vulnerable and/or cause diseases on the plants.

Good compost is needed to ensure a wide enough variety of micro-organisms to do the job of protecting the plants. In addition to the compost tea, we top-dress all the beds with a thin layer of compost one time and then keep 3–4 inches of path mulch on top of that. Path mulch is simply coarsely (about 3 inches long, up to 1 inch wide) chopped-up wood (can be bark and/or pieces of wood from branches, trunks, etc.).

The compost helps offset the nitrogen-robbing effect of the micro-organisms that digest the mulch and turn it into humus in the soil. By keeping a steady supply of mulch on the soil, weed problems are reduced, and there is no need for more fertilizer than what is present in the AACT with its fish emulsion. All of these microbes are delicate, and I've been told that any fertilizer stronger than a 10–10–10 will kill them, and, of course, many pesticidal sprays (both fungicides and insecticides) will kill the "good" microbes, leaving a clean playing field for the bad ones, which are able to return much faster without the good ones.

The science behind it is a little more elaborate, but basically what we're doing is introducing sufficient quantities of good fungus and bacteria that they out-compete the pest organisms that are always present.

At first, I could not believe the AACT treatment would be sufficient for taking care of our roses; so we tested it on one rose field. The results came so fast and so spectacular that we decided to do this everywhere. We have been very happy with the results, not to mention having a happier crew, who no longer needs to worry about getting suited up to spray dangerous chemicals.

This original test field was plagued with rose midge in several rows, as well as thrips on the white roses. Not only did the plants grow more strongly, but also both pests virtually disappeared. I think these results were likely the combination of the mulch disrupting the midge breeding cycle, and the addition of healthy organisms in the soil that will often kill pest organisms.

There's a photo in one of my books showing a fungus strangling a root-knot nematode. This fungus is one that works in tandem with plant roots to help them take up nutrients while the roots provide necessary sugars for the fungus. I've wondered if some fungus is not doing the same thing to the rose midge maggots. That photo explained something that I'd never fully understood when I gardened in sandy Central Florida, which is plagued with root-knot nematodes. I'd always been told that you can cut back on nematode problems by having rich soil. Now I know it's the good organisms that are associated with rich soil that are doing the work of protecting the plants.

At first, I could not believe the AACT treatment would be sufficient for taking care of our roses; so we tested it on one rose field. The results came so fast and so spectacular that we decided to do this everywhere.

One other thing I noticed with this program. Since we stopped using chemicals, the growth rate of the roses is much faster and stronger than previously. My hypothesis is that the chemicals actually slow the growth of plants, and so—free of both diseases and chemicals—the roses grow faster.

Rosa gallica, the 'French Rose', was the primary European species rose and gave rise to a number of hybrids. At the end of the 18th Century, new roses from China appeared in Europe. When crossed with the 'French Rose' hybrids, an exciting race was on among hybridizers, leading up to the Hybrid Teas that came to dominate most of the 20th Century.

An Accidental Sustainable
Rose Garden

STEPHEN SCANNIELLO

A beautiful feature of the original 1927 design of the Cranford Rose Garden was a lattice pergola smothered in climbing roses forming the northern border of the garden. Besides offering fragrant shade while viewing the formal rose garden, the pergola hid from view an ugly steep hillside that rose 25 feet to the Overlook, an area with benches offering a comfortable view of the rose garden below. The pergola was destroyed in a 1938 hurricane and never rebuilt, leaving an unobstructed view of the nonlandscaped hillside, a challenge for many generations of curators to come. Forty-five years later I inherited a tangled mess resulting from several decades of failed attempts to landscape this area.

THE HERITAGE ROSE FOUNDATION (HRF)—OF WHICH STEPHEN SCANNIELLO IS PRESIDENT—FOR A LONG TIME ONE OF THE BEST KEPT SECRETS IN U.S. ROSE CULTURE, IS INCREASINGLY BECOMING POPULAR. HRF PUBLISHES A JOURNAL, *ROSA MUNDI*, THAT IS RICH IN ROSE HISTORY AND AUTHORITATIVE. TO JOIN HRF, CONTACT: PEGGY MARTIN, peggyrosemartin@eatel.net. www.heritagerosefoundation. org. —EDITORS

Rough terrain and no irrigation hookups made it difficult to maintain this area in the same manner the main garden required. Despite this, a handful of rose varieties remained fighting for space with an invasive planting of *Rosa wichurana*. Blooming through the dense tangle of this prickly species were a few plants of 'Spartan', 'Redcap', and 'Pink Princess'

(Floribundas planted during the 1950s) and two plants of Brownell's everblooming climber 'White Cap'. I approached this area as more than a challenge; rather as a new frontier where I could expand the inventory of the Cranford collection.

My volunteers and I attacked with pruning shears and spades, first removing most of the *R. wichurana*, leaving only a thin border on each side to define the new planting space. We discovered a soil rich in organic material with excellent drainage and a site with perfect exposure—south-facing full sun all day long. With the center area cleared and the surviving everbloomers now placed center stage, we began adding "orphans" from the main collection—Hybrid Teas and Floribundas without name tags or provenance. Next came new shrubs of native Species, Old Garden Roses, English Roses, Explorer Roses, and numerous new hybrids from the Carefree collection ('Carefree Delight', 'Carefree Wonder', etc,). The Meidiland hybrids ('Alba Meidiland', 'Red Meidiland', etc.) were planted on the steepest slope where there used to be lawn, eliminating the need for treacherous lawn mowing. For vertical interest, cedar posts were added and planted with ramblers and climbing roses. What had once been the neglected stepchild became our favorite area of the garden to explore, offering color all season long and a winter of interesting rose hips as well. Judging by the number of visitors who wandered up through the shrubs, it was a favorite of others, too. Our new frontier soon became known as the "Hillside."

My goal for the Hillside plantings was to let these roses grow into their ultimate natural shape and size.

My goal for the Hillside plantings was to let these roses grow into their ultimate natural shape and size. Except for an annual minimal pruning (more like styling) of deadwood and rootstock suckering, these roses were pretty much left on their own. Still out of reach of irrigation, spraying, and routine fertilizer applications, the Hillside became what could be described as, in today's green gardening parlance, a sustainable rose garden.

Among the successes of the Hillside garden were:

Shrub Roses	'Carefree Delight', 'Carefree Beauty', 'Graham Thomas', 'Abraham Darby', 'Heritage', 'Sally Holmes', 'The Fairy'
Floribundas/Grandifloras	'Spartan', 'Redcap', 'Queen Elizabeth', 'Betty Boop', 'Pink Princess', 'Sadlers Wells'
Hybrid Teas	'Peaudouce', 'Maid of Honor', 'Belinda's Dream', 'Curly Pink', 'Memorial Day'
Climbers/Ramblers	'Whitecap', 'Mendocino Delight', 'Compassion', 'Paul's Himalayan Musk', 'Rhonda', 'Dr. Huey'
Hybrid Musk	'Prosperity'
Old Garden Roses	'Frau Karl Druschki', 'Rose de Rescht', 'Duc de Guiche', 'Alain Blanchard', 'Oeillet Flamand', 'Maiden's Blush', 'Mutabalis', 'Complicata'
Species	*R. wichurana, R. arkansana, R. nutkana, R. setigera*

Rosa gigantea (top) and *Rosa chinensis* var. spontanea (bottom), when crossed with each other, led to the creation of the ever-blooming Chinas and Teas that, in turn, when crossed with Western roses, gave rise to the Hybrid Teas and other modern rose classes.

The Historical Significance of Knock Out®

PAT SHANLEY

In 2000, a rose was introduced that in a short time would revolutionize rose gardening and succeed in transforming the public's image of the rose from a fussy prima donna to a friendly garden plant. That rose was Knock Out®, created by William J. "Bill" Radler.

For decades, roses had been developing a reputation as being high maintenance plants and, indeed, sadly they were. The talented hybridizers of many generations had given the rose-loving public precisely what they craved most: Hybrid Teas bred for exhibition form. In so doing, however, they had increasingly neglected and eventually forfeited every other characteristic of roses that contribute to making the rose a good garden plant. Regular spray programs became the norm, indeed a necessity, to keep these exhibition form rose plants thriving, but no one at the time thought too much about the other consequences of using these caustic chemicals. Today, however, public awareness has grown about the dangers that can come with chemicals, and, one by one, governments worldwide are banning the use of environmentally harmful chemicals. The day is fast approaching when we will no longer be able to use synthetic fungicides and other chemicals at all in our gardens.

The advent of Knock Out® changed how people garden with roses, for Knock Out® is not only amazingly disease free in just about every region

Bill Radler, regarded as the Father of Sustainable Rose Gardening because of his creation of Knock Out® and the Knock Out family of roses, in a rose field in Wasco, California. Inset: Knock Out® (image courtesy of Maria Cecilia Freeman)

of the U.S., and specifically highly resistant to blackspot where that disease is a nightmare, it is also amazingly trouble free in other respects and reliably produces flush after flush of abundant and colorful blooms over the full season. It is the first modern rose that can compete in today's landscape on a par with other modern landscape plants.

When I started growing roses, over 20 years ago, my first rose bushes were four Hybrid Teas—'Sterling Silver', 'Tropicana', 'John F Kennedy' and 'Fragrant Cloud'. I knew absolutely nothing about growing roses. I planted, watered, and fertilized them. They leafed out and produced a few blooms that first June.

The success of Knock Out® benefits all of us—the rose growers, the rose societies, the nurserymen and the botanical gardens—in renewing interest in growing roses.

Then came the heat and humidity of a New York summer—and with it blackspot. As I watched my rose plants drop their leaves, I desperately sought out a solution. I was horrified when I discovered the recommended remedy was spraying caustic fungicides every 7–10 days. I learned how unpleasant it is to don long sleeves, long pants, socks, shoes, a hat, goggles and rubber gloves for spray protection—especially in 90 degree heat with 95% humidity! I sprayed early in the day to avoid the extreme temperatures, but it was still a miserable experience.

How many people have had similar experiences and said, "Forget it! I'll grow something else"? Many, too many, learned to live without roses. So, I watched the decline in popularity of the rose, the Queen of Flowers, with a heavy heart. I used to dream of how wonderful it would be if roses didn't get blackspot and never needed to be sprayed or to receive other extraordinary special care. Then came Knock Out®—and for me it was a dream come true!

In my estimation, the introduction of Knock Out® is a watershed event that the rose world has not witnessed since 'Peace' was introduced in 1945 and before that 'La France' in 1867. It changed the benchmark against which roses are judged by the general public, and it changed how people garden with roses. From a technical standpoint, a rose of this degree of maintenance-free growing had not been seen before. Knock Out® needs no spraying to hold its foliage, and no deadheading to rebloom. It is crown hardy to Zone 5A. It blooms from May through November in the Northeast.

These characteristics have made it the dominant rose in today's nursery industry. It is used commercially, as well as residentially, and can be seen everywhere, not only in home gardens but in strip malls, corporate campuses and, indeed, any kind of landscape where consistent color and good foliage are a must. One can safely say that Knock Out® has promoted the visibility of roses. Plantings of it are everywhere—and shouldn't a great plant be in a lot of places? Knock Out® is a rose that anyone can grow. It has become a staple in gardening and, maybe as a bonus, a way to draw the public back to our wonderful hobby. And for gardeners once hooked on roses through Knock Out®, the next natural step is to consider growing other types of roses.

I learned how unpleasant it is to don long sleeves, long pants, socks, shoes, a hat, goggles and rubber gloves for spray protection—especially in 90 degree heat with 95% humidity! ... Then came Knock Out®—and for me it was a dream come true!

The historical significance of Knock Out® is far reaching. It has set the bar high for hybridizers worldwide. It is currently being used in breeding programs around the world—in France, Germany, the United Kingdom—all over Europe—and even in Asia—especially Japan. Now following on Knock Out®'s 10th year, we are seeing a return to growing roses, their incorporation into the landscape as a part of the garden and the promise, too, of a return to growth in membership for our local and national societies as rose growing becomes easier. One hundred years from now, I believe, the rose world will look back on Knock Out® as one of the most significant developments in the evolution of roses toward sustainability.

Bill Radler tells the story of Knock Out®, of how he made multiple crosses on one particular rose but only one hip formed containing one seed. That one seed germinated to become Knock Out®. When asked why he thought this phenomenon occurred then, he answered, "Because the world needed it." And the world of roses does need Knock Out®. The success of Knock Out® benefits all of us—the rose growers, the rose societies, the nurserymen and the botanical gardens—in renewing interest in growing roses. In this day of "green" thinking, Knock Out® gives credence to the idea that roses can be grown that fit into the landscape without damaging the environment. There are many more disease-resistant roses coming from the hybridizers, worldwide, and that can only help us more.

According to Radler, today's hybridizers are working toward the day when roses will no longer be something that only "rose people" can grow. "Roses won't have all the special needs anymore. The Hybrid Tea of the future will no longer be a 'Totem pole' plant, but a full plant with ample stems, shorter than the long stem roses of today. It will not require deadheading or heavy fertilization to rebloom. Work is being done to breed roses for midge resistance, Japanese beetle resistance and late spring frost tolerance." Within the Knock Out® family of roses, 'Sunny Knock Out'® is showing excellent resistance to midge. The hybridizers are also working hard to incorporate fragrance with disease and pest resistance, for who doesn't love a fragrant rose? In essence, we are going to be able to have our cake and eat it too.

Interest in exhibiting roses has also suffered with the overall decline in popularity of the "difficult to grow" rose that requires a spray program. While Knock Out® has generated a renewed interest in exhibiting the Shrub rose class, Hybrid Teas are still what serious exhibitors care about. The Hybrid Teas of the future will hopefully be plants with good disease resistance ... fuller plants, with shorter stems. When this transition comes about, the American Rose Society may well need to reexamine the judging standards for showing roses in order to better accommodate these new Hybrid Teas. But I see that as a good thing as well, as it will help to renew interest in rose shows, which benefit our hobby by educating the public on the joys of growing roses.

People no longer wish to spray chemicals to grow a beautiful garden. Roses, including Hybrid Teas, that can produce gorgeous healthy bushes that are attractive—with or without blooms—will be a wonderful addition to any garden, and the hybridizers are working on just this goal. Disease-resistant "Queen of Show" Hybrid Teas will be more popular to grow, and that could very well further the revival of membership in our societies, both local and national. A renewed interest in exhibiting roses among rose hobbyists could in turn lead to increased sales and the success of nurserymen, thus helping to generate a cycle that could give vigor and new life to rose culture in America.

All of this might emerge in time from the coming of a rose that anyone can grow called Knock Out®.

Probiotic Rose Growing

JOHN STARNES

I've been in many rose gardens over the years, and one thing has been very noticeable—the most disease—and bug-ridden ones are those subjected to regimens of toxic pesticides. "But I HAVE to spray my roses," some folks protest. But just as many women get a severe yeast infection after taking a broad spectrum antibiotic like tetracycline, with the doctor THEN trying to treat that with a new drug that kills off more beneficial bacteria in her body, the sprayed rose garden is denied having bacterial and fungal and insect allies that would fend off diseases and pests FOR the rosarian. Hence, that poor soul feels, again, that he or she "must" spray yet another toxic pesticide in a classic vicious cycle.

The healthiest and most stable ecologies in the natural world are complex, multi-tiered ones, with predator and prey creating sustainable balances. You want a FEW aphids to ensure your lacewings and lady bugs stay and do their job, and, like the human body, a healthy rose garden is teeming with beneficial bacteria and fungi that keep the pathogenic ones under control. Fungicides wipe them out, with the disease-causing ones being the first to re-inhabit the garden. Science has confirmed that a truly healthy human adult has in their digestive tract 3–5 POUNDS of living bacteria representing up to 3,000 species and varieties, and that their cell count exceeds the number of cells in the body. Seventy percent of our total immune system is composed OF these microbes And, just as many of us refuse antibiotics and, instead, ingest probiotic foods like kefir, kim-chi, yogurt, natto, tempeh, miso and more to keep our internal ecology complex and balanced, we can easily and cheaply duplicate this mindset in the rose garden and thus transition to pesticide-free organic rose gardening.

And, just as many of us refuse antibiotics and, instead, ingest probiotic foods like kefir, kimchi, yogurt, natto, tempeh, miso and more to keep our internal ecology complex and balanced, we can easily and cheaply duplicate this mindset in the rose garden and thus transition to pesticide-free organic rose gardening.

First, stop using ALL pesticides except perhaps BT (Dipel) since it is itself a natural bacteria that controls caterpillars. Switch from chemical fertilizers to natural ones like horse and sheep and poultry poop, kelp meal, alfalfa pellets, menhaden fish meal and Calf Manna (which contains several beneficial fungi and bacteria) from feed stores, Mills Magic Rose Mix, and compost. Synthetic chemical fertilizers usually lack trace elements, can harm soil organisms, and can force a plant to exude a scent that ATTRACTS insect pests.

Next, just as you would eat yogurt or drink kefir after taking antibiotics, begin inoculating your rose garden with good critters to crowd out the bad ones that cause blackspot and powdery mildew and rust. Favorites of mine include any dry compost starter (usually sold in a 1–2 pound box) plus fresh horse manure tea, compost tea, rich soil from an old growth forest or virgin meadow, plus commercial preparations of mycorrhizae that create a symbiosis with your roses' roots to better absorb nutrients. On the next page is a recipe for a brew that you can sprinkle onto your roses with a watering can, or strain and apply with a clean new sprayer that has never held pesticides. While this recipe will never be on The Food Channel, it can help ease you into pleasurable, inexpensive and nontoxic rose gardening. Enjoy.

POOP SOUP

— Fill a 5-gallon bucket with 4 gallons of well water
   or city water aged 2 days.

— Add 1 gallon of FRESH horse poop,
   stir daily for 1 week.

— Then add 2 cups Calf Manna,
   1 cup compost starter,
   2 cups good garden soil or fresh compost,
   2 tablets of Primal Defense available at health food
   stores or online)
   2 cups sugar.

— Stir, let brew for 1 day, and then sprinkle lightly all
   over your rose garden, both the plants and the soil.

Since your garden will now no longer be toxic, these beneficial microbes will multiply and create a stable complex ecology to help make rose growing a joy.

ASKING FOR ROSES

A house that lacks, seemingly, mistress and master,
   With doors that none but the wind ever closes,
Its floor all littered with glass and with plaster;
   It stands in a garden of old-fashioned roses.

I pass by that way in the gloaming with Mary;
   'I wonder,' I say, 'who the owner of those is.'
'Oh, no one you know,' she answers me airy,
   'But one we must ask if we want any roses.'

So we must join hands in the dew coming coldly
   There in the hush of the wood that reposes,
And turn and go up to the open door boldly,
   And knock to the echoes as beggars for roses.

'Pray, are you within there, Mistress Who-were-you?'
   'Tis Mary that speaks and our errand discloses.
'Pray, are you within there? Bestir you, bestir you!
   'Tis summer again; there's two come for roses.

'A word with you, that of the singer recalling—
   Old Herrick: a saying that every maid knows is
A flower unplucked is but left to the falling,
   And nothing is gained by not gathering roses.'

We do not loosen our hands' intertwining
   (Not caring so very much what she supposes),
There when she comes on us mistily shining
   And grants us by silence the boon of her roses.

—ROBERT FROST

Etiquette of the Rose Rustle

ALLISON STRONG

Rose rustling is a time-honored tradition here in Texas and, indeed, around the world! There is a special thrill in spying an old rose on a forgotten byway and bringing home a slip to root in our own gardens. In previous generations, there were perhaps more abandoned homesites and old, falling-down barns from which to scavenge these lovely survivors. Urban renewal and suburban and rural development have encroached on the wilds of the world, and, just as wildlife habitats are changing, so is the environment of rose rustling!

There are a few simple but important rules to follow each time you rustle a rose. Please attend to these rules carefully and help to maintain the goodwill of the public and the good name of the Texas Rose Rustlers. This organization does not endorse trespassing or removal of plant materials which any would-be rustler does not have the proper authorization/permission to obtain. Simply stated, any rose that is not on your own property probably belongs to someone else. It is the rustler's responsibility to investigate ownership and ask permission to visit the site and take a cutting. In the event that a rose is found "wild," please make certain that you are not trespassing on government land or property that is under the care of an absentee owner.

After learning who the correct person would be to grant permission to visit and/or take a cutting from a rose you are interested in, it is a good idea to identify yourself politely and explain the interest the rose holds for you. Tell them a little about the Texas Rose Rustlers, our mission to locate and preserve antique roses. Most people will be flattered by your interest, and gardeners are notoriously generous souls! In the event that you meet someone who is in possession of that perfect gem of a rose but who does not share your enthusiasm, they may allow you to get your cutting and move along, or they may say "NO." In this event, respect that "no" does indeed mean "no," and thank them for their time just the same. No lurking about to return after dark, no matter how tempting, either!

Carry a camera with you on your rustling forays to take photographs of the blooms, the hips, the leaves, the entire plant, and any other details of note that may provide interest, or a clue about the identity of a found rose.

It is an excellent idea to carry a camera with you on your rustling forays to take photographs of the blooms, the hips, the leaves, the entire plant, and any other details of note that may provide interest, or a clue about the identity of a found rose. Make notes about what you see in the environment, such as "growing vigorously into a pecan tree, blooming well in partial shade," or "shrub has extreme chlorosis, soil very moist and boggy."

Ask the owner questions about the plant: How long has it been here? Who planted it? Does it bloom in cycles throughout the year or just in the

THE TEXAS ROSE RUSTLERS ARE LEGENDARY. THROUGH THEIR EFFORTS, AND THE EFFORTS OF LIKE-MINDED GROUPS NATIONALLY AND INTERNATIONALLY, MANY VALUABLE "FOUND ROSES" HAVE BEEN RECOVERED FOR THE ENJOYMENT OF FUTURE GENERATIONS. FOUND ROSES ARE GENERALLY GIVEN "STUDY NAMES" UNTIL SUCH TIME (IF EVER) THAT THEIR NAMES OF INTRODUCTION CAN BE CONFIRMED. BY CONVENTION, STUDY NAMES ARE PUT IN DOUBLE QUOTES; NAMES OF INTRODUCTION IN SINGLE QUOTES. "MAGGIE" IS AN EXAMPLE OF A FOUND ROSE WHOSE IDENTITY IS STILL HOTLY DEBATED. "KATY ROAD PINK", ON THE OTHER HAND, IS AN EXAMPLE OF A FOUND ROSE WHOSE IDENTITY HAS BEEN SATISFACTORILY ESTABLISHED AS 'CAREFREE BEAUTY', A GRIFFITH BUCK ROSE INTRODUCED IN 1977. FOUND ROSES, WHICH HAVE SURVIVED LARGELY WITH LITTLE CARE, ARE PRESUMPTIVELY "SUSTAINABLE," AT LEAST REGIONALLY.   —EDITORS spring or summer? Do you ever fertilize it, and if so, with what? Avoid criticism of any kind in regard to the health, location, culture or care of the rose! Make a pleasant experience of the interaction for yourself and the rose's caretaker! Offer to root another of this rose for its owner, or offer a trade of cuttings of a different rose of your own, in exchange for the cuttings. A thoughtful gesture is to gift the owner with a small portion of your favorite rose food in an "individual serving" sized bag or box. I have created decorative wax-lined paper lunch sacks with a calligraphy marker, listing the ingredients of a mixture of dry, organic fertilizers, with the instructions "Rose Chow: just add to soil around plant dripline, water thoroughly, and apply sunshine" It never fails to get a chuckle!

Any rose that is not on your own property probably belongs to someone else. It is the rustler's responsibility to investigate ownership and ask permission to visit the site and take a cutting.

When taking your cuttings, be mindful of the health and size of the shrub, and never remove more than the plant can tolerate. Rustling some cuttings should not take the place of the annual pruning! The owner should not be prompted to wonder if the rose is going to have a hard time making it through the coming season!

Follow your visit with a thank-you note or phone call within a few days. It is important to show appreciation for the good things in life, and what could be better than the sharing of a beautiful rose?

At the Queens Botanical Garden in New York, sustainable goals are paramount. According to its mission statement:

The Garden teaches and practices sustainability in design, construction, and operations support; environmental stewardship; long-term financial viability; and the health of visitors, staff, and the community. The Garden's Master Plan of 2001 launched the Sustainable Landscapes and Buildings Project. As the name implies, the project is much more than buildings. It includwes new plants, many of which are native species; bioswales to collect storm water and reduce wear-and-tear on New York City's combined sewer system; water recycling systems; the new Horticulture/Maintenance Building; the revolutionary Visitor & Administration Center; and the transformation of our existing parking lot into a 125-space parking garden which began in September 2008.

In 2010, the Queens Botanical Garden agreed to install a Tea Rose Test Garden of 46 Tea Rose varieties donated by Roses Unlimited in Laurens, South Carolina, and the Manhattan Rose Society. The purpose of the planting was to test the hardiness of the Tea

Roses for the New York area and see which, if any of them, might be suitable for regional home gardeners.

'Faith Whittlesey', a moderately sized Viru™ Tea, is being tested for its hardiness range.

"McClinton Tea", a Found Rose that has proved popular in New Orleans public plantings, is also among the Tea Roses being tested at Queens Botanical Garden.

'Niphetos', dating to 1840, is a famous old white Tea. The clone of it being grown at Queens Botanical Garden can be traced to the Peter Beales Nursery in the United Kingdom.

It's Only Water!

*A commentary on consumption, waste,
conservation, and soil health*

BILLY STYLES AND ALAN TALBERT

Agua. Acqua. Eau. Wasser. Woda. Вода … WATER. Combine two parts hydrogen with one part oxygen, mix vigorously and there you have it … water, the miracle liquid that sustains all life as we know it. Oh, if it were only that easy, I tell myself.

Without it we perish. Since the beginning of time, water has been a source of life and, conversely, death throughout the world. All through ancient civilizations, water was considered a gift from the gods. Fountains were erected, hot baths were commonplace and gods of rain, for instance, Zeus in Greek mythology, and Tlaloc in Aztec mythology, were widely worshiped. Along with the popularity of public baths and the desire to improve personal hygiene came epidemics resulting from waterborne diseases. One of the worst famines in history occurred during the Middle Ages as a result of excessive rainfall and flooding. The old adage is true … too much of a good thing is not so good.

So, what is the current status of available fresh water in the world? Well, according to *The Rime of the Ancient Mariner,* the outlook could be better. "Water, water every where nor any drop to drink." These words came from the poem about a thirsty old sailor who was surrounded by water that could not quench his thirst. Quite frankly, this quote hits a little too close to home, given the droughts we've endured in much of the United States over the past several years.

More than three quarters (75–80%) of the planet is covered by water or ice, but only 1% of that is actually suitable for human consumption. Greater than 97% is salt water in the ocean and 2% is ice. Survival books tell us that the human body can survive for nearly two months without food, but less than a week without drinking water. We drink it daily, wash our clothes, cars and dishes with it and irrigate our landscapes with it. Some businesses even water the sidewalks and city streets with it—more on this phenomenon later. We drink it straight-up and out of fountains. We mix it with carbonation, coloring and vitamins and drink it out of plastic bottles. Drinking the natural spring variety out of fancy glass bottles was all the rage not so long ago. For all of our love affair with this colorless, odorless wet stuff, one would think that there is an endless supply sitting in a great reservoir somewhere simply waiting for us to tap into it.

Guess what? There isn't.

WHAT'S ON THE HORIZON?

Now, more than ever, responsible consumption and conservation of water need to be front page on every newspaper and online news reporting website. The unmistakable truth that one comes to is that as global population increases, the amount of water that is available for all of our uses decreases. This is currently lost on those who don't think about the gallons of water going down the drain as they wait for it to reach the perfect temperature. It should be obvious to the most naïve that, at current levels, population growth and normal usage will one day outpace our water collection capability, either because of lack of sheer volume of water or lack of adequate infrastructure to collect and store it. We basically have two choices: (1) conserve water and use it more responsibly, or (2) limit, even ration, the amount that is available to each person or family.

Sunny Knock Out

Pink Knock Out

Double Knock Out

White Out

Pink Double Knock Out

Blushing Knock Out

Carefree Celebration*

Carefree Sunshine*

Carefree Wonder

Carefree Delight

Carefree Marvel

Carefree Spirit

Cherry Parfait

Bolero

Traviata

Mother of Pearl

Easter Basket

Peach Drift

Carefree Beauty

Belinda's Dream

Caldwell Pink (a.k.a. Pink Pet)

Ducher

Duchesse de Brabant

Cecile Brunner

Climbing Pinkie

New Dawn

Mutabilis

Sea Foam

Spice

The Fairy

Reve d'Or

Souvenir de St. Anne's

Perle d'Or

Else Poulsen

Knock Out

Georgetown Tea

Monsieur Tiller

Mrs. Dudley Cross

Marie Daly

Mme. Antoine Mari

La Marne

Centennial

Sunrise Sunset

My Girl

Macy's Pride

Yellow Brick Road

All the Rage

Won Fang Yon**

Pearlie Mae

Quietness

Borderer*

Honey Sweet

Aussie Sixer***

Lady Pamela Carol

Audubon

Old Baylor

Roemer's Hip Happy

Cole's Settlement

Sweet Pea

Pink Home Run

Cinco de Mayo

Julia Child

Home Run

Cape Diamond*

Lady Elsie May**

Teasing Georgia

Benjamin Britten

Darcey Bussell

Gertrude Jekyll

Crocus Rose

Crown Princess Margareta

Marie-Luise Marjan

Pomponella Fairy Tale

Planten un Blomen

Petticoat Fairy Tale

Purple Rain

Pink Veranda

Kordes Moonlight

Grande Amore

Kordes Golden Gate

Jasmina

Felicitas

Escimo

Eliza

Caramel Fairy Tale

Cream Veranda

Brother's Grimm Fairy Tale

Aloha Hawaii

Cinderella Fairy Tale

KOSMOS

Lupo

La Perla

Laguna

Larissa

Lions Rose

Summer Memories

Red Corsair

Roxy

Rosanna

Summer Sun

Solero

WORLD WAR III ... OR IV?

Most of us assume that oil or religious fanaticism will lead to World War III. Others who understand the consequences of our gluttony of water think that perhaps more regional, national and even international conflicts will arise from disputes over water or the easy access to it. Consider that sprawling urban development in America and around the world continues to put strains on water supplies, taxing our already almost depleted reservoirs. More people taking showers, washing clothes, washing dishes, etc. ... normal usage. The onset of widespread drought conditions and weather changes like El Niño and the potential effects of global warming have made us realize that our reckless use of water over the past decades has left us in a crisis. Some areas of the world experience constant drought conditions. Over 40% of the world's population lives with constant water shortages. If we are not keenly aware of our use and begin to focus on sincere conservation efforts, we will one day find ourselves with water restrictions of a severity most of us cannot imagine. One could even suggest that our next world war may very well be over water, rather than oil. If you think that's far-fetched, go back to the ongoing drought that made news beginning in 2007 and read archived articles from the *Atlanta Journal Constitution* related to the border dispute between Florida and Georgia. This is real. We in the South may have a better perspective than those in some other parts of the country, but all, no doubt, will be equally affected when the Jet Stream decides not to favor their area.

WATER MANAGEMENT

Mismanagement of water has also been occurring for thousands of years. An estimated 69% of the water used worldwide is for irrigation. Irrigation is necessary in some parts of the world that would not otherwise be able to grow crops, but in other areas, irrigation is mainly used to produce more profitable harvests. Rapid population growth, expanding businesses and urbanization, and climate change are a few factors that affect our water supply. Because of the natural cycle of water—rain, use and evaporation, then more rain, we assume that the amount of water on Earth remains fairly constant. On the surface, this appears true, but the amount of clean, usable water needed for survival is decreasing at an alarming rate. Pollution, increases in population and our wasteful habits contribute. We have been conditioned to expect fresh, clean water to fill our glasses when we turn on the faucet. Readily available drinking water is our right, for goodness sake. Some believe that Americans are spoiled and take the path of least resistance, leaving more responsible conservation efforts to others. You know, "them," those whack-os that populate fringe groups and spend their time saving whales and spotted owls—and whining about global warming. Well, of course, I don't be-

We have come a long way since the 1980s. At the time, "green" was equated with "health," meaning "lush health," not "environmentally friendly health," as it has come to mean in the 21st century.

lieve this. I question this premise completely because I see the truth every day in the faces of our customers. It's not that the stereotypical American necessarily chose the path he is on. I don't think he slowed down long enough when habits were formed to even notice THERE ARE TWO PATHS! This is a problem of education and helping others understand the benefits of creating sustainable environments. We bump into it everyday at our store, Organic Plant Health located in Matthews, North Carolina. We talk with our customers in depth about sustainability and the true nature of plant health. The plants that appear healthy in our customers' landscapes are not healthy—they only appear healthy on the surface while the roots below are struggling. Water is not the foundation of plant health. A healthy, living soil is the foundation of all plant health. Only with a healthy, open and porous soil profile can root systems fully develop. Healthy soil and fully developed root systems allow us to reduce our dependence on supplemental irrigation—that IV drip that chemically fertilized plants rely on. We teach everyone with whom we come in contact that things are not as they seem, that easy is not better and that plant health, as they understand it, is an illusion. Then you see their faces change as they begin to understand the true factors that affect plant health and the roles that fertility, water and proper maintenance habits play in creating healthy plants. In our case, we talk about sustainable growing environments, water conservation, creating a healthier soil profile and supporting an active soil food web so that the foundation can provide the opportunity for sustainable, healthy growth. This brings me back to the two paths I mentioned a moment ago. Here's the thing … the THING IS … the path signs need to be bigger. I mean really BIG so that the choice can be made early in the journey.

MOUNTAIN GROWN

Growing up in the mountains of North Carolina, I had a spring and well water. There wasn't a water or utilities department. I never thought about water pollution, whether or not the water we used was safe, how much we were using or even that we needed to conserve it. Water always seemed an available, free, resource, and an everyday part of life. It flowed readily down clean streams and rivers. We watered our livestock with it and used it for our own needs. Sometimes the rain flooded our crops and other times it was slow to come. I began to see how harvests increased with more rain and declined when there was less. Early on as I became more serious about growing and improving plant health, I recall seeing how people indiscriminately used and wasted water. Washing cars, filling swimming pools, taking long showers, and many other wasteful habits became common indulgences. There was little or no concern about conserving water, keeping it clean, or considering that one day there may not be enough. When I became a professional, I began to see for the first time how we as a society misunderstood water and its relationship to plant health. I began to notice people consistently overwatering their plants, flowers, and gardens, wasting water around every bend. Hoses were left on, sprinkler systems ran day and night, and each time a plant looked sick they would water it more, sometimes to the point of actually killing the plant. As urban communities began to spring up, water usage increased at alarming rates. People moving from the cities to the suburbs suddenly cared more about their yards as a place of prestige and leisure. Keeping up with the Joneses, having the best yard on the block, was an aspiration many strived for. Additionally, the desire to have a lush green lawn caused consumers to look for better and more efficient ways to water their landscapes. This gave rise to the many gadgets that help to automate the watering process. Hoses and sprinklers became part of Main Street USA. Sprinklers came in many styles including oscillating, fan, rotary, fountain and even self-moving. Soaker hoses that could be placed in planting beds and gardens would slowly and evenly water small areas. Their sales exploded in hardware and box stores across America.

Another innovation to come along was the in-ground irrigation system with built-in sprinkler heads that pop up out of the ground when it's time to water. To the consumers' delight, these sprinkler systems could be set up on a timer system to automatically water lawns as often as desired, rain or shine. Homeowners rarely evaluated landscapes to determine how much water was actually needed. Apparently, they thought that the irrigation systems knew how much water the plants needed. "Just set it and forget it" became a common theme. And forget it we did. Yes, we have all seen irrigation systems watering in the middle of a rain shower and, yes, it's ridiculous. We've also seen sprinkler heads in great need of adjustment or repair; this refers back to my comment in the beginning about watering the sidewalks and city streets. We have seen it time and time again—broken sprinkler heads pointed away from the property they were intended to water—watering the sidewalks and the streets, gallon after precious gallon. This occurs frequently but was most notable at the height of the recent drought when the only businesses that could water were those with special permission from the city. By the early 1980s, 25% of all Americans had in-ground sprinkler systems. But simply watering lawns wasn't enough. Homeowners had less and less time to care for their lawns and looked for a quick fix. They wanted lush green lawns and landscapes, and they didn't want to wait for the results. We have come a long way since the 1980s. At the time, "green" was equated with "health," as in "lush health," not "environmentally friendly health," as it has come to mean in the 21st century. So along came chemical fertilizers that quickly transformed grass and gave it a vibrant, green appearance. When chemical fertilizers were introduced to consumers in the 1940s and 1950s, they were thought to be a modern miracle, but no one asked how these chemicals would affect the soil, or the waterways or water usage.

SCIENCE TO THE RESCUE ... NOT YET

We can thank a German chemist named Justus Von Liebig for the introduction of chemical fertilizers. The son of a chemist, he began his studies as a young boy. By analyzing the burnt ashes of plants, Von Liebig discovered that plants contained different amounts of nitrogen, phosphorus, and potassium (NPK). His experiments indicated that plants grow faster and bigger with more NPK, for example 10–10–10 or 17–17–17, and he went on to further develop these macronutrients. Thus began the revolution of synthetic fertilizers. Instead of letting plants grow naturally, his new fertilizer enabled farmers to grow bigger and more abundant crops. In and around the home, consumers started adopting the use of synthetic fertilizers to improve their gardens, shrubs, flowers and lawns. Homeowners, as well as farmers, were happy with these results, but it didn't occur to any of them that they were creating false growing environments, opting for short-term surge growth instead of long-term soil and plant health.

This new revolution of synthetic fertilizers was all about mass crop production. The promise of increasing the yield of harvest tenfold excited everyone. Chemical manufacturers supported and funded research, offered rewards and funding to colleges for programs, and hosted educational seminars on ways to use their products. These companies had a profound impact on agriculture. As chemical companies evolved, they continued to push their own agenda while the organic, natural approach took a back seat. Agricultural farming communities not only incorporated synthetic fertilizers, but massive irrigation systems using millions of gallons of water each year just to keep the crops alive. This practice continued for decades. Little did we know in the early days that using synthetic fertilizers actually dried out our soil and caused us to use more water just to keep the plants alive and growing. Lost in the world of modernization and ease, we just followed the crowd and went along with the current trend. Most homeowners didn't know anything about plants and their needs for survival. Along with the farmers, they were caught in a vicious cycle of fertilize—water—fertilize—water.

As all of this water was being used, underlying factors were causing severe decline in the health of our landscape. The years of synthetic fertilizer use contaminated our soil and streams, destroyed microbial life and caused chemical deposits to build up in the soil, while leaching into our waterways caused ecological damage. The result left plants unable to sustain themselves. Years of applying synthetic fertilizers and the subsequent practice of frequent, shallow watering caused soil compaction and salt-induced drought. The natural elements that promote soil health and sustainability had been destroyed. While we were concerning ourselves with improving color, growing bigger blooms, and reaping larger harvests we didn't realize that our actions were destroying the health of the soil.

WHO WATERS THE FOREST?

Have you ever wondered, "Who fertilizes the grasslands and meadows?" Or, "How does the forest survive without irrigation?" The answer is simple. If left alone, nature is supremely designed to take care of itself. When we begin altering nature for profit's sake a great imbalance occurs. For generations before the advent of synthetic fertilizers, farmers used what we now call organics in the planting fields. I can remember, as a child, mixing manure and other waste material on the farm and spreading the mixture on fields with a spreader. It was effective and increased crop yields, but it was messy and hard to work with.

J.L. Rodale reintroduced the world to organic gardening and started the return of getting back to nature in 1942 when he published a magazine called *Organic Farming and Gardening*. The magazine came out during a time when chemical fertilizers were thought of, by many, as the future of agriculture. Consequently, Rodale's thesis that the health of our soil directly affects the health of our society was widely misunderstood and often dismissed.

Those who adopted his organic approach began creating more sustainable landscapes requiring less water. Plants were actually growing more naturally and not forced to perform at unnatural levels. The use of organics has evolved since then, but synthetics have continued to be the first choice of most farmers and homeowners because of their availability and the increased crop production and harvest they initially yield. Lack of knowledge regarding the multifaceted nature of plant health contributes, too, to the prevalence of chemicals. The need for instant gratification and desire for increased profits cast a shadow on what was best for our Earth.

WHAT DO THE EXPERTS SAY?

According to a recent report* which drew on the work of 700 scientists, unless we change the way we use water and increase "water productivity" (i.e., more crop per drop), we will not have enough water to feed the world's growing population, which is estimated to increase from 6 billion now to about 8.5 billion in 25 years.

There are potential solutions. Better water storage has to be considered. Ethiopia, which is typical of many sub-Saharan African countries, has a water storage capacity of 38 cubic meters per person. Australia has almost 5,000 cubic meters per person, an amount that in the face of current climate change impacts may be inadequate. While there will be a need for

---

* *Information from the following article was used to convey some material facts about the need for water conservation:* "Comprehensive Assessment of Water Management in Agriculture," Water for Food, Water for Life: A Comprehensive Assessment of Water Management in Agriculture. *London: Earthscan, and Colombo: International Water Management Institute, 2007.*

new large and medium-sized dams to deal with this critical lack of storage in Africa, other simpler solutions are also part of the equation.

These solutions include the construction of small reservoirs, sustainable use of groundwater systems including artificial groundwater recharge and rainwater harvesting for smallholder vegetable gardens. Improved year-round access to water will help farmers maintain their own food security using simple supplementary irrigation techniques. The redesign of both the physical and institutional arrangements of some large and often dysfunctional irrigation schemes will also bring the required productivity increases. Safe, risk-free reuse of wastewater from growing cities will also be needed. Of course, these actions need to be paralleled by development of drought-tolerant crops and the provision of infrastructure and facilities to get fresh food to markets.

Current estimates indicate that we will not have enough water to feed ourselves in 25 years' time; by then the current food crisis may turn into a perpetual crisis. Just as in other areas of agricultural research and development, investment in the provision and better management of water resources has declined steadily since the green revolution. Water scientists are raising a warning flag that significant investment in both research & development and water infrastructure development are needed if dire consequences are to be avoided.

WHAT CAN YOU DO?

Although we've included some useful tips related to sustainable rose gardens and improved water management in the sidebar along with this article, we would feel remiss if we didn't give you additional practical tips for your backyard. Here are 14 tips on water management for a sustainable landscape:

(1) Populate your landscape with native plants and self-sustaining plants and understand the different plant types and their growing cycles.

(2) Create a sustainable growing environment that requires less water, by inoculating the root zone at planting—adding amendments to the soil that include endo- and ectomycorrhizae. These naturally occurring fungi attach to the root tips and enable the plant to feed on water and nutrients far outside the normal root zone. In addition, these fungi help to protect the roots from soil borne disease that can destroy the plants root mass.

(3) Improve soil health for deeper root development. Some organic fertilizers contain living microorganisms that work in the soil to increase porosity. Also, adding diverse sources of organic matter can increase microbial activity in the soil food web to boost this process. Healthy soil allows for deep root development and can reduce the need for watering up to 75% or more.

(4) Plant in the right place on your property. Soil quality, pH levels and available sun all impact the natural health of your plants. For instance, roses need 6 hours of sun, minimum, and prefer morning sun. Select the best place in your property where plants can thrive with less attention.

(5) Feed your plants appropriately. For example, roses have different needs throughout the year. Don't expect them to be at their best if you feed them the same food in the fall as you do in spring.

(6) Apply fresh mulch to help retain moisture.

(7) Understand the natural water patterns in your area and plant accordingly. Do you normally get enough rain to feed your plants or do they require significant irrigation?

(8) Water only in the early morning hours to prevent rapid evaporation.

(9) Avoid overwatering and underwatering. Make sure you check your soil for the moisture depth. Just because the ground is dry on the surface doesn't mean that it's dry several inches below the surface. A standard coring tool will enable you to check moisture levels a foot or more below the soil surface.

(10) Use a rain gauge to monitor how much water is applied to eliminate wasteful runoff.

(11) When watering roses, do not water the plant—drench the soil taking special care to keep the plant dry. Foliar "splashing" can increase the occurrence of disease and easily spread blackspot from one plant to another.

(12) Supplemental irrigation should come from stored water containers such as rain barrels. Minimize artificial irrigation unless absolutely necessary and under your complete control—limit the use of automatic timers.

(13) Stay away from chemical or synthetic fertilizers. These products only cause your plant to require more water and only address the top growth and development of the plant. They do nothing to improve root structure or soil health and these two things are critical to reducing water use.

(14) Limit the use of pesticides and chemicals. Using excessive chemicals to achieve false results will lead to decline and the ultimate downfall of the urban landscape. Proper usage will actually build the plants' immune system and help it to protect itself from disease.

CONSERVATION EFFORTS

Water conservation has become an important part of our daily lives today. Current city water restrictions have forced homeowners in most areas to use less water and become more aware of their usage. Watering lawns on specified days of the week and prohibiting car washing have helped to conserve water through times of drought, but these first-line efforts are not enough to prevent serious shortages. The average American uses approximately 160 gallons of water each day. A lot of this is wasted through leaky faucets that waste up to 100 gallons a day, flushing the toilet using 5–6 gallons of water per flush, or running 5 gallons of water down the drain while we brush our teeth. Wasting water is just one of the problems. Pollution has destroyed many of our freshwater sources. Industries release over 197 million pounds of toxic chemicals in our waterways on an annual basis. Other chemicals such as phosphorus, a main component of fertilizers and detergents, have recently been shown to contaminate waterways.

Water Conservation Meets the Sustainable Rose Garden

Growing roses and promoting sustainability in the landscape can be very rewarding as long as you follow a few tips regarding soil health and plant care and maintenance.

1. **Plant roses properly and in an hospitable location.** Roses like to receive lots of sun, at least 5 to 6 hours or more per day otherwise they may become "sun-starved." Hoping and wishful thinking cause some gardeners to plant what they believe are heavy shade-tolerant roses under trees or in other low-sun areas. Even if these roses (Hybrid Musks for the most part) grow, they produce very few blooms. The unvarnished truth is that roses, when planted properly in the right location, will grow more robustly and require less water.

2. **Do not restrict airflow to your roses.** Do not plant roses too closely to each other or to nearby structures. Roses planted without adequate air movement are more susceptible to disease, and, therefore, more likely to suffer decline. Healthy roses require less water.

3. **Mix roses in with other plants in garden beds.** Roses aren't just for the formal *Rose Garden* anymore. Use some variety in your planting and put roses all over your landscape. As long as you have healthy, active and well-prepared soil, adequate sunlight and proper drainage, roses can be happy in a variety of settings.

4. **Prepare beds properly with plenty of drainage**. You can use a variety of organic amendments to allow for efficient air, water and nutrient movement through the soil. An open soil profile allows for greater root development, which also reduces the amount of supplemental irrigation.

5. **Do not use chemical fertilizers on your roses.** Chemical fertilizers do nothing to promote soil health or aid in root development. You will actually have to increase watering when you apply chemical fertilizers.

6. **Feed your roses organic fertilizer regularly**—every 60 days or so during the growing season, depending upon the amount of rainfall you get and the condition of the soil. Roses that are fed consistently are more resilient. They will be less affected by variations in temperature and weather or insect and disease infestation. Healthy roses require less watering.

7. **Use slow release organic fertilizers.** Fertilizers with slow release nutrients and diverse sources of organic matter provide long-term feeding for the plant as well as the soil. It's also helpful to apply a fertilizer that contains beneficial fungi such as endo- and ectomycorrhizae. These fungi attach to the root tip and form a symbiotic relationship with the plant: the plant provides the fungi with carbohydrates, and the fungi send out tendrils that reach far outside the root zone supplying the plant with necessary water and nutrients.

8. **There is a pattern forming regarding soil health and water conservation.** Soil Health = Root Development = Sustainable Growing Environment = Reduced Watering.

9. **Apply organic mulch 2–4 inches thick around the plant**. This keeps the soil surface temperature more consistent and provides a bit of moisture retention for the plant. Remember to fully cover the base of the plant with mulch in the winter to protect if from the elements. Mulch adds an element of stress resistance, which reduces the amount of water required.

10. **Resist the temptation to water at all**. If you must water, do so early in the morning—never late in the day or at night, which opens the door to disease.

Proactively maintain your plants: Observe them regularly and catch insect and disease infestations early. Use an organic fungicide/insecticide whenever possible. These actually help build the immune system of the plant and increase their disease resistance in the future.

The awareness of contamination has given birth to the no-phos move-ment, which promotes managing and conserving freshwater and reducing the amount of chemicals we use. Many of us are looking for new ways to reduce water use and to reuse water. Homeowners can capture water with rain barrels or similar water-holding chambers to reuse within the landscape. By placing an object in the toilet tank to displace water, you can reduce the amount of water used on each flush. Taking short show-ers versus drawing a bath, which uses about 36 gallons of water, will also reduce consumption.

There are also many proponents of using gray water for irrigating land-scapes. Gray water is non-industrial wastewater generated from domestic processes such as dishwashing, laundry and bathing. Gray water usage could help conserve a tremendous amount of drinking water. However, there are many restrictions and guidelines to adhere to when incorporat-ing gray water into your landscape watering protocol. The average con-sumer may not have the background or knowledge required to maintain these guidelines, so it's best to speak with a professional or someone in your local government before making this decision. Some detractors of using gray water counter that the common detergents, soaps, and cleaners used today do not support the use of gray water and, therefore, greatly reduce the amount that can be used safely.

Conservation and choosing to grow with sustainability in mind is a choice. For all of our sakes, we hope you make the right one.

Join the Revolution. Gro-Organic!

Fire Ants versus Molasses

BETTY VICKERS

FINAL SCORE: MOLASSES 1, FIRE ANTS 0

Once upon a time, I decided to move my compost pile. This was no big deal. My compost pile is small, contained within a Shepherd's bin (4x4-foot pvc-coated wire). I rolled my wheelbarrow over to the side of the bin and commenced to transfer its contents to the wheelbarrow. When I was about a third of the way into the bin, my fork uncovered that stuff of nightmares—fire ants. Millions of fire ants!

Molasses is the best product in the world to spread over acreage. The bacterial activity it creates is stunning, and it will greatly advance any organic program …

I dropped the fork and went to the garage, where I picked up the dried molasses. Returning to the bin, I unceremoniously dumped the dried molasses, probably a quarter of a bushel in quantity, onto the compost. It was loose and fluffy, and I sort of shook it around over the top. Then I returned to the wheelbarrow, took its compost to the new location, and turned it into the new pile. That took five minutes, after which I returned to the original compost pile, trying to figure out what to do next.

But there was nothing to do. The fire ants were gone. All gone, and they did not come back—not in that pile (which I then removed), nor in the new pile, which was nicely blended with the dried molasses.

I doubt that I killed a single fire ant—not that I wanted to do so. I am very much of the "live and let live" philosophy, and I'm perfectly happy to have fire ants in my garden, so long as they do not sting me or those I love, including Izzy the Cat. They may (and do) destroy/chase away all the termites they want.

I presume the fire ants in my compost pile moved downward into their massive subterranean world. (I understand that they maintain a network that extends from Texas to Alabama, where they first came off the boat.) So they could, and did, return to my garden another day, but never to my compost pile.

DRIED MOLASSES

Dried molasses is a byproduct of the refining of sugar cane. It is composed of the cane detritus and the "bottom of the barrel" sugar residue (the less-than-food-grade molasses). It is cattle feed and, as such, can be found in feed stores.

Molasses is the best product in the world to spread over acreage. The bacterial activity it creates is stunning, and it will greatly advance any organic program—so it can now also be found in nurseries (at much higher prices). Feed stores offer bags of 40–50 lbs for less than $20; or you can purchase a smaller bag of 2–4 lbs at a nursery for $5 or more.

Friends who live in big cities outside of Texas complain that they have no feed stores. This is very sad for them. However, a feed store is unnecessary for anyone with a small patch to garden. Liquid molasses will work well. Buy a jar of molasses at the grocery store, dilute it (a tablespoon of molasses to a quart of water), and pour it over the mound.

Some recommend the addition of "orange oil" (cold press D-limonene), which is very effective, indeed. But don't use it if you want earthworms—and who doesn't?—because it kills them, too.

Sustainable Rose Growing and the Breeding of New Roses: The View from India

VIRU VIRARAGHAVAN

Sustainable rose growing is a subject which deserves to be center stage in the warm Indian climate, and, indeed, in all other warm climates of the world, where disease problems are at their worst. What do we mean by "sustainable rose growing"? "Sustainable" in the broad sense means "something which can be maintained" and for the environmentally conscious—as all of us rose growers should be—it means "maintenance without adverse environmental impact."

Unfortunately, standard rose-growing practices in India are quite often the very reverse of sustainable, burdened as the Indian rose grower is with growing roses, created in temperate climates, under tropical conditions. Ask a keen rose grower in India whether you can grow roses, and the response will be an enthusiastic "yes," but further enquiry will reveal the amount of exertion involved—weekly combination sprays with fungicides and insecticides. The environmental impact of such practices is significant, and it is no surprise that rose growing is confined to the real enthusiast or keen exhibitor.

The pioneering rose hybridizer, B. S. Bhatcharji, put the matter in simple words—he was writing in the 1930s—that rose growing is for the

239

pleasure of raising beautiful flowers under normal care. As a hands-on horticulturist, he meant by "normal care" that there was no need to display the over-enthusiasm of the rose exhibitor, but at the same time you could not expect to grow a rose without giving it the care which you would bestow on raising tomatoes or cauliflowers in your vegetable patch.

If we are to have easily grown roses—such rose varieties as can be grown under normal care—the basic requirement is growing roses which have reasonable resistance to fungus problems. Here again a note of caution is very much required. Rose breeders should not fall into the trap of striving for roses with that mirage "immunity," but look to develop such plants which have the capacity to recover from infection without the use of fungicides.

It is well to remember that the rose in a tropical situation has to compete with many other beautifully luscious tropical plants, which are endowed with lovely evergreen foliage. It therefore becomes imperative to create roses which have equally beautiful evergreen foliage ...

Rose varieties touted as immune to fungus problems have an alarming habit of suddenly becoming vulnerable as the fungus evolves faster than the rose's capacity to defend itself. A case in point is 'Baby Love', which was completely resistant to blackspot in my tropical mountain climate—with almost constant moist cool weather—no summer, no winter. A laboratory for breeding blackspot!! Sure enough, after the fourth year, 'Baby Love' succumbed completely to blackspot, and now performs much worse than less acclaimed varieties.

The capacity to recover from infection is a feature of many of the heritage roses, which is why they have lasted so long. Many heritage rose varieties, even under adverse conditions as in the tropical parts of India, can be grown without fungicide protection. A case in point is how the favorite garland rose, R. Edward, which is grown over several thousands of acres in India, will contract both mildew and blackspot but come back victorious, and flower in delightful profusion every time.

We now come to another basic question. Is disease resistance linked to adaptation to specific climates? Can there be a universal great rose, or do we have to satisfy ourselves with roses adapted to climatic regions? Sadly, regional adaptation seems to be the rule. Even the great rose 'Peace' is quite unhappy in the Indo-Gangetic plain of northern India, where otherwise spectacular roses can be, and are, grown. But some of the shrub roses have wider adaptation, e.g., 'Prosperity', 'Carefree Beauty', 'Belinda's Dream'.

The performance of the tropical *R. clinophylla* and the sub-tropical *R. gigantea*, the two species with which I am working, illustrates the point. *R. clinophylla* was planted in the sandy and saline soil of Madras (now called Chennai) on the south-eastern coast of India, in a garden quite near the sea, where the water had also become quite salty, owing to excessive pumping. Amazingly, the rose was quite happy despite very little attention, no sprays, no manures, and only the occasional watering by a rather erratic gardener. The Madras climate, warm and humid

*In addition to the foliage factor and disease resistance, the forcing conditions provided by tropical heat have to be taken into account. We need roses in the Tea–*R. clinophylla *line which are bushy and evergreen, and gigantea hybrids of manageable size.*

almost throughout the year is one of the worst rose-growing climates in India, but this rose has fresh green foliage and makes a nice bush.

When *R. clinophylla* was grown in the hot dry climate of Hosur, near Bangalore, in peninsular India, it again adapted itself remarkably well. One plant is 15 feet high and 10 feet across, in spite of the competition from the greedy roots of the nearby hedge.

But *R. clinophylla* in the cool moist mountain climate of my Kodaikanal home in southern India, under my personal care, is clearly not very happy. Mind you, this is a climate in which the average rose thrives.

On the other hand *R. gigantea* is a spectacular success in Kodaikanal. Some of my plants have climbed about 40 feet into the cypress trees, flower

Girija (right) and Viru Viraraghavan of India at the World Federation of Rose Societies meeting in Sakura, Japan, in 2006. They also received the Great Rosarians of the World Award at the Huntington Botanical Garden in California in 2006.

'Lotus Born', a pink Viru™ Tea Rose, will be introduced in the United States in 2011.

'Faith Whittlesey', a white Viru™ Tea, was the first of these moderately sized new Tea Roses to reach the U.S. It is named in honor of a former U.S. Ambassador to Switzerland who also received the International Friend of the Rose Award in New York in 2010.

R. clinophylla (R. lyelli type) in the wild, growing on a field boundary in Oriya Village, Mount Abu, in India, reaches immense proportions. Inset: *R. clinophylla* blooms. Another form of this warm-weather species, related to *R. bracteata*, has been used to create a new series of "clinophylla hybrids," three of which have reached the U.S.: 'Silver Dawn', 'Ganges Mist', and 'Pat Henry'. (Girija Viraraghavan is in the foreground; images are from the Indian Rose Federation Annual, 1993)

profusely, and never, but never, get mildew or blackspot. Naturally, no spraying is feasible on a 40-foot-high plant.

If the rose is a plant essentially adapted to climatic regions, we clearly have to hybridize roses for each region to get the optimum results. For the warm climate rose grower there is no doubt that a separate line of breeding, separate from the breeding lines in temperate regions, is essential.

What should be the basis for such focused breeding? Obviously, we have to start with heritage roses well adapted to such climates. Of these, the Chinas like 'Louis Philippe', 'Craimoisi Superier', 'Archduke Charles', and 'Old Blush'; Tea Roses like 'Duchesse de Brabant', 'Mrs. B. R. Cant', 'Rosette Delizy', 'Madame Falcot' and 'Mrs. Dudley Cross';and some of the Bourbons—R. Edward, 'Maggie' ('Eugene E. Marlitt'?) 'Souvenier de la Malmaison', stand out in various warm climates ranging from peninsular India, southern United States, Puerto Rico, the West Indies, Bermuda, Brazil, and parts of Australia. Many of the Noisettes and a few of the Hybrid Perpetuals, for example, 'Frau Karl Druschki' and 'Paul Neyron', are similarly well adapted., as also some miscellaneous Shrub Roses like 'Prosperity' etc., mentioned earlier.

Rose breeders should not fall into the trap of striving for roses with that mirage "immunity," but look to develop such plants which have the capacity to recover from infection without the use of fungicides.

Among the relatively modern roses, the extra-vigorous ones—'Queen Elizabeth' and 'Montezuma', for example, are able to cope better with the warmth (but the average Hybrid Tea or Floribunda is very short-lived, indeed).

Such roses, as well as *R. clinophylla* and *R. gigantea,* form the basis for the new breeding line which is being developed. At this comparatively early stage of breeding it is well to remember that the rose in a tropical situation has to compete with many other beautifully luscious tropical plants, which are endowed with lovely evergreen foliage. It therefore becomes imperative to create roses which have equally beautiful evergreen foliage—such roses as are beautiful even when not in bloom, if the gardener in a warm climate is ever to grow roses. As it is, very few roses are being grown in these climates.

In addition to the foliage factor and disease resistance, the forcing conditions provided by tropical heat have to be taken into account. We need roses in the Tea–*R. clinophylla* line which are bushy and evergreen, and gigantea hybrids of manageable size. Some of the new roses raised with this approach are already proving to be good performers in warm climates. We could mention Tea roses like Faith Whittlesey™ and Garnet Crest™; the

Is disease resistance linked to adaptation to specific climates? Can there be a universal great rose, or do we have to satisfy ourselves with roses adapted to climatic regions? Sadly, regional adaptation seems to be the rule.

Hybrid Clinophyllas™, Silver Dawn™, Ganges Mist™, and Pat Henry™; the gigantea Tea, Alister's Gift™; and the Hybrid Giganteas like Naga Belle™, Evergreen Gene™, Amber Cloud™, and Golden Threshold™ (the latter three being climbers), as being well adapted. I confess that Amber Cloud™ and Golden Threshold™ could hardly be described as growing to a manageable size, but other good qualities justify inclusion. They are glorious in large gardens.

Further developments in the line include bringing in the foliage of *R. laevigata*, so well adapted to warmth and endowed with perhaps the most beautiful of rose foliage. The use of *R. roxburghii* also suggests itself, as such hybrids could well grow to the dimensions of small trees, and be the substitute for flowering cherries in the tropics.

The warm climates of the world, including many rapidly developing countries have so far been denied new roses which can be grown sustainably. And we rose breeders have to strive hard to change this situation so glaringly contradicting the claim that the rose is the world's favorite flower.

The Provence Rose, as depicted in J. Duke, *The Compleat Florist* (1747), might have been a chance seedling that occurred almost two centuries earlier in Holland. It is among the earliest hybrid roses still grown. All hybrid roses before the second half of the 18th century assuredly arose as "chance" seedlings. Controlled pollination was only beginning to be understood at that time and did not become widely practiced with roses until the latter half of the 19th century.

Sustainability Genes: Breeding the Blackspot-Resistant Rose

VANCE WHITAKER

They reside within every living cell of the rose plant. Tightly packed within chromosomes, their tiny message is written in long strings of code called DNA molecules. And though they are too small to be visible to the naked eye, their impact is huge. They are called sustainability genes.

The traits of every rose are controlled by its genes. Color, form, vigor, the machinery of photosynthesis—all aspects of the rose are governed by its genetic blueprint. Traits that affect sustainability are

Infection is optimal at about 68°F. It is no wonder, then, that the relatively cool and humid evenings of late summer are when blackspot runs rampant in the garden.

no exception. Any gene that helps a rose endure environmental stresses such as heat, cold, and drought and thrive with minimal inputs such as water, fertilizer, and pesticides could be included.

Through several years of research at the University of Minnesota, I have become acquainted with a particularly fascinating set of sustainability genes called disease resistance genes. In particular, I have observed the effects of genes that make roses resistant to blackspot disease. By learning how these resistance genes work, we can devise strategies for breeding the blackspot resistant rose.

WHAT WE'RE UP AGAINST

Blackspot disease is the most important disease of roses grown outdoors. While other fungal diseases that attack roses such as powdery mildew, downy mildew, rose rust, cercospora leaf spot, and spot anthracnose are certainly important, none has the reputation of blackspot. This is mainly due to its amazing ability to defoliate the plant, stimulating the leaves to yellow and then drop. As a result, many synthetic fungicides are sprayed to combat blackspot. But in an era of increasing environmental consciousness, the use of pesticides is becoming less and less accepted. Both the release of chemicals into the environment and the cost and time associated with spraying are contrary to sustainability ideals.

The importance of blackspot disease, along with increasing environmental concerns, has made genetic resistance a worthy topic of research. In places like Germany, Great Britain, Minnesota, and Texas, research efforts are underway at several major universities. In the following sections, a synthesis of new findings will be presented. It will become clear that by understanding how blackspot fungus infects roses and how roses combat infection, it is possible to develop effective breeding strategies for blackspot resistance.

KNOW THINE ENEMY

Blackspot is caused by an infection of the fungus *Diplocarpon rosae*. Unlike some of the less-discriminating fungi such as the causal organism of powdery mildew, *D. rosae* only infects members of the genus *Rosa*. It is primarily spread through asexual spores called conidia that are transported in water droplets and that require the presence of free water to germinate and infect. When visualized under a light microscope, the conidia are clear and two-celled. Both cells may germinate, sending out a germ tube that directly penetrates the leaf surface. Infection is optimal at about 68°F. It is no wonder, then, that the relatively cool and humid evenings of late summer are when blackspot runs rampant in the garden.

Though blackspot is caused by a single fungal species, there is diversity within this species. Studies with molecular markers have shown that *D. rosae* collected in North America and Europe has considerable genetic diversity, and this diversity appears greater than some other related fungi. Why is this important? To use an analogy, as a human species we differ in such aspects as our height, eye color, hair color, and a myriad of other genetically governed traits. *Diplocarpon rosae* is also a diverse species, and isolates of this organism differ in their ability to infect roses.

In 2004, 50 *D. rosae* isolates were collected from across Eastern North America. Fourteen of these isolates were individually inoculated to a group of 12 roses. The results separated these isolates into three "races" based on their ability to infect the selected roses. The following table shows a subset of the results to illustrate the concept of race. Race A was collected from Texas, race B was collected from Wisconsin, and race C was collected in Minnesota.

Races can be differentiated from one another based on their ability to infect certain rose hosts. This is why a rose that is resistant to blackspot in one location may be quite susceptible in someone else's garden. Even within a single garden, the races that are predominant will vary over time. As a result, resistance is unpredictable. The cultivar 'George Vancouver' might appear completely resistant to blackspot in a location where it is exposed only to race A but could be severely spotted in a location containing races B or C. Therefore, from field performance alone, it is difficult to know the true resistance of a rose cultivar.

D. ROSAE RACE			
Rose	A	B	C
'George Vancouver'	R[1]	S[2]	S
Honeybee™	R	R	S
Love & Peace™	S	S	R
'Chorale'	S	S	S

[1] *Resistant*
[2] *Susceptible*

At the University of Minnesota, races from North America and Europe have been obtained in collaboration with other researchers and are being stored in liquid nitrogen at extremely cold temperatures to ensure that they will remain available to the wider research community for years to come. These races are used in lab tests to determine the resistance of roses to specific races in a controlled and repeatable fashion. Droplets of spore suspensions are inoculated to detached leaves inside of sealed plastic containers. Within two weeks, symptoms are well developed on susceptible roses, and white masses produce from the surface of the lesion. On completely resistant roses, no visible signs of the disease can be observed. (SEE PLATES 18 AND 19)

HOW RESISTANCE GENES WORK

So far, we have discussed blackspot disease from the perspective of the pathogen. But what causes some roses to be resistant to some races and susceptible to others? The genes responsible for these drastic effects are called race-specific genes. These genes produce a protein product that helps the plant to sense the presence of the pathogen. When the pathogen is sensed, changes within the protein initiate a complicated cascade of defense responses. In roses this may involve killing off several of the leaf cells at the point of infection. Since *D. rosae* requires living host cells in order to survive and infect, this halts the spread of the disease. Think of this strategy as a "scorched earth" warfare strategy. In other cases, chemicals are exuded that kill the spores when they land on the surface of the leaf. Think of this strategy as chemical warfare. The important point is that the race-specific genes in roses allow them to sense the presence of some races of the pathogen but not others. The result is either complete resistance or complete susceptibility.

A convenient aspect of these genes is that they are usually single dominant genes. Thinking back to basic genetics, this means that if you cross a rose with a race-specific resistance gene to a susceptible rose, at least half of the seedlings will contain the resistance. That's nice for the breeder.

The downside is that the gene is only specific to a subset of the possible races. Also, the complete resistance conferred by that gene puts pressure on the population of *D. rosae* to adapt. Remember, this is a genetically diverse fungal species. If a particular isolate has the ability to overcome the race-specific gene due to a genetic mutation, this fungal isolate will have an advantage in survival and reproduction and could become more predominant in the garden.

Studies with molecular markers have shown that D. rosae *collected in North America and Europe has considerable genetic diversity, and this diversity appears greater than some other related fungi. … Isolates of this organism differ in their ability to infect roses.*

Fortunately, race-specific resistances conferred by single genes are not the only kind of resistance. Other kinds of resistance are present in roses in which some infection of the pathogen occurs, but the spread of the disease is slowed and minimized. This is called partial resistance. By inoculating roses with blackspot and measuring the diameters of the resulting lesions, large differences in lesion sizes among roses can be observed. A method that we have used in our research program is to grow potted roses in a greenhouse to maintain them free of blackspot disease. A spore suspension is sprayed onto leaves that are bagged to maintain free water for 2 days.

After 11–14 days in a greenhouse maintained at a high humidity, lesions are well developed, and their diameters can be measured. Lesions in our experiments have ranged from less than 1 millimeter to over 6 millimeters in diameter. Such large differences can have a dramatic effect on levels of blackspot disease throughout the growing season. Larger lesions usually produce more spores, which are spread by rain or irrigation water to nearby uninfected leaves. These spores penetrate the leaves, resulting in more lesions that in turn produce more spores. Over weeks and months, this process results in an exponential increase in disease. Small lesions help slow disease progression by limiting production of spores.

A nice advantage of partial resistance is that it is usually not race-specific. It is also advantageous in that it puts less pressure on the pathogen population to adapt, since some survival and reproduction of the fungus does occur. The downside is that partial resistance is not as simply inherited as race-specific resistance. It is usually controlled by multiple genes, making its inheritance more difficult to predict.

A RESEARCH-BASED STRATEGY

Based on knowledge of how different types of resistance genes work, we have developed a strategy at the University of Minnesota to find and utilize these resistance genes in the most effective way possible. First, a collection of blackspot races from around the world is maintained in liquid nitrogen storage. These isolates are periodically retrieved from storage and inoculated to detached leaves in the lab. The presence or absence of resistance is rated to determine what major genes might be present. For susceptible roses, lesion diameters are measured to determine the level of partial resistance that is present once major genes have been overcome. This strategy is currently being used to assess the resistance of rose cultivars that are included in the Earth-Kind® rose trials. In the future, roses being considered for inclusion in the trials could be prescreened using this method.

Not only is this an excellent way to evaluate cultivars, but it is also an excellent way to evaluate potential parents in a breeding program. Parents can be chosen to combine different race-specific genes into the same rose, a strategy called gene pyramiding. For example, Love & Peace™ which contains a single gene for race C resistance was crossed to 'Folksinger' which contains a single gene for race A resistance. Since these are both dominant genes, some progeny were obtained in the first generation that contained both genes and were resistant to both races. Parents may also be chosen so as to combine race-specific and partial resistance in the same rose. If the major gene is overcome, underlying partial resistance can limit the spread of infection. The progeny can be tested for partial resistance by inoculating with a race that is known to overcome the major genes. For example, seedlings from the cross of 'Folksinger' x 'Chorale' were inoculated separately with races A and C. Some seedlings were completely resistant to race A, containing the resistance gene from 'Folksinger'. Of the seedlings resistant to race A, all became infected with race C, but some contained partial resistance to race C that limited lesion size. The most valuable seedlings resulting from this cross are those that contain complete resistance to race A but also contain an underlying partial resistance to race C in case the race A resistance gene is overcome.

WHAT HOPE IS THERE FOR THE BACKYARD BREEDER?

At this point the backyard breeder might be getting a little frustrated. "I don't have a collection of characterized blackspot races," you might say. "I don't know what races are present in my garden, so how can I accurately screen parents and seedlings?" To this I must admit that you are partially right. Our collection of races and inoculation methods allow such accurate screening not possible elsewhere. However, keep in mind that the information gained from such research yields usable information. For example, we have established that 'George Vancouver' is resistant to race A and that Love & Peace™ is resistant to race C. If you plant both roses as checks in your garden and find that Love & Peace™ remains resistant while 'George Vancouver' is susceptible, it may be that race A is not present in your garden. So while the whole collection of races in your garden is unknown, it is possible to gather clues as to what races might not be present. For more information on roses that can be used as "checks" in your garden, please see our article in *Plant Breeding* (Whitaker et al., 2007). In addition, a much larger collection of roses that are included in the Earth-Kind® trials are being screened with races A, B, and C, and the results will be published in the near future.

In a breeding program ... parents can be chosen to combine different race-specific genes into the same rose, a strategy called gene pyramiding. ... Parents may also be chosen so as to combine race-specific and partial resistance in the same rose.

THE BLACKSPOT PLAYGROUND

A good screening environment for potential parents and for seedlings produced by the backyard breeder should be a hospitable environment for blackspot, a blackspot playground! In order for the effects of disease resistance genes to be obvious, heavy disease pressure is a must. This means no fungicide sprays or sanitation. But also take positive steps to promote disease. Overhead irrigate, if possible, to maintain free water on leaves and stems. Collect blackspotted leaves from infected plants, soak them in water for a few minutes to collect the spores, and spray the spore solution on your plants. Do this late in the evening so that free water will remain as long as possible.

In the example I gave above, a particular garden did not appear to contain race A, based on a lack of infection on Love & Peace™. How should you seek to introduce this race into your garden? The most direct method would be to collect blackspotted leaves from Love & Peace™ from a friend's yard or a public park and make a spore solution to spray. In fact, to promote blackspot diversity, why not begin by collecting blackspotted leaves from multiple cultivars in multiple locations in your area? Keep in mind, however, that the transport of blackspot across state lines without a permit from the USDA is illegal and should not be attempted.

STRATEGIES FOR SUCCESS

Once a suitable screening environment is created, the first decision a breeder faces is to choose good parents. Perhaps it is obvious, but it must be stated: choose resistant parents to get resistant progeny. As was previously mentioned, most disease resistance genes are dominantly inherited. Very few disease resistance genes in plants are recessive. Therefore, if neither of the parents exhibits resistance, it is extremely unlikely that any of the progeny will be resistant. When choosing parents that are partially resistant, the same principle holds true. Also consider the fertility of the parents. Differences in ploidy and other reproductive barriers can significantly reduce hip and seed set. Ploidy should also be considered to avoid a "genetic dead-end". If a tetraploid and a diploid are crossed to create a sterile triploid, further progress in breeding can be limited.

Before making a cross, also consider the size of the population that will be required. It is tempting to make a few crosses among desirable parents and germinate copious quantities of seed, hoping that the laws of statistics will bless you with one or two promising seedlings with the right combination of traits. But it is much wiser to adjust population size according to the goal you are trying to achieve. If you are crossing a rose containing a major resistance gene with a susceptible rose to obtain resistant seedlings, perhaps only 30 or 50 seedlings need to be grown. A resistant seedling from this generation may then be crossed with a rose containing a different resistance in the next generation. If a partially resistant rose is being crossed to a susceptible rose, a larger population size may be warranted. In our research we have found that crosses of this type predominantly yield seedlings that have resistance comparable to or worse than the susceptible parent. Due to the multigenic nature of the resistance, only a few seedlings will have partial resistance comparable to or better than the more resistant parent.

> *If you plant both roses as checks in your garden and find that Love & Peace™ remains resistant while 'George Vancouver' is susceptible, it may be that race A is not present in your garden. So while the whole collection of races in your garden is unknown, it is possible to gather clues as to what races might not be present.*

SUSTAINABILITY GENES

Genetic resistance to blackspot disease is complicated by the complex relationship between plant and pathogen. Thankfully, new research is shedding light on the invisible weapons that roses use to defend themselves against fungal attackers. As the nature and mechanisms of these weapons are increasingly understood, breeding strategies can be employed to use them more effectively. Indeed, sustainability genes are the key to breeding the blackspot resistant rose.

ACKNOWLEDGMENTS

I would like to acknowledge Dr. Stan Hokanson, Director of the Woody Landscape Plant Breeding and Genetics program within the Department of Horticultural Science at the University of Minnesota for the initiation and direction of this research. Thanks also to Dr. David Zlesak for reviewing this manuscript. The work described herein was performed in collaboration with Dr. David Zlesak and project scientists Steve McNamara and Kathy Zuzek. International collaborators include Dr. A.V. Roberts and Dr. Thomas Debener.

REFERENCE

Whitaker, V.M., K. Zuzek, and S.C. Hokanson. 2007. Resistance of twelve rose genotypes to fourteen isolates of Diplocarpon rosae (rose blackspot) collected from eastern North America. Plant Breeding 126:83–88.

A Century (or Two)
of Hybrid Musks*

JEFF WYCKOFF

The origin, naming, and development of the Hybrid Musk class of roses, a family that now consists of over 175 varieties, are features of a tale that has a number of interesting twists and turns. In some ways it compares to that of the origin and naming of the Hybrid Tea class, another somewhat ill-named family that defies all attempts to assign a more botanically correct label thereto (as the United Kingdom's Royal National Rose Society discovered some years back with their "Large Flowered" label, now basically obsolete).

The relationship between the Hybrid Musk family and the musk rose *R. moschata,* often described as tenuous by various authors, might better be termed remote. Were we to apply the "Six Degrees of Separation" concept to *R. moschata* and either 'Danaë' or 'Moonlight', Joseph Pemberton's first two Hybrid Musks from 1913, we would discover eight degrees of separation, as illustrated by the family tree (see next page).

This parentage chart is based on information from *Modern Roses XII* *(MRXII)*, and it is apparent that *R. moschata* could have entered the picture later than documented here. For example, both of the unknown pollen parents on the right of the chart could have had lines to the musk rose,

---

* *SEE PLATES **22** AND **23** for images of Hybrid Musks.*

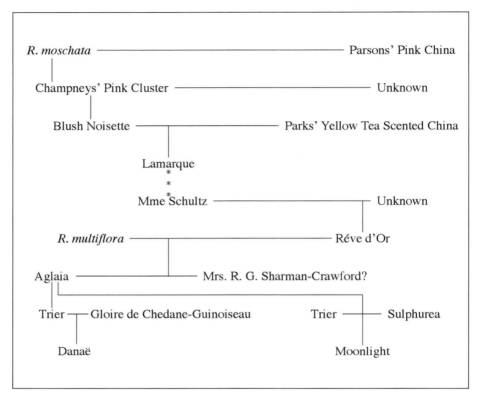

while 'Mrs. R. G. Sharman-Crawford', a pink-blend Hybrid Perpetual from Dickson's in 1894, is listed as only a possible pollen parent of 'Trier'. Finally, *MRXII* lists "no parentage found" for 'Mme. Schultz', an 1856 Noisette from Jean Béluze; its inclusion here as an offspring of 'Lamarque' is based on a paper given at the Columbia, South Carolina, ARS National Convention by Dr. Charles Jeremias in 1992. This shaky family tree, coupled with the eight degrees of separation noted above, make the *R. moschata*–'Moonlight'/'Danaë' relationship both tenuous and remote, so where did the name "Hybrid Musk" come from, and who was responsible for this interesting misnomer, at least with regard to the roses of Pemberton?

In *The Makers of Heavenly Roses,* Jack Harkness gives us the following account:

'Moonlight' was his first Gold Medal rose, and in reporting its success, which occurred at the Autumn Show on 9 September, 1913, the Rose Annual questioned whether it was a Hybrid Tea, or, as some people thought, a Hybrid Multiflora. Joseph continued to advertise his roses as Hybrid Teas, until Courtney Page, secretary of the National Rose Society, reviewing the new roses for 1917, classed 'Pax' as a Hybrid Musk, with these words: "When I first saw this rose in the early part of June I immediately recognized an entirely new break, and on referring to my notes made on that occasion I find the following: 'A new Hybrid Musk of the first order, very strongly perfumed—real musk.'" He described the colour as pure white, tinted lemon in the bud, with prominent golden anthers. ... In 1919, Pemberton adopted the term Hybrid Musk.

Why Page considered 'Pax' to be an "entirely new break" is unclear, particularly considering the appearance of 'Danaë' and 'Moonlight' (the latter with its Royal National Society Gold Medal in tow) some 4 years earlier. All three roses are in the creamy-white to light yellow range, all have lightly petaled, "semi-double" blooms, and Peter Beales rates both 'Danaë' and 'Pax' as being only moderately fragrant. Perhaps Page caught 'Pax' on a warm day when the musk odor was particularly strong, or perhaps he had his mind made up already, as his statement "a new Hybrid Musk" would seem to indicate.

Another account relating to the establishment of this new class has the Reverend Pemberton showing up at an NRS National Show sometime in the mid-teens and wishing to enter his roses as Hybrid Teas, which he then considered them. The person in charge of entries for the show (perhaps Mr. Page himself?) refused to allow them in as Hybrid Teas, and, noting an apparent resemblance to *R. moschata* (whether through the form or the fragrance of the blooms is unclear), suggested they be entered as "Hybrid Musks."

The relationship between the Hybrid Musk family and the musk rose R. moschata, *often described as tenuous by various authors, might better be termed remote.*

In any case, Hybrid Musks they became, leading to an interesting anomaly in the 1921 NRS Annual, wherein an article by H. R. Darlington entitled "The Hybrid Teas of the Past Ten Years" includes reviews of

'Danaë', 'Moonlight', and 'Pax', stating of the last: "… has creamy white flowers resembling Moonlight, but slightly fuller and larger. The foliage is not quite so attractive, nor does it grow so strongly as that variety, which I prefer of the two, but it makes quite a good garden plant."

The very next article in the Annual, authored by Pemberton himself, entitled "Some of the Best New Roses of the Last Ten Years," reviews both 'Moonlight' and 'Pax' as Hybrid Musks, and says of the former:

If Joseph Pemberton can be considered the Father of the Hybrid Musks, then Louis Lens, the Belgian breeder best known for the classic white Hybrid Tea 'Pascali', must surely be deemed the "King of the Hybrid Musks." Lens introduced a staggering total of 54 …

"Moonlight, Hybrid Musk (Pemberton 1913) A perpetual flowering cluster shrub rose. Flowers, white flushed lemon. One hesitates to include any of one's own raising in this list, but one does so at the Editor's request. To show the esteem in which the writer holds it, it will suffice to list it here without further comment."

This same issue carries a black and white photograph of 'Vanity', an NRS (it was to become "Royal" at a later date) Certificate of Merit winner from 1920. 'Vanity' represented somewhat of a new direction for Pemberton and his Hybrid Musks, from the relatively small plants and pastel blooms in small clusters from previous years to a large plant with deep pink blooms borne in large sprays, features that would turn up in some of his later varieties such as 'Nur Mahal' (which incidentally has a near-identical parentage to that of 'Vanity': 'Château de Clos Vougeot' [a red Hybrid Tea] x seedling).

In all, Pemberton is credited with introducing 28 varieties of Hybrid Musks, of which some 21 are still in commerce somewhere in the world, according to the 2007 *Combined Rose List*. He is also listed as having bred some 20 Hybrid Teas, of which only a couple are still in commerce, including 'The General', a medium red from 1920 with no parentage given, and 'I Zingari', an orange-scarlet near-single from 1925 named after an Australian cricket club that is still in existence today.

Whatever their heritage, Pemberton's roses were not the first to be designated as Hybrid Musks. Perhaps the earliest use of this name is to be found in William Paul's seminal 1848 book, *The Rose Garden*. Paul divides his encyclopedic list of varieties into two groups: "Summer Roses: Blooming In May, June, and July," and "Autumnal Roses: Blooming From May Till November." In the former, his Group XIX is labeled "The Hybrid Musk and other Hybrids," so it is difficult to determine specifically which of the 10 varieties therein he considers Hybrid Musks and which "other hybrids." However, he does say, rather enigmatically: " 'Madame d'Arblay' and 'The Garland' partake of the nature of the Musk Rose, although possessing but little of its peculiar odour." Both of these are now classed as Hybrid Multifloras, as are two others of his group of ten. Of the rest, one is now a shrub, another an Ayrshire, and the remaining four are extinct and do not appear in *MRXII*.

Paul's "Autumnal" group of musks, Group XXXVII, is labeled simply "The Musk Rose" rather than "The Hybrid Musk," as we would expect from a group that supposedly bloomed well into the fall. The dozen varieties in this group deserve enumeration, as their present classifications shed some interesting light on the Hybrid Musk family as a whole.

"THE MUSK ROSE"

PAUL'S NAME	CURRENT APPROVED NAME	CLASS — DATE OF INTRODUCTION (MRII)
Blush, or Fraser's	'Fraser's Pink Musk'	Noisette,1818
Double White	'Double White'	Hybrid Musk, before 1629
Eliza Werry	(Extinct)	
Eponine	'Eponine'	Hybrid Musk, before 1835
Fringed	(Extinct)	
New Double (Ranunculus)	'Ranunculus Musk Cluster'	Hybrid Must
Nivea	Probably 'Aimée Vibert'	Noisette, 1828
Ophir	'Ophir'	Hybrid Must, c. 1835
Princesse de Nassau	'Princesse de Nassau'	Noisette, 1835
Rivers	'Rivers Must Cluster'	Hybrid Musk, before 1846
Rosine	(Extinct)	
Tea-Scented	Possibly 'Ruga' (aka Tea-Scented Ayrshire)	Ayrshire, before 1820

As the progenitor of the Noisette family, 'Champneys' Pink Cluster' has *R. moschata* as a seed parent. So it is understandable that three of Paul's reblooming musks are now classed as Noisettes. Had it not been for the development of its offspring, 'Champneys' Pink Cluster' would it-self likely be classified today as a Hybrid Musk. However, perhaps more important is the clear indication that first- and perhaps second-generation offspring from *R. moschata* were in existence early in the 19th century (and before) and that Courtney Page did not just pick this classification out of thin air with 'Pax'.

Whatever their heritage, Pemberton's roses were not the first to be designated as Hybrid Musks. Perhaps the earliest use of this name is to be found in William Paul's seminal 1848 book, The Rose Garden.

John (Jack) and Ann Bentall, for years Pemberton's gardeners and the inheritors of much of his unfinished breeding work following his death in 1926, are often slighted as presumably having put their names on roses already in Pemberton's "pipeline." However, in an article in the Summer 2007 edition of the *White Rose News*, the bulletin of the RNRS Yorkshire Rosarians, Jim McIntyre sheds some new light on their output of, among other roses, seven Hybrid Musk varieties:

> With so much of his work carrying on after his death the question has to be asked if Pemberton was a one-man hybridizer or did he rely on a small team. What influence was Florence [his sister]? What part did John Bentall play in the decision-making? Hazel Le Rougetel revealed at the Historic Roses In-ternational Conference at Cambridge in 1997 that, at a meeting she had with his son Jack, he had said that it was his mother Ann who took over during the 1914–18 war when the, as yet unnamed Hybrid Musks were beginning to make their mark.
>
> So, was she the powerhouse behind the operation? Certainly many of the rose introductions once credited to her husband are now being given to her. A clue stands out if one looks at the names given to the Pemberton roses. Only one seems out of place and that is 'Nur Mahal'. There are several stories about this princess, one of which was that she strewed rose petals on

the water and noticed an oily film from which she ultimately captured rose perfume. However Pemberton explained the name at the time simply by saying that she was a clever woman who successfully managed the affairs of her rather weak emperor husband. Draw your own conclusions.

George C. Thomas probably has more of his roses grown in America today than those of any other hybridizer. Of course, 98% of these are 'Dr Huey', springing up like weeds from the rootstock of winter-killed hybrids. Of over 60 varieties attributed to Thomas, 37 are named "Bloomfield _____"—and of these 10 are Hybrid Musks. Certainly 'Bishop Darlington' ('Aviateur Bleriot' x 'Moonlight') and 'Bloomfield Dainty' ('Danaë' x 'Mme. Edouard Herriot') are his most enduring, but it is interesting to look at the parentages of the rest of his output in this family as well. Of the nine remaining Bloomfields, 'Danaë is used as a seed parent four times and a pollen parent twice, while 'Moonlight' appears as a pollen parent once, as it does in another of his Hybrid Musks, 'Mrs. George C. Thomas'. Two Bloomfields plus a final Hybrid Musk, 'Cascadia', have no Hybrid Musks (nor 'Trier') as an immediate parent.

The additions to the Hybrid Musk family from W. Kordes Söhne consist of 15 varieties, bookended by 'Eva' in 1933 and 'Lavender Lassie' in 1960. Once again, it is illustrative to look at the parentage of this array, not only to see which varieties Kordes considered particularly productive parents, but also to ascertain how much further away the Hybrid Musk family was moving from its progenitor (or at least namesake), *R. moschata*.

'Eva' is classed as a red blend and is described by Peter Beales as a "lesser-known cultivar [that] is well scented. Dark green foliage on a fairly tall-growing plant." Its parentage is 'Robin Hood' x 'J.C. Thornton', the former a Pemberton Hybrid Musk and the latter a red Hybrid Tea from Bees. 'Robin Hood's' parentage is listed as: seedling (presumably a Hybrid Musk seedling) x 'Miss. Edith Cavell', a red Polyantha. 'Eva' became Kordes' "brood mare," as it were, for the next 10 years, serving as seed parent for 6 of the 10 Hybrid Musks introduced during this period, as well as pollen parent for 2 others.

Offspring included the still-popular 'Erfurt' as well as 'Sangerhausen', a deep pink that then became the seed parent for both 'Nymphenburg' and 'Grandmaster' in 1954. 'Lavender Lassie', Kordes' most popular and last Hybrid Musk to date, can claim 'Eva' only as a maternal grandparent.

The fecundity of 'Eva' is tempered by the fact that her offspring, while nominally Hybid Musks, possess bloodlines that are even further diluted. Assuming the best, that 'Robin Hood's' seedling pollen parent is a direct descendant of 'Trier', then 'Eva's' children would be 11 generations removed from *R. moschata*. Considering that this is about the distance children born today are removed from George Washington, we can see that family relationships are getting ever more tenuous.

If Joseph Pemberton can be considered the Father of the Hybrid Musks, then Louis Lens, the Belgian breeder best known for the classic white Hybrid Tea 'Pascali', must surely be deemed the "King of the Hybrid Musks." Lens introduced a staggering total of 54 Hybrid Musks, all within the last 25 years, beginning with 'Poesie' in 1982. Virtually all of these 54 were registered in a group in 2000, likely because of Lens' failing health (he died the following year). As might be expected, Lens' output involved a wide variety of crosses with a disparate group of parents: species, Hybrid Multifloras, Chinas, Polyanthas, and many other types are to be found in his breeding lines. Of interest here, however, is that, unlike those of Kordes, many of his parents and "half-parents" (i.e. [A x B] x C, wherein both A and B could be viewed as seed half-parents) were Pemberton's and Bentall's Hybrid Musks, while some nine of the 54 hearken back to 'Trier' as either a full or half seed parent.

The fragrance of the Hybrid Musks, coupled with their above-average disease resistance, repeat bloom, and abundant colors, should keep them in the forefront of nursery catalogs and websites for some time to come.

By far the most popular parent in Lens' Hybrid Musk breeding was 'Ballerina', Bentall's immensely popular introduction from 1937, unfortunately with unknown (or unreported) parentage. 'Ballerina' appears no fewer than 20 times in Lens' output, fairly evenly distributed among seed and pollen, parents and half-parents. Pemberton varieties to be found in his breeding lines include 'Moonlight', 'Kathleen', Felicia', 'Vanity', and 'Robin Hood'. In all, 32 of the 49 of his Hybrid Musks for which parentage is given contain a Hybrid Musk parent or half-parent.

As a cross section of Lens' Hybrid Musk parentage, we might look at his four varieties named after composers:

'Puccini' light pink [(*R. luciae* x unknown) x (Ballerina x Robin Hood)]

'Ravel' pink blend (*R. multiflora adenocheata* x Ballerina)

'Sibelius' mauve (Mister Bluebird x Violet Hood)

'Verdi' mauve (Mister Bluebird x Violet Hood)

'Mister Bluebird' is a mauve Miniature from Ralph Moore, while 'Violet Hood' is Lens' own shrub, a cross of 'Robin Hood' and 'Baby Faurax'. *R. multiflora adenocheata* is a recently recognized variant of *R. multiflora*, described in *MRXII* as "flowers deep bright pink, fading lighter, single, borne in clusters, slight fragrance."

While Lens' Hybrid Musks are not widely available in North America, they are becoming more and more popular. At present, a total of 16–17 varieties are carried by mail order nurseries, the likes of Hortico, Rogue Valley Roses, and Vintage Gardens.

Similar to other rose families, Hybrid Musks have waxed and waned in popularity over the past century. While they may not be experiencing a 21st-century renaissance, there are certainly more Hybrid Musk varieties available from more nurseries worldwide today than ever before. A comparison of the *Combined Rose List*s of 1988 and 2007 show that, for examples, 'Eva' has gone from 5 to 20 listings, 'Danaé' from 9 to 33, and 'Ballerina' from 26 to well over a hundred. This surge of popularity is also reflected in ratings in the ARS' *Handbook for Selecting Roses* where, between 1987 and 2008, 'Eva' went from not even being listed to 7.8, while 'Danaé' and 'Ballerina' both went from "%" (insufficient reports) to scores of 7.7 and 8.7, respectively. Nursery catalogs and ARS and

RNRS publications from the middle of the 20th century would need to be scoured to determine the status of the Hybrid Musks during that time, but I suspect they never really went out of favor with knowledgeable rose growers.

While Courtney Page may not have done proponents of accurate botanical nomenclature any favors with his assignment of the name of Hybrid Musk to an emerging family that might better have been consigned to the Hybrid Multiflora class, he undoubtedly raised public awareness of this group and likely ensured its perpetuation with the rose-buying public with this fortuitous choice of words. The term "musk" has long been associated with fragrance, owing to its historic use in perfumery. Any number of plants and animals, to include *R. moschata*, have been given the name of "musk" because they are perceived to emit an odor akin to that of musk-based perfume. This connection between the name and the fragrance in roses has been reinforced by a variety of literary references, as exemplified by the following two extracts:

> The coming musk-rose, full of dewy wine
> The murmurous haunt of flies on summer eves
> — Keats, *Ode to a Nightingale*

> O'ercanopied with luscious woodbine
> With sweet musk-roses, and with eglantine
> —Shakespeare, *A Midsummer Night's Dream*

It seems evident from the foregoing examination of breeding lines that hybridizers, as probably did Courtney Page, have bestowed the name Hybrid Musk on their creations based primarily on fragrance (with a secondary nod perhaps given to plant habit) rather than on parentage. Given the relative nature of both quality and quantity of fragrance in roses, plus the likelihood that the great majority of rose growers would never have had an opportunity to smell the aroma of the true *R. moschata*, it would further seem that any significant aroma would have qualified a new shrub variety as a potential Hybrid Musk in the eyes — or rather the noses — of the buying public. Just as breeders today trade off established names like

Peace, Knock Out, and Simplicity with new introductions that may have little or no genetic connections to the originals, so the name "Hybrid Musk" would have been one that resonated well with rose growers.

With disease resistance being the overriding concern for rose breeders nowadays, fragrance has, despite catalog descriptions to the contrary, taken a seat firmly in the background. The fragrance of the Hybrid Musks, coupled with their above-average disease resistance, repeat bloom, and abundant colors, should keep them in the forefront of nursery catalogs and websites for some time to come. Probably the largest selections of Hybrid Musks in North America are carried by Rogue Valley Roses and Vintage Gardens, while Pépinières Louis Lens in Oudenburg, Belgium (who, according to the *Combined Rose List* does export) may hold the record with some 74 varieties, mostly Lens' own, but with a small selection of others.

Contributors

Lynne Chapman—Co-author, *Tea Roses: Old Roses for Warm Gardens,* safrano.rose@gmail.com.

Brian Debasitis—Soil ecosystem consultant and owner of Mauby All Natural, San Jose, California, bdebasistis@mauby.com.

James Delahanty—Writer and rosarian, Ventura County Rose Society, California, jjjzdelahanty@earthlink.net.

Noelene Drage—Co-author, *Tea Roses: Old Roses for Warm Gardens.*

Di Durston—Co-author, *Tea Roses: Old Roses for Warm Gardens.*

Alice Flores—Rosarian, nurseryman, and member of Heritage Roses Group Board, aflores@mcn.org.

Maria Cecilia Freeman—Artist, botanical illustrator, Santa Cruz, California, mcf@mcf-art.com.

Steve George—Professor and Extension Horticulturist, Texas AgriLife Extension Service. Creator and National Coordinator of the EarthKind® Environmental Landscape Management Program, george3@tamu.edu.

William A. Grant—Garden writer, photographer, lecturer growing roses on Monterey Bay, California, grant@ebold.com.

Gaye Hammond—gayeh@LPM-triallaw.com, 5020 Montrose Blvd., 9th Floor, Houston, TX 77044, 281-458-6116.

Derald A. Harp—Associate Professor, Horticulture, Texas A&M University—Commerce, Derald_Harp@TAMU-Commerce.edu.

Pat Henry—Co-owner, Roses Unlimited, Laurens, South Carolina, RosesUnLMT@aol.com.

Janet Inada—Owner, Rogue Valley Roses, info@roguevalleyroses.com.

Jeri Jennings — Editor, *Rose Letter;* Editor, *Gold Coast Rose Society Newsletter,* heritageroses@gmail.com.

Jenny Jones — Co-author, *Tea Roses: Old Roses for Warm Gardens.*

Peter E. Kukielski — Rockefeller Curator of the Peggy Rockefeller Rose Garden and Rose Collection, The New York Botanical Garden, pkukielski@nybg.org.

Wayne Mackay — Professor and Director, University of Florida, wmackay@ufl.edu.

Marjorie Marcallino — Curator, Roosevelt Island Rose Garden, Mdmhilo@aol.com.

Michael Marriott — Lecturer and Manager, David Austin Roses, United Kingdom, MichaelM@davidaustinroses.co.uk.

Clair G. Martin III — Shannon Curator of Roses and Rose Collections, The Huntington Botanical Garden, San Marino, California; Chairman of the Great Rosarians of the World™, cmartin@huntington.org.

Karl Mckoy — "Wet soils" rose gardener and Curator of Roses, Queens Botanical Garden, New York, kmckoy@queensbotanical.org.

Hillary Merrifield — Co-author of *Tea Roses: Old Roses for Warm Gardens,* hmerrifield@gmail.com.

Dan Mills — Co-owner, The Weed Patch, Fairfield, Florida, tuckermills@netscape.com.

Barbara Oliva — Curator, Sacramento Historic Rose Garden, California, boliva@macnexus.org.

William M. Patterson — Co-owner, Roses Unlimited, Laurens, South Carolina, RosesUnLMT@aol.com.

Gary Pellett — Co-owner, Newflora LLC info@newflora.com.

Jill Perry — Curator, San Jose Heritage Rose Garden, California, oldtearoses@hotmail.com.

Ellen Spector Platt — Author of 10 books; writes blog, *www. gardenbytes.com*; Secretary, Manhattan Rose Society, New York City, mlark@earthlink.net.

William J. Radler — Rose hybridizer; Great Rosarians of the World 2008 Honoree, wradler@wi.rr.com.

Ron Robertson — Owner, Garden Valley Ranch Roses, ron@gardenvalley.com.

Stephen Scanniello—President of Heritage Rose Foundation, steprose@ mac.com.

Pat Shanley—Founding President, Manhattan Rose Society; ARS New York District Director; Chairman, ARS Marketing & Membership Committee; Chairman of the Great Rosarians of the World®—East, Locust Valley, New York, pshanley@aol.com.

John Starnes—Rose hybridizer and garden writer, Tampa, Florida, johnastarnes@msn.com.

Allison Strong—Texas Rose Rustler, allisonstrong@rocketmail.com.

Billy Styles—President & Co-Founder, Organic Plant Health, Charlotte, North Carolina.

Alan Talbert—Vice President & Co-Founder, Organic Plant Health, Charlotte, North Carolina, alan@organicplanthealth.com.

Betty Vickers—Trustee & Secretary, Heritage Rose Foundation; Editor, *The Yellow Rose,* journal of Dallas Area Historical Rose Society; Chair, Library Committee, American Rose Society, vickers.b@ sbcglobal.net.

Viru Viraraghavan—Rose hybridizer; Co-editor, *Indian Rose Annual;* Great Rosarians of the World 2005 Honoree, Kodaikanal, India, girija.vira@gmail.com.

Gene Waering—Vice President & Program Chairman, Manhattan Rose Society, New York City and Jacksonville, Florida, gwaering@gmail. com.

Marilyn Wellan—Former President of the American Rose Society & Great Rosarians of the World 2009 Co-honoree, Alexandria, Louisiana, roseusa@suddenlink.net.

Billy West—Co-author, *Tea Roses: Old Roses for Warm Gardens,* bjkwest@gmail.com.

Vance Whitaker—Assistant Professor of Strawberry Breeding and Genetics, University of Florida, vwhitaker@ufl.edu.

Jeff Wyckoff—President, American Rose Society, kjwyckoff@comcast. net.

David Zlesak—Assistant Professor of Horticulture, University of Wisconsin—River Falls; rose hybridizer, zlesak@rocketmail.com.

Picture Credits/Sources

TEXT AND ARTICLE COLOR SECTION

Brad Braaten, color section (International Friend of the Rose Award, Pl. 2)
Lynne Chapman, color section (Close Look at Tea Roses, Pl. 9)
Lynne Chapman, Hillary Merrifield, Billy West, 222
Maria Cecilia Freeman, 55, 56, 210 (inset)
Margaret Furness, color section (Close Look at Tea Roses, Pl. 10)
William A. Grant, color section (International Friend of the Rose Award, Pl. 3)
Derald A. Harp et al., color section (Earth-Kind® Trials)
Stan Henry, 92, 93
Jeri Jennings, 104, 110
Jenny Jones, color section (Close Look at Tea Roses, Pl. 7)
Ann Kugel, color section (International Friend of the Rose Award, Pl. 1)
Peter E. Kukielski, 118
Marjorie Marcallino, color section (Roosevelt Island Rose Garden)
Gary Pellett, 167
William J. Radler, 212
Ellen Spector Platt, 179, 181, 182, color section (Chocolate and Roses) (photos and text © Ellen Spector Platt)
Pat Shanley, 2
Vintage Gardens, Gregg Lowery, color section (Hybrid Musks)
Girija and Viru Viraraghavan, 242, 243
Gene Waering, color section (various)
Billy West, color section (Close Look at Tea Roses, Pl. 4)
Vance Whitaker, color section (Sustainability Genes)
Paul Zimmerman Roses, color section (Hybrid Musks)

COLOR SECTION FOR SUSTAINABLE ROSE VARIETIES

Page 1, Radler—courtesy of Conard-Pyle
Page 2, Radler/Meilland—courtesy of Conard-Pyle
Page 3, Meilland—courtesy of Conard-Pyle
Pages 4–6, EarthKind®—courtesy of Gaye Hammond
Page 7, Lim—courtesy of Bailey Nurseries
Page 8—courtesy of Chamblee's Nursery, Roses Unlimited Nursery
Page 9, Shoup—courtesy of Michael Shoup
Page 10, Carruth, Noack, Bedard—Photos by Gene Sasse© 2010 Courtesy of Weeks Roses
Page 11, Austin—courtesy of David Austin® Roses
Pages 12–16, Kordes—courtesy of W. KORDES' SÖHNE and Newflora™

Special thanks to: Steve Hutton & Jacques Ferare of Conard-Pyle Co. and Star® Roses, Gaye Hammond and the whole EarthKind™ team, Terry Schwartz & Sarah Parker of Bailey Nurseries, Michael Shoup of The Antique Rose Emporium, Maxine Gilliam of Weeks Roses, Michael Marriott of David Austin® Roses, Maya Polscher of W. Kordes' Söhne, Chris & Gary Pellett of Newflora™.